The Online Writer's Companion

JY 13 '17

A Complete Guide to Earning Your Living as a Freelancer

P. J. Aitken

ALLWORTH PRESS
NEW YORK

Allworth Press books may be purchased in bulk at special discounts for sales promotion, corporate gifts, fund-raising, or educational purposes. Special editions can also be created to specifications. For details, contact the Special Sales Department, Allworth Press, 307 West 36th Street, 11th Floor, New York, NY 10018 or info@skyhorsepublishing.com.

20 19 18 17 16   5 4 3 2 1

Published by Allworth Press, an imprint of Skyhorse Publishing, Inc.
307 West 36th Street, 11th Floor, New York, NY 10018.

Allworth Press® is a registered trademark of Skyhorse Publishing, Inc.®, a Delaware corporation.

www.allworth.com

Library of Congress Cataloging-in-Publication Data is available on file.

Print ISBN: 978-1-62153-528-7
Ebook ISBN: 978-1-62153-529-4

Printed in the United States of America

TABLE OF CONTENTS

INTRODUCTION

I don't consider myself to be particularly tech savvy, but I'm not completely clueless either. I was an Internet child, a loner who spent his days and nights battling with a 56k modem and hogging the phone line. I was born in 1985, so I'm still fairly young (although my gray hairs and the noise I make when I sit down would beg to differ), but in my teenage years it was still considered "geeky" to use computers, and I became a whizz kid purely because I knew what RAM stood for (or so they thought) and that a "hard drive" was not something be giggled at.

I lost my way somewhat over the years, but I like to think that I knew a little more about the net than most.

Fast forward to 2012. I had been writing for many years, mostly as an aspiring novelist whose only purpose was to write a novel, find an agent, and then repeat when that process inevitably failed. Toward the end of the year I decided that enough was enough. I had won short story competitions and had seen many stories published in magazines, but I was broke and I was going nowhere. I self-published, and to cut a long story short, it went rather well for me. I was making more money than I had ever dreamed of and my work was finally being read.

I didn't want to spend all of my days writing novels though—creativity is a fleeting thing and I had gaps in my schedule that needed filling. I was also worried that my books would stop selling and I would be left with nothing but the regret that I didn't make more of the opportunity when I had the chance. So, I decided to freelance, and that's when my lack of Internet knowledge surfaced.

I knew nothing about the websites that will be the focus of this book. I actually resorted to *Craigslist*, better known for producing serial killers and posts that make the human race look like an experiment in absurdity and sexual perversion. I found jobs that offered pennies, including one that paid $50 a month for what amounted to two articles a day. I figured I needed the experience—I needed something on my CV other than doodles and the words "Published Author," and I was sure that my experience as a novelist would get me that job and others like it.

As it happened, I didn't get the job, and I'm thankful for it. After that, and thanks to a chance Google search, I discovered Freelancer. This is a website that is devoted to freelancers of all professions, a community where people post jobs for writers, artists, programmers, and more, and one that deals with hundreds of thousands of dollars' worth of projects a week. This opened my eyes, exposing me to sites like Fiverr, People Per Hour, and to an entire industry I never knew existed.

This was a gold mine for me, a realization that I didn't need to "settle" for shitty jobs on Serial-Killers-R-US. After a little more searching, I discovered Elance. I thought that it looked like the best one out there, and I was right. There were over 300,000 writers on Elance, all competing for millions of dollars' worth of projects, and in eighteen months I had made it into the top five. I also branched out into other sites, trying not to keep all of my eggs in one basket, which is very important in this industry, as discussed later (**see Section 16.3 on page 252**), but Elance always remained my main site, my main source of income away from my books. Elance then became Upwork, and in the changeover I remained one of the most sought-after and most highly rated writers, earning even more money than I had earned through the success of my novels.

In this book I will tell you how I went from a clueless idiot who didn't know these sites existed to a leading freelancer at the very top of the industry, and I will show you how you can do the same. I didn't use anything but hard work and common sense, and I'm confident that anyone can do what I did with the right guidance. This isn't a self-help book; it isn't a golden ticket. I'm not going to tell you that it's all about positivity and eating your greens, and I'm certainly not going to tell you the "secret" that will have clients queuing outside your door—although I can tell you how to make them interested in you. Making it as an online freelance writer—and any sort of online freelancer for that matter—requires a lot of hard work and commitment. In fact, being reliable and hard working will do much more for you than being a great writer ever will.

This book will show you the basics. It will tell you what sites to use and how to get the most out of them; how to make an eye-catching profile; how to set your price in a highly competitive market; how to find the right projects and the right clients; how to outsource; and how to increase your score and your reputation. It will also look at blogging and content websites, an industry that all freelance writers should consider getting involved with on a part-time basis. To round it off, I have included sections on tax, investments, and other resources. This is more than just a book about freelance websites; it's a book that will guide you into the life of an online freelancer. It will help you to succeed in that role and ensure you live comfortably with the sort of financial security that every career deserves, but one that isn't usually given to freelancers.

There is a lot of content to sort through, a lot of tidbits, guides, tips, and more. To make things a little more accessible, I have included small references to later chapters within the text, and there is a "summary" section at the end of all chapters, highlighting the key areas. There is also a comprehensive index at the back of this book that will help you search through the content, which means you can keep the book to hand when you begin your career and even beyond that. Despite all of this, the best way to read *The Online Writer's Companion* is from the first page to the last. That way you will learn everything you need to know about working in this environment. Once you've done that, read through again, taking time to go through each chapter as it corresponds to your current situation. On this second read, you should pay more attention to the references in brackets, visiting the pages and chapters mentioned, before going back to where you were.

0.1 — MY JOURNEY AND YOURS

I don't like to brag. Actually, I probably do, at least a little bit, but I'm sure you don't want to listen to it. However, my own situation is incredibly relevant to this book. I wouldn't have written it and I certainly wouldn't have been able to publish it if I hadn't come a very long way in a very short time. It wasn't easy and I made a lot of mistakes on the way, but those mistakes shaped me and my career and they allowed me to better understand this industry.

I occasionally work under a pen name, so you might not find me on these sites, but for the purposes of being entirely open, I have worked on most of the sites mentioned in this book. In the early days, my work was split between Elance and oDesk, and when those sites merged, I focused on that one platform. I worked on anything I could get, from editing and proofreading jobs—not my strongest suit—to writing comic book scripts, film scripts, academic essays, press releases, memoirs, website content, and social media posts. I have written blog posts and articles on everything from kitchen refurbishment and animal welfare to gambling, sports, home brewing, dieting, medieval history, and chemistry. But for a select few of these subjects, I knew very little about what I was writing before I was given the job.

As I shall relate in this book **(see Section 19.1 on page 292)**, it pays to understand a lot of things about a lot of subjects. It pays to be a general knowledge geek, but it also pays to take anything you are given. In my opinion, this is what defines a freelance writer, and it is also what makes them successful.

I once worked with a decent writer on a series of sport articles. They were all related to his favorite sports and he did a good job writing them, earning a respectable fee. When that work dried up, I found some other work for him relating to a different sport. I assumed he would take it, but because he knew little about it, he turned it down. The same happened when I offered him other articles on everything from blackjack to casino gambling. You simply can't do this. If you wait to be given work on a single subject, if you reject all other work that comes your way, you're not going to earn enough money to be a full-time freelancer. This is the twenty-first century, and we all know how to use Google, so take the job, do your research, and get paid. As far as all of your clients should be concerned, you know everything about everything and you have no weaknesses.

There are a lot of poor freelancers on these sites, a lot of unprofessional and even rude workers. Do not think that just because you're not the best writer in the world, you can't make it here. That is something I have heard from many talented writers over the years, and time and time again I've told them that while the best-rated writers are very good at what they do, the majority are useless. These are the ones you're competing against, certainly in the early days of your career, and if you can write and work better than they can, then you're halfway there.

Anyone can do what I did. I was lucky enough to have success as a published author prior to my freelancing career and I used that to my advantage, but that was not necessary to anything I did. You can make it regardless of your experience and—to a lesser extent—your ability. After all, we're all here to learn and to improve, and as long as we don't overprice our abilities, then clients won't have an issue hiring us.

The reason so many others fail, the reason so many quit, are suspended, or struggle to get jobs, is because they jump in headfirst. I was very cautious when I began and I was so wary of failing, of making the slightest mistake and suffering as a result, that I played

> **Freelancing Categories**
> There haven't been a great number of studies done on online freelancing, but the surveys that have been done suggest that between 65 percent and 85 percent of freelancers identify themselves as writers. Coders and web designers are also common, with graphic designers making up the numbers. The second largest group seems to be neither of these, though, and is composed of freelancers who work in multiple categories, such as writers/designers who also do admin work.

it very safe. Over time, I learned a lot about this industry and was able to make a lot of money, but I also made a lot of sacrifices. If you want to earn more than $100,000 in a year, if you want the acclaim and respect that goes with it, then you need to work long hours. If you are given a difficult job, you need to stick at it. If you are given a short deadline, you need to stay awake until you complete it. I once limited myself to just four hours sleep a day in order to finish a project that required 140 hours of work in a single week. What's more, in my first year I worked an average of fifteen hours a day, seven days a week. I very rarely left the house, I turned down parties, get-togethers, and holidays, all because my clients needed me. You could say that I was (and still am) a little too obsessed with money, and my family and friends would certainly say that, but you have to be. It's all about the money, about getting the most out of your time and your clients, about having enough to live on, having enough to afford a break from work, having enough to invest or to pay your taxes. Maybe I was obsessed with money, but you will be too.

Of course, after those years I pretty much burnt out and was in dire need of a break, but still, because of that work I was able to live comfortably. I had a list of contacts who would give me work when I needed it, and I am now in a better position than I have ever been.

If you are prepared to make a commitment, to make sacrifices, and to work very hard, you can make a truckload of money and you can establish the sort of contacts that all writers dream of. I have worked with literary agents, publishers, billion-dollar companies, and million-dollar entrepreneurs. I have worked with several celebrities, including ones with more than ten million followers on social media—the sort of exposure that you just can't buy. I may have burnt out, but I have a lot to show for it. And I'm not just talking about money, which is a first for me.

Thanks to my early mistakes, my cautious attitude, and my sacrifices, I can try and make life a little easier for you. This book should ensure that you avoid becoming a nobody; it should ensure that you are not suspended, that you do not receive bad feedback that will end your career before it begins, and that you will get jobs that are right for you. This book is a short cut to success, but you still need to put in the hours if you want to make big money.

Online freelancing is an exciting career, trust me on that. You get to write about everything and anything; you get to do things you've always wanted and things you thought you would never do. It's not all about the money either. You get to learn so much, to work with clients all over the world, and to befriend many of them. You get to create your own hours, work from home, and spend time with your children, your partner, or your pets—and if any or all of them annoy you, you can tell them you have an urgent deadline and retire to your home office.

There are downsides, don't get me wrong, and when you're working all the hours you can get then you might curse me for ever getting you into this industry. It will change you, it might lower your opinion of the human race, and it will certainly destroy your creativity. But it will also strip you of the self-doubt that many writers have about their work. It will help you to stop caring about what others think. Your focus will be the money, and nothing else. For a writer looking to make an easy income and to improve their writing and their chances of success, there is nothing better.

Part 1

THE BASICS

"... begin your journey as a freelance writer,
one that involves a lot of caffeine, a lot of sleepless
nights, and a lot of anger directed at clients who
only deserve it 95 percent of the time."

Chapter 1
THE PLATFORMS

Hemingway, the short-tempered master of the succinct, said that "We are all apprentices in a craft where no one ever becomes a master." This applies to freelancing as much as it does to novel writing. The environment changes too much to ever truly master it, but that's not the goal of many and it's certainly not the point of this book. I'm sure all of you will settle for being the Hemingway of freelancing, making the money, getting the respect, building a worthwhile career, and enjoying a drink or five while you work.

Before we get into the nitty-gritty of what it takes to reach those drunken heights, we'll take a look at all of the sites that we will be focusing on throughout this book—excluding the aforementioned portal of sin that is Craigslist. You should try to stick with one site in the beginning, using the methods outlined later to build a profile and to find long-term clients and big projects, but once you have established yourself, then you can branch out into others. Not all of them are worth your time, but that's just my opinion and it would still pay you to check them all out.

1.1 — FREELANCER

Freelancer like to call themselves the "biggest" freelancing website on the net. I don't know whether this is true or not, but I do know that size doesn't matter (so I'm told) and that when it comes to freelancing there are several things that are way more important.

You want a website you can trust, a website that will have your back when a client is trying to pull a fast one, and a website that processes payments quickly and easily. If those are hurdles and freelancing is a race, then Freelancer is Oscar Pistorius on the day he forgets his gym kit.

The Basics

This website just feels . . . cheap. It is poorly put together, very messy, and a pain in the ass to navigate. They're surrounded by freelance programmers and designers, so you'd think they'd ask for a little help in making their site look a little less like a high school design project, but they haven't.

The customer support is slow and they (and their system) don't make a great deal of sense, as I will explain a little later. As an example of this, you can take "tests" on Freelancer that will reward you with badges to show your efficiency in everything from grammar to creative writing and a host of other subjects. It seems like a good idea, and at the very least it gives you something to do when you're bored, but these tests aren't free. In fact, they cost 5. Not $5 or £5. They cost 5 in all currencies.

You can change the currency on your account with a simple click, and when you do this you will notice that those tests go from 5 pounds to 5 rupees. For the uninitiated, 5 rupees is about $0.08, while 5 pounds is about $8. Quite a difference.

Whether this fault still remains at the time of writing is irrelevant (for reasons that will soon become apparent, I refuse to go back to the Freelancer site in order to check). The fact is that it was there and it remained there for a long time. I did email them asking about it, but they didn't reply, maybe hoping that if they ignored me, I would go away. At least they got that right.

There are some unique features on Freelancer, including "Contests," but as with a lot of this website's features, they are heavily geared toward the client and leave the freelancer exposed. Basically, if a client needs something small like a logo, layout, design, or even a short piece of writing, he or she will post something that resembles a normal job. The difference is that instead of applying with query letters and credentials, the freelancer actually completes the job and submits it to the client with no promise of payment. The client waits until the submission period is over and then selects the best submission, paying the agreed-upon price only to the "winner."

Platform Reviews
Sites like Guru, Freelancer, and Upwork tend to accumulate bad reviews on review sites such as Site Jabber. If they were e-commerce sites, you'd run a mile and could be forgiven for doing so. However, it means nothing in this industry. The freelancers and clients who have had good experiences tend not to leave reviews, but the ones who have a beef with the site, whether because of a suspension or a bad experience, will do their best to express their discontent. These review sites are best ignored.

While great in theory, this is so flawed I am amazed it has been in use for so long. Clients have no obligation to pay you anything, and if they feel like it, they can take your submission and everyone else's. What's more, in many cases the winning amount is very small, barely enough to justify the time you spent working, and far from enough when you consider that you only have a one in thirty or one in forty chance of actually being paid.

The Cost

My first gripe with Freelancer comes at the beginning of the job. Upwork and Guru take their cut when you are paid, but Freelancer take their cut as soon as the job begins, usually from your credit card. That means that not only are you 10 percent down before you even start, but if that client then fails to pay you, it's *your* problem and it's up to *you* to claim that money back. While this might be acceptable for small jobs, what happens on the bigger ones? If you pick up a large contract for $10,000, then you're $1,000 down before you begin, which many freelancers cannot afford.

Freelancer also require a long wait before they release payments. This only applies to your first withdrawal, but having to wait fifteen days is a touch excessive. Add to this the amount of time it takes to complete the job and for the client to pay you, and it means that you could be waiting more than four weeks for your first payment, even though you already paid Freelancer 10 percent of that payment from your own pocket.

I have also spoken with many clients who have had issues with withdrawals, and I've experienced one myself. After the fifteen-day wait, I tried to transfer the money to my bank account. Following another short delay, Freelancer contacted me to say they needed to verify security information before they could proceed. They didn't need this information from me, though; they needed it from my client. I was forced to wait another week or so as they tried to contact my client, who had actually been ignoring them. If I hadn't known the client, and if he hadn't been nice enough to respond to those emails and verify that information when I personally requested it, I wouldn't have been paid. This is frustrating to say the least, but when it happens after the system has confirmed the payment, after you have released the work, after the job has been finalized, and a long time after you have paid your 10 percent, it is incredibly worrying.

I did ask them what would have happened if the client had chosen to ignore me and them, and their response was to reassure me that I "might" have been able to get my 10 percent back, with the other 90 percent presumably going back into the client's pocket.

Personal Experiences

I have another personal issue with this company. I once applied for a job that offered an hourly payment of around $30 an hour—at the time I was building up my Freelancer profile and getting used to the way it worked. The client hired me and then messaged me (an Instant Messaging system is used to work out the details of jobs) and told me that the job was actually for $0.01 for 500 words and that the hourly fee was to "be ignored." This would have worked out at around $0.04 an hour, $0.10 if I was really fast.

When I picked my jaw up off the desk, I politely refused and told him it wasn't for me after all. His words at that point were, "Come on, you might as well. I need the work done," which is as viable as it is sane. I then closed the job down.

He had changed the scope of the job, not I, yet moments later I received an email from Freelancer telling me that it was against their terms for me to reject too many jobs, and if I did it again within a set time frame, my account would be suspended. It should be noted that "too many jobs" was defined as two, because that was the first time I had done that. When I argued my case, they ignored me.

For someone who has achieved a lot of five-star ratings and made a lot of money in this industry, I do get into a lot of sticky situations. That will become apparent even before this chapter is over, but it should be a warning sign for you. I'm easy to please and I don't ask for much, and if I can have so many issues with these sites, then many others will as well. Add to this the fact that Freelancer uses a very messy layout and is heavily geared toward clients—many of which exploit freelancers—and you have a platform that I would only recommend as a last resort.

I'm not here to pick sides and I don't want personal grievances to sway you; but at the same time, it's only right that I am honest about my experiences, and none of my experiences with Freelancer were pleasant. Things might be different for you, and not everyone who has used this site shares my opinion.

1.2 — GURU

Guru holds a strange position in this market. It is one of the most recognized freelancing platforms and the one that many freelancers and nonfreelancers have heard of, yet it is actually very small in comparison to the others. There isn't a great deal of jobs here for writers, but it is a good site and I recommend it. I just wouldn't recommend that you spend all of your time there.

My partner—a woman who is infinitely more talented than I am but can never know—uses Guru and she loves it. She is a designer, not a writer, and therein lies the only problem with Guru: it is not ideal for writers. There simply aren't as many jobs on the site as there are elsewhere, and although it ticks plenty of other boxes, including a few unique features, this is a deal-breaker for full-time freelance writers. If you're a part-time freelancer, and if you work in other areas (such as design and programming), then it should be okay, but for writers it's unlikely to give you more than a handful of jobs.

The Cost

You need to pay for a premium membership if you stand a chance on the Guru platform. Fortunately, this doesn't cost much, and as it greatly reduces the amount of money they take from you at the end of a job (a fee just shy of 5 percent), it will pay for itself in the end. In fact, with this option, Guru take the smallest cut of any freelancing platform, and for full-time freelancers the savings can really mount up. For a freelancer earning $50,000 a year, the difference between Guru and Upwork/Freelancer is $2,500, a fraction of which will go to paying monthly fees.

On Guru the emphasis is always on the freelancer when it comes to paying service fees, which makes this a cheap place to be a client.

The Benefits

One of the things I like about Guru is the fact that freelancers can off-set bad feedback. There is enough advice in this book for you to avoid bad feedback, but sometimes mistakes are made and it is inevitable. There are also a lot of idiots in this world, and once you start freelancing, you'll realize that many of them operate as clients on freelancing websites (obviously, all of my clients are genuine, amazing, lovely people . . .). You won't be able to erase all of the bad feedback you get, but you can tell Guru to "ignore" some of the bad feedback if you have a lot of good feedback. Think of it as a karmic overflow. If you work tirelessly to stack up that five-star feedback and then bump into someone who gives you one star, you have enough overflow to make his comments disappear.

Guru, like Upwork, also allows freelancers to rate clients at the end of a job, which works to promote a balance and doesn't give the client any power over the freelancer. This is the case with most platforms nowadays, but it wasn't always so, with Elance (which no longer exists) being the biggest offender in the past.

Guru is very easy to navigate. It is very well designed and neat. This is a professional environment, and unlike Freelancer and their emulation of a 1990s Geocities site, Guru looks like it was designed by people you would trust with your financial and personal details, people with whom you would be happy to do business.

The Downsides

As mentioned already, the main downside is the lack of jobs for writers. I can't stress how difficult it is to get yourself established on these websites, even if you have a lot of worthwhile credentials. Clients want to work with freelancers who have good feedback and a long history of successful jobs, which leaves new freelancers in a bit of a catch-22 situation. There are, obviously, ways around this, and that's what this book is all about. However, many of the first few steps are trial and error, and when there are such a limited number of jobs to apply for, it can prolong that process.

There aren't many downsides, which in itself is a plus, but the one mentioned is a pretty big one. You could also say that Guru is quite expensive, going from the fact that you need to pay what amounts to one of the most expensive monthly fees at $40 a month for the premium service. For the most part, this is only going to be an issue for those working very few jobs and for very little money. In many ways this is a plus, as it stops a flood of cheap and cheerful freelancers from joining the site, and therefore stops those clients who expect the earth but don't want to pay for it (you will be introduced to *those* clients at some point, and they'll make you hate them, yourself, and all of humanity in the process).

Personal Experiences

I joined Guru after establishing myself on oDesk and Elance, back when those two were separate entities. But I never really got going.

As I will discuss a little later (see Chapter 4.0: The Right Price), your first job needs to be a specific type of job, which can mean rejecting 95 percent of the ones available. On Upwork that might give you five to ten jobs a day to apply for, but on Guru you'll be lucky if you find one. Finding a suitable job to apply for is just the start, and when you consider that you'll be rejected nine times out of ten in the beginning, that first step can be a long way away.

I would still suggest that you try to get established on the Guru platform, but don't invest too much of your time in it. Take it slowly, follow the instructions laid out in this book to set up your profile, apply for jobs, and start earning. While your account steadily builds on Guru, you can focus elsewhere, on the biggest and best platform of them all: Upwork.

1.3 — UPWORK

Most sites claim to be the biggest, but Upwork would probably hold that title officially. I'm not going to say that it has the best layout or features, because while I do believe that is the case, I have devoted a lot of time to this platform over the years so that could be down to familiarity. From the perspective of a freelancer, in regards to ease of use, safety, and availability, it is the best. It also has the most jobs. While many of these are simply not worth your time (with clients expecting a lot of work for very little money), there are many glittering diamonds amongst the coal.

The Cost

Upwork uses a system of "Connects," which we will discuss in more detail a little later (see Section 5.1 on page 94). You can join for free and apply for between thirty and sixty jobs a month using these Connects. However, to get the most out of the service, you should look to pay the $10 monthly fee for a premium membership. This definitely applies to those looking for full-time work and for those quoting a premium themselves, because jobs will be harder to come by and this membership will allow you to apply for many more of them.

Upwork takes a cut from all jobs. This used to be a flat 10 percent, but then they incorporated a sliding scale. At a maximum of 20 percent, they take a lot more than any other platform, but this is only for the first $500 you earn from a single client. After that you'll only pay 10 percent on your earnings up to $10,000 and 5 percent on everything above $10,000. Unlike Freelancer, who will take their cut even before you're paid, Upwork will simply snip a bit off the top when the client releases the money to you. Many clients will pay you extra, covering Upwork's fees without you asking, but this doesn't apply to all and you should never expect to be paid these fees. From a client's point of view, it is not part of the equation. They are not told, "The freelancer will get this amount." There is no two-stage billing process where they try and cheat you by taking away your 20/10/5 percent, which is what many freelancers seem to believe. If fees are mentioned and paid, great; if not, keep your mouth shut. You don't want to sound greedy, or like someone who is trying to squeeze extra money even after the terms have been agreed upon.

When you withdraw money from Upwork, you will be charged $1.99, and you can withdraw as often as you like. There are also small VAT charges, brought in after the merger of oDesk and Elance.

> **Big Ambitions**
> When Upwork was founded in mid-2015, merging Elance and oDesk into one platform, they were generating over $1 billion in revenue, and their goal was to turn this into $10 billion by 2021. The first few months were not pretty, with the site suffering constant lag, downtime, and glitches. Luckily, by the fall of 2015, these issues were smoothed out and they are well on course to meet their targets.

The Benefits

I have discussed the flaws in the Freelancer setup, flaws that make it very difficult for freelancers, and I have also mentioned how Guru has very few jobs. The beauty of Upwork is that there are no such issues.

It is not perfect—nothing is—but it is the best platform around. There are more jobs, more worthwhile clients, a better payment system, and a better messaging system. There are also Top Rated and Pro programs, which offer big bonuses for the best freelancers (**see Section 2.2 on page 30**), and the Connect system beats any other system when it comes to applying for jobs.

This is where you can make the big bucks, whether you're a writer, designer, or programmer. This is where you can get yourself a worthwhile reputation, where you can connect with some very useful and very powerful people. Don't dismiss the others just yet, but if you want to emulate my success and that of the wealthiest online freelancers, then focus your attentions on Upwork.

The Downsides

Upwork is very slow when it comes to processing payments. When a client releases money, you need to wait for up to a week before it clears in your Upwork account. From then you can withdraw it to your bank account, after which you will wait another week or so. For someone living hand to mouth, relying on this money to pay the rent and to buy food, this can be tricky. If you account for it, however, and if you always anticipate a delay, then you should be okay.

Another downside is that there are a lot of useless jobs and demanding clients. For the sake of your own sanity, they need to be avoided. You wouldn't believe the tat that goes through this site on a daily basis—the jobs that people create, the things they expect you to do. As I write this, I average about twenty job invites a week on Upwork, 90 percent of which are absolutely ridiculous. My last invite was from someone who wanted to pay me $200 to write, and I quote, "Flawless full-length novels that will become bestsellers and achieve five-star Amazon reviews."

The high fees are a downer for some, but this is fairly standard across the industry, and they get a little less extortionate as you earn more. Upwork can also be difficult to reach over the phone. When they were known as oDesk, they had a phone number on their "Contact" page that didn't work for about two years. Seriously—it was disconnected. That seems to have changed though and they do care a little more than they used to. Still, you shouldn't rely on them and you shouldn't need to contact them very often. This is not an online shop; you're here to work and most of the time you're on your own.

Personal Experiences

In a way, this is the site that made me. It is very different now to when I first joined, but the changes that have been made over the years have been mostly beneficial. In the days of Elance, there was a ranking system that I used to full effect: I moved to the very top and was listed as the "best" writer from the United Kingdom and the fourth best overall. I was also listed as the best individual writer for a period. I was even ahead of many of the highest-earning companies, although this was because I was doing the work of a company for many months.

On Elance I didn't have any major issues. I did have a few problematic clients, including the worst client I have ever had the misfortune to do business with—a man who took my politeness and my professionalism and exploited it like a high school bully. This was a man who was bitter and alone (and not without reason), who took his anger out on anyone who crossed his path—mostly me. It was very early in my career and I ignored the warning signs. It did teach me a few valuable lessons though, both about these sites and about the levels to which some people will sink.

Aside from this, I have not had any major issues with the Upwork format—although *slight* issues and frustrations due to blips on their part have been in plenty supply.

I had a bigger issue with oDesk, though, which is the platform from which Upwork directly emerged. I worked with a very friendly Nigerian man who was new to the site. He was verified, but he had no work history. It was still early in my career and I was prone to making mistakes. The first mistake was to agree to work with him when he had no profile history (the importance of which we will discuss later), but I would then be proved right in my assumptions that he was a nice, genuine man.

He wanted me to write a book for him, and knowing that I was running a risk because of his lack of work history, I asked for some of the money upfront. He paid, no problem there, but then he was suspended—and for some reason, I was taken down with him.

For two weeks I tried to get some sense out of oDesk, and for two weeks I received nothing but apologies in reply. I was working on Elance at the time so I didn't lose too much work, but all of the invites I had sent were taken away and my jobs were suspended. As it happened, I had only recently decided to spend more time on oDesk and to build my profile there, but I did have a few completed jobs and a flawless record.

After two weeks, I aired my grievances on Twitter, and immediately, along with another apology, they reinstated my account, but never gave me an explanation. They did, however, reiterate that I shouldn't work with unverified clients, perhaps suggesting that it was all my fault. Of course, they neglected to realize that while the client had no work history, he *was* verified. He had been verified weeks earlier. By them. They had given him a big tick, the green light. And in doing so they had told everyone on the platform that he was an official client and that there would be no problems. This was equal to them patting me on the back, saying, "We've got you covered," and then throwing me under a bus.

From what I could gather, they had issues with the fact that my client had a joint British and Nigerian passport, and that he was making such a big payment upfront. They never fully explained what happened to me and why I was taken down with him, and as far as they were concerned they didn't need to tell me.

Unless you class a joint Nigerian/British passport as "dodgy," which I definitely do not, there was nothing suspicious about this client.

He was a lovely man, raised and educated in the finest schools in England—a huge success back in Nigeria. But for some reason he was dismissed. He was given the chance to go back, but after that, who would bother? This was a scary experience for me, knowing they could take everything away from me even though I had done nothing wrong. It stopped me working on oDesk and it made me despise the platform. But when they merged with Elance, I had no choice but to return.

Luckily, the merge created better customer support, much more like Elance than oDesk. I have had no issues with them since and am happy to let bygones be bygones.

1.4 — FIVERR

There seem to be as many sites with the same format as Fiverr as there are sites with the same format as Upwork, Guru, etc. These work a little differently from the ones mentioned above, and while they do allow for members with more varied talents to join up and earn a living, it's equally hard to make it to the very top and the money you make on your journey is nowhere near as much.

Think of them as a marketplace, one with thousands of sellers and buyers, like eBay, only instead of flogging overpriced tat that only seems like a good idea at two o'clock in the morning after one too many glasses of wine, they sell services. Known as "gigs," these services range from voice-overs to essay writing and more. There are even women who will pretend to be your girlfriend for a day . . . so I've heard. This sounds fun, and that's the problem, because that's all it is for most people.

There *are* some people who make money from these sites, and the trick to doing this is in the "extras." Like the tempting bars of chocolate you can't help but grab as you wait in line at the super-market till, these extras are there to tempt you when you've already committed to making a purchase. A voice-over expert offering ten seconds of his time for the mandatory $5 gig might offer extras for more time, different voices, added music, different formats, etc., turning $5 into $50 before you realize it. As an example, I used this site to pay an artist to sketch a caricature of my father for his birthday. The artist was brilliant yet he offered to do a simple sketch for $5. By the time he enlarged it, added color, added extra objects, and completed it in super-quick time, I paid closer to $50. I also tipped him to the value of a couple of gigs, because the work was brilliant. This means that although he was selling himself short to begin with, working for what probably amounted to $5 an hour (of which Fiverr takes 20 percent), in the end he received $60 for less than two hours' work.

Low Numbers
While it has been reported that some sellers can earn a six-figure salary on Fiverr, the odds are against you. You need to turn yourself into a product in order to succeed, and like all successful products, it's all about finding something that takes up very little of your time, can be sold in bulk, and has a high mark-up. I have yet to find a writer who can make more on Fiverr than on less restrictive platforms.

For me this site and others like it were not made for professional writers. In the case of Fiverr though, it can be great for artists and perfect for voice-over artists. They can find a "starting point" to serve as a $5 gig, something that will interest buyers but won't take them a great deal of time to complete. They can then offer extras, which is where they will make their money. As a writer, this is not plausible. Unless you can find a surge of buyers that need fortune cookies or tweets written, then this is not a good use of your time.

On sites like People Per Hour, you can set a respectable price for your service, whatever it may be. Unfortunately, Fiverr is much more popular, and because the starting price is always $5, you can guarantee that there is always someone undercutting you somewhere. If you struggle with the other sites on this list and want something to ease you into the world of online freelancing, then by all means give Fiverr and sites like it a go; but if you're looking for a serious full-time or part-time job, and one that will put you in touch with clients at the very top of many industries, then it's not worth your time. Likewise, if you're not confident in your abilities as a writer and think what you have to offer is more in line with a "gimmick" than with professional work, then Fiverr might be a better fit.

1.5 — ELANCE/ODESK/UPWORK

If you began your freelancing career during or after 2016, then there might be a degree of confusion regarding some of the site names you've probably seen bandied about. Basically, what is now Upwork used to be two different sites, neither of which were initially called Upwork. Confused? Just think yourself lucky that you weren't a member of these sites when those changes were made, as they caused a lot of anger and frustration.

The two different sites were known as oDesk and Elance, respectively. In fact, when I first proposed this book, that's how things were. Like many freelancers, I had accounts on both oDesk and Elance, although I used Elance much more than oDesk. On oDesk, there was no such thing as "Connects." You were allowed to apply for twenty jobs a week, and that total reset at the beginning of the following week. This had its benefits, namely the fact that you didn't need to pay any sort of membership fee in order to have an active oDesk account.

However, that's where the benefits ended. The jobs on oDesk were very poor. Clients simply didn't pay a lot of money, because there was a glut of freelancers willing to work cheaply and things were setup to cater for them. It was almost unheard of to get a job for more than $20 an hour. In fact, oDesk had a three-tiered payment system. Clients could state whether they wanted Level 1, Level 2, or Level 3 freelancers to apply for their jobs. These were "Entry Level," "Intermediate," and "Expert." The problem with this is that to qualify as "Expert," they only needed to be offering more than $16 an hour, which, as you can imagine, messed up clients' perceptions and expectations.

oDesk also took a higher cut than Elance, and they took five times longer to pay you your money.

End of an Era
Founded in 1999, four years before oDesk, Elance was considered to be the superior platform by many freelancers, myself included. This is where the biggest and best jobs were, but oDesk created more volume and more revenue as a result. This is why, following the merger in 2013, the owners stuck with the oDesk platform, building upon this to create Upwork before then discarding Elance altogether.

Elance was the perfect site back then, so when the owners of Elance merged with the owners of oDesk, freelancers like myself became concerned. Initially, they promised to keep the two sites separate, but that didn't last. They turned oDesk into Upwork, changed to a "Connects" system, and then, several months later, announced that Elance would merge with Upwork before disappearing.

So we said good-bye to Elance, and while many of us hoped we would also say good-bye to oDesk, it merely changed its name. It's not all bad news though. oDesk, now Upwork, is not as bad as it once was, as it is heavily influenced by the many freelancers and clients that joined from Elance. Big jobs and respectable clients are there in numbers, although you have to wade through those offering $1 an hour in order to find them.

So now you know. There is no reason to bemoan the loss of oDesk, because what it turned into is far greater than what it ever was. But you can feel a little sorry for the loss of Elance, knowing that while things are very good as they are now, they used to be a lot better.

1.6 — MY ADVICE

Upwork is the best platform for freelance writers. This is where you should devote most of your time and effort, because building a solid profile here will reward you with endless job requests and a number of good clients who know the value of good writing.

Guru is also worth a look. In fact, to begin with, you'll find that Guru and Upwork offer you the most. These are premium sites that require monthly payments for access to the best features. This stops a flood of lower-quality workers from joining, the ones that will undercut you by a seemingly impossible sum and then produce work that is incomprehensible (proving the point that you really do get what you pay for). Many of these come from what are known as "writing farms," writers in very poor countries working for very strict bosses. The bosses get pennies for the jobs and therefore have very little left to pay the ones who actually complete them. These people need to work just like the rest of us, and I don't begrudge them for that. The issue I have is with the clients who hire them, paying them pennies and hassling them to produce high-quality work, which they know is impossible. Those clients then have skewed values, and when it comes to hiring native writers, they expect to pay an amount that makes minimum wage look like a lottery win.

This mentality thrives on Freelancer, and it used to be dominant on oDesk as well, but since merging with Elance and becoming Upwork, that is no longer the case—at least not to the extent that it once was. Generally, Upwork and Guru have fewer cheap and cheerful writers and have therefore created an environment where quality is expected, appreciated, and valued.

Upwork should be considered when it comes to outsourcing. Not because it is the best, but because it is easier to use and to find good freelancers. Try to avoid turning into one of *those* clients, though. By all means negotiate a deal, as I will discuss in the relevant chapter on outsourcing **(see Chapter 11.0: Outsourcing)**, but never expect the best when you hire the worst, don't turn into a slave driver, and always show your appreciation to those who deserve it. I've been guilty of leaving bad feedback in my time as a client, but I have encountered the worst of the worst. I can ignore the simple things, including the occasional missed deadline and even poor writing—and I have seen a lot of this—but some of the freelancers I have hired do not deserve to be called "writers." They give honest and talented freelancers a bad name. Surprisingly, these freelancers are not in short supply, and when you consider that these are your competition, that these are the guys that have been hired before you and will be hired after you, you can understand just why clients appreciate quality and professionalism so much. And we're not talking about writers working for pennies in poor, non-English-speaking countries. We're talking about British, Americans, and Australians who must have bribed or cheated their way through school, because I wouldn't have passed a nine-year-old with the level of English competence I have seen in many adult "writers."

Freelancer could also be considered when it comes to outsourcing, but this is not the right platform for freelancers just starting out. There is a lot of risk involved and no security offered from Freelancer themselves.

First things first: join Upwork. Guru and the others can wait. Once you have your Upwork account, you can move onto the next chapter and you can begin your journey as a freelance writer, one that involves a lot of caffeine, a lot of sleepless nights, and a lot of anger directed at clients who only deserve it 95 percent of the time.

Options for Jobs Outside of Freelancing Platforms

Escrow.com: This works like the escrow payments on Upwork and other platforms, and anyone can sign up. The fees are steep, but you can choose which party pays these fees and you can also split them. *Suited for bigger jobs.*

PayPal/Other Web Wallets: While accessible, you run a risk of the client initiating a chargeback and taking the money and the work. This needs to be done within a certain timeframe, so you're safe if you go beyond this. A fee is charged per transaction, but this is minimal. *Suited for smaller jobs.*

Cash/Wire Transfer: If the client lives nearby, ask for cash; but if possible, ask for a wire transfer instead. It's secure and very difficult to reverse. You may be charged a fee for this, so it is not a viable option for small-paying jobs. *Suited for medium- to high-paying jobs.*

Cheques are not safe and they are certainly not guaranteed; **credit cards** can be costly to accept and the buyer can also initiate a chargeback; **Western Union** is a possibility, but the people who insist upon this method straightaway usually have ulterior motives, and it doesn't have the best reputation either (through no fault of its own).

Platforms

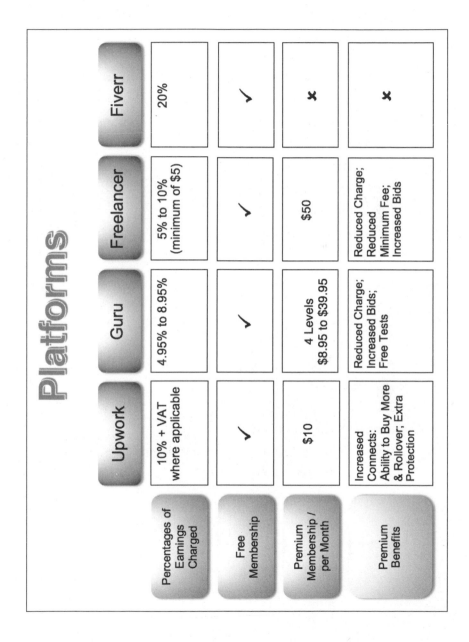

	Upwork	Guru	Freelancer	Fiverr
Percentages of Earnings Charged	10% + VAT where applicable	4.95% to 8.95%	5% to 10% (minimum of $5)	20%
Free Membership	✓	✓	✓	✓
Premium Membership / per Month	$10	4 Levels $8.95 to $39.95	$50	✗
Premium Benefits	Increased Connects; Ability to Buy More & Rollover; Extra Protection	Reduced Charge; Increased Bids; Free Tests	Reduced Charge; Reduced Minimum Fee; Increased Bids	✗

Chapter 1 Summary

- Upwork was formed from a merging of the two biggest platforms: oDesk and Elance.
- Upwork is the best site for writers.
- Freelancer should be avoided; Guru should be considered.
- Most clients will expect to pay very little and still get a lot, but there are some honest, decent clients who understand the value of good work.
- Use Upwork to outsource.
- There are a lot of poor writers and unprofessional freelancers out there, and this is your competition.
- Besides Upwork and Guru, few other platforms are worth it for freelance writers.

See Also:

- *Top Rated, Featured, and Pro (**page 30 – 2.2**)*
- *The Right Price (**Chapter 4.0**)*
- *Tips for Other Freelancers (**page 107 – 5.8**)*
- *Connects (**page 109 – 5.9**)*
- *"Offline" Clients (**page 120 – 6.5**)*
- *Outsourcing (**Chapter 11.0**)*
- *Don't Put Too Many Eggs in One Basket (**page 252 – 16.3**)*
- *Researching a Job (**page 292 – 19.1**)*

Chapter 2

SETTING UP YOUR PROFILE

When it comes to creating a profile, all freelance platforms are the same, as are the benefits a good profile can bring. You need a solid profile that looks professional, displays your skills, and attracts clients. It's not just about looking good to the clients who view your profile either. A big part of being successful is making sure that your profile is at the very top for any given subject. If someone submits a job with keywords such as "article writing," they will be shown a number of profiles that match those keywords. This applies to most platforms, and if your profile makes it there, then the number of job invites **(see Section 3.7 on page 65)** you receive will go through the roof.

Upwork is the biggest site and the main focus of this chapter. They have a Top Rated program as well as a Featured and a Pro program. To make it onto these, you need to tick a few boxes, which we'll look at soon. First, we'll cover the basics. You need to be completing jobs and receiving five-star feedback before you will even be considered for the Top Rated program, so the very first step is to create a profile that will help you get those jobs.

Demographics

According to a number of surveys conducted on online freelancing, the average freelancer:

- is female;
- is aged between twenty-five and thirty-five;

- works at least three hours a day;
- is concerned about instability more than anything else;
- has at least a high school education;
- lives in the United States, United Kingdom, or India;
- and is more interested in payment than the quality of the client, the quality of the work, or anything else.

2.1 — PROFILE CREATION

With some degree of variance, all platforms will ask you to complete a number of sections, but you don't have to complete each of them. In fact, on Elance, where I worked more than any other site and where I made it to the very top of the rankings, my profile was only 90 percent complete. This also carried over into Upwork. That's not to say that you can be lax about this; some sections are more essential than others and cannot be skipped.

Verification

If you believe the sites themselves, then the verification process is essential to getting a job and making it as an online freelancer. This is nonsense. I have never been 100 percent verified on any platform, simply because I have always written under a pen name and verification on many sites requires photo ID. Some sites will also ask for Skype calls, proving that you are the person in the picture. Again, none of this is essential and clients won't care whether your identity has been verified or not. Saying that, if the verification process requires a simple connection to your social media account, or if it's more about ensuring you have a legitimate bank account to pay for your membership and to withdraw money to, then go for it.

Profile Picture

I had a few issues with my profile picture in the beginning. I used a picture I had used as an author photo, one where my face was hidden, and it didn't stop me from getting jobs. However, two different sites asked me to change it and they both suspended my account until I did. It seems that the freelancing sites take this more seriously than clients do, although the rules differ from site to site. On Guru you can get away with a generic image; on Upwork you will need a picture of you and it needs to be professional; on Freelancer, well, who cares.

Find a picture of you that looks professional. You don't have to be smiling, but it's not going to do you any favors if you have a face like a slapped arse. It doesn't really matter if you're looking at the camera or not, but don't snap the back of your head. Use some common sense here, which is to say that no one wants to see you topless, no one wants to see a mirror selfie, and no one wants to see holiday snaps. Don't worry if you have a goofy smile or if the picture doesn't capture you at your best; this is not a dating site and it's good to show your human side (unless your human side happens to be grumpy, in which case try and smile).

Overview/Description/Summary

This is where you need to sell yourself, which is something that many struggle with. Next to writing a synopsis, this is the bane of every writer's life, but it's also one of the most important pieces of your profile. It is the first thing that a prospective client will read, and on many sites it will also be included with any proposals that you submit.

Don't go overboard. Don't tell your life story. Don't try to be "hilarious" (humor is subjective, and while you might make a few clients laugh, you'll make others think twice). Keep it simple, but be sure to get across all of what makes you a good choice for any job.

If you are a published author, mention it. If not, don't say you are an "aspiring author." You don't want clients to think you have been trying and failing to make it as an author, even if that's exactly what's been happening. They might want to hire you to write a book and they will want that book to be published; and while it is never that straightforward, if you highlight the fact that your work has been rejected by publishers time and time again, they'll think it wasn't to the standard needed. There are also many amateur writers trying to make it on these sites, writers that have some spare time after school or work and want to give writing a bash. There is nothing wrong with this, but most clients don't want to hire people like that. They want professional writers, people dedicated to what they do, people who have spent many years learning the craft. They don't always want to pay a professional rate and there are clients out there who think professional authors should be thankful for $5 an hour, but without exception a client will always hire a professional writer ahead of an aspiring one.

If you don't have the credentials needed to make this statement, there are ways around it. If you used to enjoy writing when you were twelve and you're now thirty-two, you can say that you've been writing for twenty years. You haven't been writing professionally in that time, but this is still an honest statement and from this most clients will make the assumption that you're a professional writer. Also, remember that the term "published writer" doesn't necessarily just include novelists. Be wary of too much exaggeration though, because most clients are not stupid. Think of your overview like a CV that will be read before every interview—you can polish the truth, but as soon as you start to tweak it, you could dig yourself a hole that you'll struggle to get out of.

I've always said that writing credits carry more weight than educational ones, but still, if you have a master's degree or higher in something like literature, language, or creative writing, then include it. If it's in something else, don't, but still highlight the fact that you have been in higher education for "X" amount of years attaining a degree, all in an effort to improve your skills and build for your future. If you don't tell them otherwise, then they will make the assumption that your degree is in literature or creative writing.

Education

I usually leave this part blank, simply because I don't have a long list of degrees, diplomas, and accreditations. So, don't worry if you don't have a lot to go here—if I can make it without any impressive qualifications, then so can you. If you do have plenty to go here, then be sure to only mention what is relevant and impressive. There is no harm in mentioning degrees not associated with literature or writing, but this is often the last place a client will look, so it should be succinct and not be packed with a long list of every single thing you have ever achieved.

Finished high school and college? Great, so has 95 percent of the other people fighting for the same jobs as you. You have a degree in sports sciences? This is not the place to brag. Show that you are academic, show that you are used to academic writing and that you are professional, ambitious, and learned, but don't go over the top. Creativity can often be culled by the educational system, years of rigidly sticking to strict guidelines and writing endless essays about useless topics can do that to people. Still, while such an academic career is not necessary to becoming a writer, there are those who emerge all the better for it and clients understand this as much as anyone else.

Background

Again, this is a topic that might worry some people. What if you've just finished school, what if you've been working menial jobs, what if, what if. Don't worry. I had the same issue. I had little education. After deciding to become a full-time writer at age eighteen, and living the proceeding years in near poverty, I did nothing until I eventually made it. Still, there are ways around this.

I personally highlighted my work as a self-published author, expanding that until it sounded like I hadn't just spent a year or two being incredibly lucky. This is where all of your writing credits come into play. If you have self-published, mention it. Talk about the book, the process. Mention the marketing and the sales. If the sales weren't that impressive, don't talk figures. If you have ever been published in a magazine or a website, talk about it. If it's not very impressive, be vague; if it is, be exact.

As with the Education section, do not include useless info. It's okay to mention that you volunteer for a charity in passing if it is relevant ("During my work for [xxx], a children's charity, I have compiled a number of press releases and other written material."), but if not then it just looks like you're bragging. You are here to impress with your writing skills, not your personality. There are ways that seemingly unrelated jobs can be linked positively to freelance writing, but if you can't find that link, no one needs to know.

Unless this is your very first step in trying to make it as a writer, or any other kind of freelancer, you'll probably have something to discuss here. If not, simply expand on your Overview (mentioned above). Talk about yourself; mention projects you are working on right now. For instance, I'm currently cowriting a children's book with a close friend and a freelancer designer. If I were to write about this, I would mention "I am piecing together a series of children's books, along with a talented writer and a celebrated graphic designer. This is due for completion very soon and should be published next year." You have no guarantee it will be published, or even if you will decide to self-publish it, but if that's your goal, then mention it.

If you're in this position, be very careful. I've known writers to say something along the lines of "I do not have any writing credits yet, but I am confident in my abilities and my parents/friends also tell me I'm a great writer." Perhaps understanding the problem with this approach, one writer even added that he knew his parents were not "just saying that," because they were very honest people. If you honestly have nothing to go in this section and are resorting to this sort of cringe-worthy nonsense, just leave it blank. Like everything in your profile, it can be built upon in time, when the jobs come in and your CV is expanded.

Portfolio

You need a portfolio, regardless of which site you're using. This is where you showcase your talents. Don't fill this with endless documents and text, though; your job is to tempt the client, not bore them. If you have published a book before, post the cover. In fact, if you have been involved with any stage of publication of a book, a comic book, a play, a film, or anything else, then post a cover, a movie poster, or any other graphic. Ideally, you want a few of these in your portfolio, as they serve to break up the monotonous text that you also need. This should come in the form of MS Word documents. Don't worry if you don't use Word, neither do I—your word processor should be able to convert **(see Section 6.2 on page 116)**.

Don't post entire novels. Create a new document, cherry-pick the best paragraphs from your best novels/short stories, and post them under headers that list the title and the genre. If you are using ghostwritten work, then ask for permission first and be sure to tell them that you only plan to use short excerpts. They probably won't let you post the whole thing, but prospective clients won't read this much anyway. Create different documents for different genres and styles. So, as well as a collection of paragraphs from novels, post snippets of nonfiction or ghostwritten work and post samples of product descriptions. You can post full articles, as these will come in handy later (as we'll learn soon), but be sure to post your very best work. If posting more than one article, make sure they are on completely different topics and/or in completely different styles.

Don't compromise here. Find your best work in as many genres and styles as possible. If you don't have any previous work to display, don't worry. You will be able to build as you go, completing jobs, posting snippets of them, and then replacing them when you do something better. You'll still need something to begin with, though, so post some extracts from unfinished novels, and if you don't have any, then write some from scratch. Write an article or two as well and complete some descriptions for products you use every day. This will showcase all that prospective clients need to see.

If you're a writer, don't be scared to post unpublished work you haven't copyrighted. This is a genuine concern for designers, whose work can be picked up by Google images and stolen at will. But it seems that this concern is most common in unpublished writers. Believe me, people are not trawling the Internet hoping to steal snippets from amateur writers. All novice writers go through this period early on in their careers, and while all professional writers will roll their eyes every time they hear a writer voice this concern, the truth is that we were just as paranoid at one point. Unless you have a one-in-a-billion idea that makes everyone's eyes flash with dollar signs when they see it, then you will be okay with posting sentences or paragraphs of your work.

Tests

You will find tests on most sites. These are important, but you shouldn't waste too much time on them and you should also be very selective about which ones you show on your profile. We will discuss tests in more detail later in this chapter.

2.2 — TOP RATED, FEATURED, AND PRO (UPWORK)

When oDesk and Elance announced they would merge into Upwork, the Top Rated program was one of the things they used to soften the blow for established freelancers. Luckily, I and a number of other freelancers qualified immediately, after which we were introduced to the Featured and Pro programs, which we'll also look at. First though, let's discuss what you need to be Top Rated. The following was taken directly from the Upwork site:

1. A "Job Success" score of at least 90 percent
2. Twelve-month earnings of at least $1,000
3. An account in good standing with no recent account holds
4. A 100 percent complete profile with photo (90 percent for free-lancers who brought their profiles over from Elance)

5. Up-to-date availability (if unavailable now, set a date estimate)
6. At least thirty days of work history on Upwork (not required for freelancers who brought their profiles over from Elance)

These things are very easy to achieve. Providing that you follow the advice laid out in this book, then numbers one, three, and four should not be an issue. Numbers two and six will come naturally as you work, assuming you don't sell yourself far too cheaply. In fact, never mind twelve months—you should be aiming to make $1,000 in a month when you start out; after a few months, you should look to earn that in a week. In time, when you have established yourself as a full-time freelancer who can be respected and who can deliver professional work, then you should aim for at least $2,000 a week.

As for number three, I have already mentioned that there can be issues with suspensions that happen for no reason. I experienced this with oDesk, but that was cleared up quickly and it clearly had no bearing on my Top Rated status (although there was a period of six months between my suspension and attaining that status).

As well as a badge to show everyone that you are a Top Rated freelancer, you will also see an increase in the number of invitations you get. Upwork will then provide you with a personalized contact number. This is the most important part, because in the days of oDesk there was only one contact number and it didn't work. There are also a number of other perks, with more added as the site grows.

After being a Top Rated member for a couple of months, I received an email from Upwork regarding their Featured Freelancers program. This sounded promising, but it didn't seem to lead me anywhere and in all honesty, I'm not sure if it is still active. My profile needed one small tweak with the photograph before it was ready to go. Apparently the centered headshot of my face looking directly into the camera needed to be replaced with a centered headshot of my face looking directly into the camera. I think he just wanted to give me something to do. The conversation I had regarding this wasn't completely wasted though, as I managed to get a full list of the specifications needed to become featured:

- **Photo:** This needs to be professional and friendly. It should also be a headshot—one that is centered.
- **Title:** You need a short and sweet title, one that describes who you are and what your talents are. This means that "Published Fiction Writer" would work, despite only being three words. Try to aim for less than six words.
- **Overview:** We have already discussed the perfect Overview, one that is succinct—limited to just a few paragraphs—and discusses your credentials and your skills.
- **Skills:** This is rarely flagged when it comes to being Featured, but you should still focus on including as many skills as possible. If you don't think you have many more than "writer," then type "writer" and see what comes up on the automatic search. You'll find everything from "article writer" to "content writer," and most freelancers will include both of these and everything else in between.
- **Portfolio:** If you follow the advice mentioned earlier, you should be okay here. Include images for that eye-catching effect, like book covers, comic book covers . . . that sort of thing. Include a few snippets of your very best writing, rather than full novels or short stories.
- **Links:** Upwork will ask you to link other accounts to your profile, including social media accounts. This is not essential. I have never done this and it was not mentioned to me during the Top Rated or Featured discussion. Still, if you have them and use them professionally (not advised for personal accounts), add them.
- **Employment History:** As long as you include something here, then you will be eligible for the featured program. If you were previously unemployed, there may still be something you can add. Did you self-publish anything? If so, use the name of your self-publishing company, or make one up. If you wrote articles for a website or a company, write down the name of that

company/website. Try to find some employment history that is relevant to your skills.

- **Qualifications:** Again, as long as you have something, then you might be okay, but be sure to write a description in the "optional" space, because you won't qualify for the Featured program if you don't.

I'm not really sure how relevant the Featured Freelancers program will continue to be and if it will even be active by the time this book is published. I have my suspicions that they were just trying a few things out and weren't entirely happy with this one. What I am confident of, though, is that the Upwork Pro program will continue to grow, becoming a big part of this platform.

I had to jump through even more hoops to be a member of this program, but it does seem to be worth it. Upwork Pro is basically an exclusive group of freelancers (numbering just a couple of hundred as I write) that Upwork have personally vetted. They want big brands and businesses to use their platform, and they know that they have to make life easier for them if this is going to happen.

So, the goal of Upwork Pro is to give big clients a small pool of reliable and skilled freelancers to choose from. Those freelancers still apply for jobs the usual way (there is an extra section on the "Job Search" screen for these jobs), but their proposals are first screened by Upwork. They ask a bunch of questions, set some strict requirements, and funnel the very best freelancers to the client. This is a great way to get bigger and better clients, ones who have no issue paying for good writing—but they are very selective.

I was lucky enough to be chosen, though, and this is the process I went through:

1. **First Email:** The first I heard of this program was in an email. From what I can gather, they sent these emails to a large section of the community, and I'm not sure if they focused on those with extensive and positive work histories, those who were members

of the Featured Freelancers program, or what. These emails were not personalized and they asked everyone to complete a form on the website. I believe that these forms are still there and that anyone can apply to this program using them.

2. **Form:** The form asked me for my username and other details, as well as a few words on why I believed I was a good fit for this program. It also requested some information that was already on my profile, including samples of my best work.

3. **Second Email:** I was told that I had passed the first step and was asked to send in some more samples. Which I did. I was then told that I needed to arrange a voice call with one of their recruitment specialists.

4. **Voice Call:** A few weeks later I sat down for a Skype session with a lovely American lady. She asked me a few basic questions and I did my best to impress her. This was actually where I learned about the program, because until that point I had gone with the flow and hadn't paid attention. As soon as I was being scrutinized by someone from halfway across the world, I felt it was time to start paying attention.

5. **Acceptance:** Another week or so passed before I received an email to confirm my acceptance into the program.

In my first few weeks I only saw a few jobs posted, but the clients were very big, so I could certainly understand the benefits of this program. As it happens, I had a full schedule and didn't really have any desire to apply for more jobs. The only reason I jumped through all of those hoops was because I thought that it might be important and that it might make for an interesting chapter in this book. But as Upwork grows and attracts more big clients, this could prove to be a very useful program.

It would be a waste of time to apply straight away, but if you complete a few jobs, get some good feedback, and build some strong relationships, and if you think that you have something that others do not, then by all means apply.

2.3 — TESTS

On Upwork, Freelancer, and a number of other platforms, you can complete a range of tests to show off your skills. On Upwork, these tests are free, which is how it should be. The same goes for most other sites. On Freelancer, you need to pay $5 for each one. Nothing on Freelancer is ever straightforward, though; at the time of writing, and for the last year or so, the fee is actually 5 in whatever currency you choose. I have already explained the flaw in this **(see Section 1.1 on page 3)**, and if it remains as you are reading this, then simply go to My Profile and, under Currency, change it to Indian Rupees. As you can see, 5 INR is a lot less than 5 USD. It shouldn't remain, because a few years have passed between the publication of this book and first noticing this issue, but it wouldn't surprise me.

> **Essential Upwork Tests for Writers**
> US Basic English
> UK Basic English
> English Vocabulary Test
> Content Writing
> Creative Writing Test (Fiction and/or Nonfiction)

The tests themselves are usually the same, or very similar, regardless of the freelancing platform you use. The rules are also the same.

Do not take and display tests that are irrelevant to the jobs you are applying for. If you're a writer, then no one needs to know you are also skilled in programming, design, or website building. Focus on the basics first. Take tests in grammar, punctuation, and spelling. There will be tests for both British English and US English, with Australian English tests also used on some sites. Take all of these. If you score less than 4.5 out of 5, don't display that result on your profile. Instead, keep retaking the test—you may need to wait for a few weeks—and only display the results when you have scored well.

If there are no test results on your profile, then clients will assume that you didn't take the tests. And that assumption is much better than the knowledge that you only scored 3 or 4 out of 5 in a Basic English test. The foundation of every writer should be an advanced understanding of English, and if you don't have this and the clients can see that you don't have it, then they won't hire you.

Of course, most of the time, it won't matter. A lot of clients simply don't care about these tests. Before Elance became part of Upwork, it utilized a ranking system, and scoring well in a few tests was a good way to move up the first few levels of this system. That system disappeared in the changeover and no other platform has it. There are other benefits to these tests, though. On Freelancer, you need them to apply for some jobs and to make your profile standout. On Upwork, they come in handy if you pay any attention to the communities and the skills categories (which I don't). On most sites, clients can also search by completed tests, telling the system to only invite freelancers who have attained a certain level on a certain test.

There are a few clients who give priority to them. I asked ten of my clients if they even noticed the tests, and only one of them said they regularly paid attention to them, while another admitted to doing so in the past when hiring a freelancer. Basically, they are not as important as they once were, but they are still a part of the process and you should still complete a few tests when you first sign up. The benefits may not be big or obvious, but for something that takes a few minutes of your time, it's worth it.

Additional Upwork Tests for Editors
English Spelling (UK Version)
English Spelling (US Version)
US English Grammar Test
UK English Grammar Test
Chicago Style Editing Skills
MS Word Test

Focus on the basics, take your time. These are not difficult tests and you should be able to complete them easily enough using some basic skills. However, you can also use Google, dictionaries, and other programs at the same time. You will have plenty of time. This is cheating, but it's cheating that no one will care about and the system won't pick up on. However, if you find that you need to cheat in order to attain respectable scores on basic tests, you're going to run into a lot of problems down the line.

2.4 — UNDERSTANDING THE LAYOUT (UPWORK)

To begin with, and to save confusion further down the line, you should try and familiarize yourself with the setup. Excluding Fiverr, People Per Hour, and other gig-based platforms, the majority of freelancing sites operate in the same way and with similar setups. So, even though I'll focus on Upwork, you'll still find these sections on other sites.

Upwork is constantly changing and this book will attempt to reflect that, but it's not always possible, so please refrain from swearing at me if this is a little dated. Swear at Upwork instead—they probably deserve it more.

My Stats

This section will show overall feedback score, which is the average of all job feedback scores; your responsiveness, which is how quick you are to respond to invites; and your application success, which looks at how many jobs you applied for and how many times those applications generated profile views, interviews, and hires (compared to the average). Early on, it's worth paying very close attention to your stats. Not only will clients base their opinion of you on these stats, but it's also good to know whether your applications are getting you anywhere. If you find that clients are not even glancing at your profile, then you should think about changing your proposal; if they are looking at your profile but not interviewing you, then change your profile; if they are interviewing you but not hiring you, improve your conduct in the interview.

Don't worry about the "Long-Term" client percentage early on; this will be low to begin with, but it will increase as you progress. You should also try to keep your response rate high, replying to all invitations, even if it's just to reject them outright. If you are slow or nonresponsive, this will work against you with future invites.

Availability

This is somewhat unique to Upwork and allows you to showcase your availability—in terms of hours per week, part-time, full-time, etc.—on your profile. Always keep this on at least thirty hours per week, even if you don't have that much free time. You won't be required to stick to this, and if a client asks you to work full-time to fill hours you don't have, you can just tell them that you don't want to devote so much time to a single project. It's easy to shut up shop as a freelancer—to ignore all interest and all invites when you have a full schedule—but if you do, in a month, a week, or even a day, you could finalize your last deadline and then realize you have no other jobs to turn to. Keep clients interested in you, keep the invites coming—even if you won't be available for a few weeks or months. Plan ahead, because the only thing worse than having too much work is having none at all.

Saved Jobs

Ignore this. I have no idea why it's there. It's completely useless. If you want to save a job so you can apply later, bookmark it. Clients can hire within minutes of posting the job, so really you should be applying to the jobs that interest you immediately. There is no need to "save" a completed job as a reference, as it will remain in your history anyway.

Work Diary

If you have any ongoing hourly jobs and are using the Time Tracker for these, this is where your activity will be stored. If you "accidentally" load Facebook while you're clocked in, only for the app to take a screenshot at that exact moment (it happens to the best of us), you can go here to delete that screenshot. You will notice that your activity is also tracked, but you can ignore this. Any client with a couple of brain cells to rub together will understand that this means nothing for many jobs, because it only tracks keystrokes and mouse clicks, ruling out many proofing, critiquing, and researching jobs. Your pay will not be reduced if your activity is low.

Get Paid

To withdraw your earnings, you need to click on the main header and then the subheader listed under "My Jobs." On the right-hand side you will see your current earnings, followed by a "Get Paid" link.

If those earnings have yet to clear, then nothing will show and you won't be able to withdraw. Payments are discussed in more detail later **(see Section 5.2 on page 95).**

Contracts

Your current contracts will be listed here, but this is not something you need to pay much attention to unless you lose track.

Messages

This system has changed a few times over the last couple of years, and as I write, it looks a little too much like Facebook for my liking. Clients can see when you are online and you can see when they are online. But just because it works like Facebook doesn't mean you can be casual. You still need to be professional and formal. Bear in mind that as soon as you press "Enter," you will send the message; to avoid spamming your client's email inbox with notifications, turning one message into ten, be sure to press "Shift" and "Enter" simultaneously.

If you're not a fan of this setup, simply change your notifications so that you receive an email every time you get a message, and then respond to that email. Your reply will be converted and sent through the instant messaging system, and as long as your emails are not sent with added signatures, advertisements, or anything similarly superfluous, the client won't know the difference.

Reports

Although this is one of the four main headers, it's not something you will find useful and it's certainly not something that you need. You should have committed to memory everything contained here.

Settings

You can find the Settings page by clicking on your avatar in the top right corner of the screen, and it'll also show under User Settings when you enter the payment screen. Here you will find details on your membership and your Connects; tax information (including VAT numbers and

W-8Ben forms); profile information; notification settings; and contact information. If your tax information is correct, then the only thing you need to concern yourself with in the beginning are your notifications. We'll look at self-employment taxes a little later **(see Chapter 20.0: Taxes)**, but this section has nothing to do with your personal taxes.

Mobile Site

There was never a good mobile app for oDesk or Elance, and Upwork didn't have one for a while either. This changed a year or so after the merger, and you can now download an app for your phone. I personally don't use this and don't see a need for it. I work from my laptop and I can converse with clients using my phone's email when I'm not working. If you are used to using a phone or tablet more than a desktop or laptop, and if you've only just started out and are spending more time interviewing and applying than you are working, then this may be ideal. Just try to avoid text-speak. I've had several clients and freelancers send me rushed, half-assed messages because they have been using their phone. It doesn't give the right impression.

2.5 — W-8BEN

If you are based outside of the United States, then you will need to fill-in and submit a W-8BEN form. As far as forms from the IRS go, which are often mind-numbingly tedious, this is incredibly straightforward. This form is just one or two pages, and you only really need to include your name and address and then tick a few boxes. However, you may also need to include a TIN, which will be used in place of a Social Security Number.

This is where it gets tricky, but not by a great deal, as you simply need to complete another form. You can find more details on both of the forms you need on the IRS website: www.IRS.gov.

I'm not sure just how essential these forms are, as I have never been required to submit them to Upwork or to any of the two sites that became Upwork. I also know of many non-US freelancers who have made a living on these sites and have never submitted this form. As it happens, my work as an Amazon author also required the W-8BEN form, so I already have one (along with a TIN) but they have never asked for it.

My advice would be to sign up, get started, apply for some jobs, and continue as normal. Don't worry about this, don't even think about it. When it comes time to withdraw, then go through the motions and see what happens. You'll probably find that the money gets to your account, no questions asked. If not, then you can apply for your TIN (which will be sent within a few weeks) and then print off and fill in the W-8BEN. Worst-case scenario: you have to wait up to six or seven weeks before you can make your first withdrawal. If you can't afford to take that chance and if you'll be relying on immediate payments to cover rent and bills, then sign up for a TIN as soon as possible. By the time you have won and finished your first jobs, and by the time that money has cleared in your account and Upwork have requested a completed W-8BEN, you should be ready to give it to them.

Chapter 2 Summary

- Be meticulous when creating your profile, cover every section, don't get too personal, don't brag, and only mention skills, experience, and qualifications that relate to the jobs you want to apply for.
- Keep a close eye on your stats; do all it takes to make these pristine.
- Make being a Top Rated freelancer an early goal, and work toward Upwork Pro.
- Never showcase basic test scores on your profile unless you scored top marks.

- Don't put too much emphasis on tests, but look to complete some in your free time.
- Familiarize yourself with the layout of the freelancing platform, but bear in mind that many sections are superfluous.
- Prepare to submit a W-8BEN form (and apply for a TIN) if you work on Upwork and are a non-US resident.

See Also

- *Freelancer (page 3 – 1.1)*
- *Top Rated, Featured, and Pro (page 30 – 2.2)*
- *Tests (page 35 – 2.3)*
- *Invites (page 65 – 3.7)*
- *Payment (page 95 – 5.2)*
- *Software (page 116 – 6.2)*
- *Taxes (Chapter 20.0)*

Chapter 3
APPLYING FOR JOBS

Strangely enough, this is usually the first step for many aspiring free-lancers. You can jump straight in at the deep end if you want, but if you apply for jobs without a decent profile and portfolio, then you're not going anywhere. Once you have created that perfect pro-file, taken a few tests, posted a portfolio, and gotten to grips with the site, then you should move onto this section.

I'm as impulsive as they come. I'm always rushing into things, and that's exactly what I did when I first started. As a result of this, what followed were a couple of weeks of wasted Connects, wasted time, and wasted opportunities. Only when I took a step back, slowed down, and fixed everything mentioned in the previous chapters did things begin to work out for me.

3.1 — SEARCHING FOR A JOB

There are two things that you should do for every job that you want to apply for, particularly in the beginning. The first is to ensure that the client is paid up and verified. Not all clients who don't meet these targets are out to screw you, but it's not worth the risk. For a client to be verified, they simply need to have added an active bank account, PayPal account, or credit card. This is essential because it means they will be able to pay you. If they have not, then you have no recourse if they decide to take the work you completed and not pay you for it. Clients like this can also get you suspended, as I mentioned previously when dealing with one such client on oDesk **(see Section 1.3 on page 10)**. There is a box you can check on Upwork (and other sites) that eliminates all unverified jobs from your search, which is advised early on.

I also suggest that you only work with clients who have completed a handful of jobs. I'll explain why this is important soon, but it means that if you are using Upwork, you should uncheck the search option that says "No Hires."

You can also limit your search to certain categories of jobs, from copywriting and creative writing to ebooks and more. If the skills you have are very specialized, then find the one that fits and tick the box. Most writers, and indeed most freelancers, should be able to cover all jobs under the writing category. For the sites that include translation jobs under writing, as opposed to its own category, then you might want to deselect this. There are a lot of translation jobs, and if this is not your area of expertise, they'll just get in the way.

On Upwork, there is also a search function that allows you to choose between beginner, intermediate, and expert jobs and payments. Bear in mind that intermediate, when it comes to writing, is merely $15 an hour, while expert typically qualifies as anything over $20, though some clients seem to think it means anything over $10. If you want to make it as a full-time writer and you also have the skills to do so, always check the option for expert jobs only.

Now you're ready to search.

The default search should be for the most recent jobs (listed from newest to oldest), so the further along you go, then the further back you will go. Bear in mind that while some jobs remain open for sixty days or more (depending on the site), the client will generally lose interest after five days. If they have not hired anyone by then, they won't hire anyone at all. Save yourself some time and don't apply for anything that is more than five days old. As you advance, limit this to two days, restricting yourself to clients who will look to hire quickly and get things done immediately.

If a client is still interviewing for a job that is more than a few days old, there's a good chance they'll just waste your time, spending several days or weeks discussing the project with little intention of hiring you. This might sound harsh, but trust me: if you give some clients an opening, they will strap you down and beat you senseless with their bullshit for days on end.

Don't overextend yourself to begin with. Don't try to apply for every job. Stick to those you think you will be able to complete relatively easily, those that you will enjoy. Always look at the titles and the budgets. You don't need anything else at this stage. This is all you need to find out if the client is taking the piss or not.

As an example, with some paraphrasing, this is what I came up with on a recent search:

Edit a Novel — 60,000 Words ($30 to $60)
Write a Steamy Romance eBook ($1 per 250 words)
Experienced Writers Needed. Top Pay!!! Not to Miss!! ($500 to $1000)
Ghostwriter for Memoir (Not Sure)

This was on Upwork, where "Not Sure" is relatively common in place of a fixed price budget. Now, looking at the above jobs, you'd be crazy and desperate to take the first two. Not only are they offering to pay what amounts to pennies an hour, but clients who offer so little are typically more demanding, more obnoxious, and will leave worse feedback. You might think that the third job is the best, but 99 percent of jobs with titles like that come from a handful of clients using the same or similar profiles. They sound okay, until you click the link, read the details, and discover they're paying the same, or even less, than what is offered on the second job.

Highest-Paying Writing Jobs

- **Grants & Business Plans:** Highly specialized, but pays more per word and per hour than any other job. Requires more research and experience than actual writing ability.
- **Academic Work:** Essays, dissertations, and even nonfiction typically offer big payments because the client can't allow for any mistakes. These jobs require high-quality writing and a lot of research.
- **Specialized Fiction:** Writers of horror, crime, literary fiction, and a few other genres are rare on these platforms, and good writers are even rarer. Add to this the fact that many authors work quickly and these jobs can pay up to $150 an hour.

No self-respecting client looking for a professional writer will create a title like that. It's akin to early Internet advertising—you almost expect to see it proceeding the words "Work from Home."

The fourth job is the most interesting one here. The client wants a memoir **(see Section 10.4 on page 168)**. The chances are they have never written or commissioned one before. They are probably new to the site and there is a good chance that if they receive an offer from a talented writer, they will be willing to fork out the extra cash and hire them, rather than accept one of the many cheap offers they will undoubtedly receive. Of course, there is one issue with this client. If we suppose that they are new (most jobs of this manner come from new clients), then they've had no previous jobs and left no previous feedback.

This is a big issue because this is your next step. Once you click the interesting links (I like to line them up, opening all in new tabs, before looking at them in more detail once I've finished my search), then you should check the client's history. You're not looking for the feedback that freelancers have left them; rather you're looking for the feedback that they have left freelancers. Early on in your career, bad feedback can destroy you. If I had received bad feedback from my first jobs, I would have never been able to make a career out of this.

You only want to deal with clients who leave five-star feedback on a regular basis. This applies to most clients, but there are those who never leave anything better than four stars, and even those who think three stars deserves gratitude. This is crazy, and I can only assume they are treating freelancers like books or films. "Yes, they're okay, but they're not the best ever. I mean, they're not Stephen King or Philip K. Dick, so they don't deserve the full five stars."

Of course, just because they have left five stars for others doesn't mean they will automatically do the same for you. That's not what you're expecting. You simply want a client who will leave you the best marks after you have put your heart and soul into your work and delivered the best you possibly can.

Of course, some clients have just dealt with very poor writers. I can testify to this myself. I have left bad feedback before as a client, and ironically, my client history is the sort of history that would turn me off as a freelancer. This is because I had one freelancer who actually mocked me from his first message to his last. I have no idea why, and I was nothing but polite to him. At the time I had left nothing but good feedback and this, combined with my politeness and the fact I didn't say anything negative when he produced poor work or was rude, meant that he thought I was a pushover. I also had a client who spammed me when I "dared" to tell her to rewrite something. I had asked for a review and she gave me a copy and paste of an article stolen from the net, and then had the nerve to defend it and insist on payment. She followed this with a barrage of angry messages, a one-way rant that expressed a lot of anger and suggested that she wasn't very good at taking criticism. I also had someone who I commissioned for original artwork, only for him to Google the keyword I gave him and steal the first picture he saw.

Lowest-Paying Writing Jobs

- **Spinning:** Whenever you see this word, run a mile. Spinning is an automatic and very cheap process, discussed in more detail later **(see Section 10.2 on page 164)**.
- **SEO Articles:** I have had several jobs in this category that paid very well, but the majority pay next to nothing. Always be wary of jobs that

emphasize SEO more than good writing, as they will be more interested in how many keywords you can stuff in than your writing ability. These jobs tend to go to low-rate writers whose talents lie in online marketing (on a very small scale) as opposed to writing.

- **Erotic/Romance Fiction:** Even the most popular books in these genres are not particularly well written, and there are indie e-publishers (who hire freelancers to write books for them) who take this for granted and commission very poorly written books. Clients will expect to pay no more than $0.01 per word on average for work in this genre.

These all deserved, and all got, less than five-star feedback. I am a fair man, and I have left a lot of five-star ratings before and since. I also understand how hard this job can be, so I have left a lot of five-star ratings even for those whose quality of work deserved much less. However, I cannot tolerate rude, obnoxious, insulting, and unprofessional freelancers.

Even though it was all justified, early on in your career my client profile is the sort of thing you need to avoid. I'm not a bastard, but I'm the exception, because most of the time when you see such a history, it means the client is already predisposed to leaving you bad feedback before the job begins.

So, if that is the case, then why is the memoir job mentioned above, and the other jobs like it, such a promising prospect? Well, the simple fact is that you can't write a memoir in a few days or a few weeks. The process should take you at least six months, and often up to a year. This is because you need time to gather information, to write, to let them review the work, to edit, to proof, etc. I have started three such jobs, and I have finished none of them. Memoirs are fads. They are something that people think they want for a few days, something that they pump money into, and then lose interest in a few months down the line. The first job I had like this is still ongoing. The book was good, the client was happy, and the work was all but paid for; but she had a full-time job to attend to, and as time went on, her responses became slower and slower. She needed to provide me with info to continue, and that meant spending time remembering, writing, and researching, before passing this info on. This was time she didn't have, so in the end I received several thousands of dollars for work I didn't complete on a job that has remained open for three years.

The second job was suspended after two payments, before the client even saw what I had produced. He gave me a small upfront payment, seemed excited to get started, and then changed his mind before reading a word. The third I backed out of, after discovering the client was a needlessly bitter, angry person who I didn't want to work with.

A memoir is a long-term project and one that will probably never be finalized. And even if it is, it'll be so far down the line that you'll no longer be a new freelancer treading carefully, but a full-time freelancer who couldn't care less about feedback when an offer of money is on the table.

3.2 — PROPOSAL

When I was still learning the ropes, it was not unheard of for me to send forty-plus proposals and to get nothing in return. Using the Connect system **(see Section 5.9 on page 109)** on what is now Upwork, there was a period in which I used my monthly quota and then spent another $100 on additional Connects, before eventually landing a job or two. Of course, there are some techniques to make this process easier and to ensure you don't need to use as many. As time goes on and your rating improves, it will also be easier. At my highest ranking, I didn't need to apply for jobs because invites and long-term clients saw to that. However, I did it nonetheless to see how much easier it would be: for every five proposals I sent, I received three replies expressing genuine interest.

Freelancing sites will tell you to personalize your proposals and clients often ignore you if you do not. But just how realistic is this? In the beginning, with all of those job invites to send, personalizing your responses can be a full-time job. There are ways around this though.

The first thing you need to do is to choose carefully. We discussed this in the previous chapter, but it is worth reiterating here. The second is to create a form proposal, something that can be used time and time again, and to then personalize it. Let's use the following as an example:

Dear Client,

I am an experienced freelance writer and a bestselling author of fiction and nonfiction. I can write in many styles and understand many different forms of English, specializing in US and British. I am still new to this site, but I have been writing for many years and have covered countless topics in that time.

My price is $00.xx per word, or I can work for the hourly fee quoted on my profile. I work very fast and am always available for a discussion if need be.

If you have any further questions, please don't hesitate to contact me.

Regards,

[Your Name]

When you find a job that you want to apply for, and one that passes the tests discussed in the previous chapter, you should skim-read the details, taking onboard only what is essential. Some clients like to rewrite *War and Peace*, and while this might be essential info for completing the job, it will be repeated later (trust me). You can also read it when you are being offered the job.

If the client signs off with their name, then use that when applying and when messaging them. If they do not, just leave the "Dear" bit out. I like to include "Hi" or "Hey" if they seem friendly. This, and the importance of matching a client's tone, will be discussed later in this chapter. After that, look to add a new sentence to your form proposal that is based on the job.

Do not, under any circumstances, simply rewrite the title. I have seen this a lot as a client, mostly from nonnatives speakers who perhaps don't understand the nuances of the language enough to see how wrong it is. This is why, on a job I created to ask for "Talented and Creative Freelance Writers for Ongoing Projects," I received proposals that began, "I believe I am very skilled at Talented and Creative Freelance Writers for Ongoing Projects and am the right person for the job."

If it's a travel job, mention your experience writing travel articles and provide links. If you don't have experience, focus instead on your love of travel and your writing ability. There are also niche jobs that are often very easy to get, because all it takes is a joke or a humorous story that relates to what the client is offering.

As an example, one of my first jobs was writing tea blend descriptions for a start-up company. I could see he had a passion for his product and I also happen to love tea. So, I used a standard proposal and I also mentioned my obsession with tea, including a joke and then following it up by telling him I would be happy if he paid me in tea. Don't overdo it and don't try too hard when trying to be funny. It's very tricky, very subjective, and therefore very easy to get wrong; but if it's light, inoffensive, and simple, you can't go wrong. The trick is to seem friendly and to make them smile, not to make them laugh out loud.

You still have to write from scratch, but only a paragraph, and sometimes only a sentence. If the client has taken the time to write a long description, then spend some time giving them a little more in your proposal. If they are brief, and include little detail, then simply include something like, "It sounds like an interesting job. I have written about [Job Type] before and really enjoyed it, but I need a little more information before I can give you an exact quote." It shows that you have read the proposal, and if they are interested, they will most likely send you a message with more information.

You will also find that you can use the same "personalized" proposal for more than one job. This is why it is important to search for the jobs that are of interest to you and open them all up in new tabs before applying for them all at once. If there are several travel sites needing content, send them the same proposal that mentions travel. I'm only using travel as an example—although there are many such jobs available—but the same applies to jobs that require editing and proofreading, jobs that require fiction or nonfiction ebooks, etc.

Most clients attach a lot of weight to personalized responses, because most freelancers don't send them, thinking they don't have the time. This is nonsense. If you're simply spamming job applications, then you'll get nowhere, and, like myself when I first began, you'll be spending a fortune on Connects, applying nonstop, and getting only rejection in return. In time, you will also get a feel for the jobs that are more likely to generate interest, in which case you can spend more time on writing proposals for them, while limiting the time you spend applying to other jobs.

3.3 — PRICE

It is important to stick to your guns; do not drastically lower your fee just to secure a job. By all means let the client negotiate, and work for a little less if it's still an acceptable amount of money, but never cheapen yourself. Not only will you struggle to make a living working for a basic rate, but clients who pay such small amounts also tend to be more demanding. This is counterintuitive but the simple fact is that these clients are reluctant to spend anything so when they do, no matter how small it is, they expect a lot more for it.

There is an example I can use here from my own experience. I once took on a job writing descriptions. The client seemed okay and he ticked many boxes; however, the payment was not great. Still, I was in need of work and it seemed simple enough. I worked out that each description would take me five minutes at the most, and as he was offering $2 each, that would be $40 an hour. As soon as he gave me the job, he threw a dozen parameters and restrictions at me (this will happen a lot). All of a sudden, a five-minute job turned into a thirty-minute one.

I didn't want to disappoint or to cancel the job, so I persisted. I worked all day and I gave him twenty-five descriptions. He then decided that he wanted something else done to them that he had not told me about, and he expected me to go through all of the descriptions and spend another thirty minutes on each of them. At this point I gave up. I hadn't slept and he was offering me a grand total of $50 for ten hours of work.

I politely declined, canceled the job, refused a meagre payment (he insisted on paying me $15 for my time, insisting that he did have a heart, even though you would need a microscope to see it), and walked away. I have since talked with half a dozen freelancers who work for as little as $5 an hour and they have reported that 90 percent of clients who pay so little are just as absurd and demanding. From personal experience, I can say that the majority of clients paying upward of $30 an hour are reasonable people, people who may ask you to do extra work, but will likely pay you for it.

If you ever get tempted into drastically reducing your price simply because some work is better than no work, remember that that isn't always the case. Give yourself a lower limit, the lowest amount you would be happy to work for, and never go below it. Do not give yourself a higher limit: your goal is to make as much money as possible. As you work more and gain more prestige, your price will just keep rising.

Freedom and Insecurity
Most freelancers choose this career path because of the freedom it gives them to choose their working hours. But the main worry they have, and the main reason many of them quit, is because of the instability and the lack of security. You can't have it both ways and need to understand that hard times will come, but with hard work and persistence, you'll get through.

I am often asked the exact price that freelancers should quote per word and per hour, but in truth it all depends on your experience and your abilities. It's also complicated and forever changing, which is why the entire next chapter is devoted to it **(see**

Chapter 4.0: The Right Price). I earned an average of $0.06 per word in the beginning, but I went as low as $0.04 per word. However, I can write and edit at least 2,000 words an hour, so while this worked for me, it might not work for someone who can only manage 500 words an hour.

If you are new, are not a successful or published author, and have no credentials, you will struggle to get more than $0.03 a word to begin with. As time goes by, you might be able to stretch to $0.10 a word. If you want to go higher, you'll need some credentials outside of freelancing—you need something more than what shows on your profile and your history. The only exceptions to this rule concern grant writing. If you have the experience, history, and ability, you can earn thousands for just a few thousand words, but only if you can get results.

You should also understand your own abilities. Be truthful with yourself. I have met a lot of writers who seem to think they have what it takes but struggle to write a single sentence that makes sense. I knew one such writer who tried his best to get $0.05 a word, despite only being offered less than $0.01 per word. When someone finally took the bait and agreed to pay him $0.05, the work he delivered was so poor that they canceled the job and filed a dispute. He could have made a decent part-time wage as a subpar writer earning $5 or $10 an hour, but he thought he was worth more than he was and that was the end of him.

Of course, he is one extreme, and there is another. There are very talented writers out there who don't think they have what it takes, writers who are constantly worrying about the quality of their work. These writers will work for peanuts, never believing they are worth more. If this sounds like you, if clients are commending you and if you have nothing but five-star feedback, then take things up a level.

This certainly doesn't apply to all writers. As a rule of thumb I find that the writers who claim to be the best are often overestimating their true abilities, whereas the writers who downplay their work are often worth their weight in gold.

3.4 — INTERVIEW PROCESS

I'm not here to tell you to follow me and copy everything I do and have done. It worked for me, though, so it might work for you as well. One thing I do that I am confident no other freelancer does is to give priority to new clients. Let's imagine that, all at the same time, you're working hard on a project for a client who is neither short term nor long term, you have a long-term client to respond to, and you have also just received your very first question (initiating an interview) from a new client. Who do you focus on first?

Anyone else will probably tell you that you should finish the job you're doing, connect with the long-term client, and then reply to the interview. I prefer to drop everything and answer the interview question. This is how you get new jobs, and it's how you please new clients and add them to your list of favored clients. They want to hire someone who responds to messages quickly, someone who's on the ball. If you reply a day or two later, you might miss the chance. Always give priority to new clients by answering questions and sending replies before you focus on your actual work. After all, it is this communication that will give you jobs and good feedback and will ultimately establish long-term relationships.

Regardless of which site you use, the first step in the "interview process" is to receive a message from the client regarding the job. They will never just give you the job based on your proposal and will almost always discuss it first. I can only recall two occasions in which they offered me a job straight away, and I was so wary of taking the job without a discussion that I ended up messaging them while leaving the invite open.

If they ask for a sample of your work, send them one. It doesn't matter how many samples you posted on your proposal, many clients will still ask for more at this stage. If they try to negotiate the price, then let them **(see Section 4.3 on page 81)**. Some clients will ask for a free sample, that is, something you write there and then. This is against the rules of many freelancing platforms and it also doesn't bode well for any future relationship. They can't respect you or your work very much if they are asking you to work for free to "prove yourself," especially when you have half a dozen samples already on your profile.

Instead, I like to wait for them to offer to pay me for a sample (which many clients do) and then tell them a variation of the following:

> How about this. I will write the sample for you, but you don't have to create the job or pay me. If you like it, then we can go through the motions, you can release the payment for the sample, and then we can get started on the job. If you don't, then we part ways and you don't waste your money on work you don't like or can't use.

This sounds like it's benefiting the client, but it's benefiting the freelancer just as much. If you complete a sample and they don't like it, not only will they not hire you for the job, but they'll probably leave you bad feedback as soon as they release payment. It's not worth it for the sake of a few dollars. If you're a good writer and trust in your abilities, then nine times out of ten you'll get the job. I have gone through this process dozens of times, and there have only been two occasions on which I didn't get the job. The first time was because the client insisted on a three-hour Skype phone call; the second time was because I couldn't understand what the hell he wanted. This method will not only clear things up, but it will also introduce you to the client and the job, and it will let you know what his or her personality is like, what he or she requires, and how fast/slow he or she is at responses and payments. If at any point you get suspicious and want to back out, then you can, and your profile won't suffer.

Of course, not all jobs are this simple. Clients tend to fall into several groups, and while the above does cover one of those groups, it doesn't tell you the whole story. So, let's group the clients together and discuss how to approach each of them.

3.5 — UNDERSTANDING CLIENTS

How you approach the interview process depends on the individual client. Certain methods work with certain clients, and for some clients, it's best just to turn tail and get the hell out of there. I don't want to dehumanize all clients; after all, I act as a client myself on freelancing platforms and you probably will as well **(see Chapter 11.0: Outsourcing)**. This is just a useful way of understanding different business and personality types, and at the end of this section you'll also find a table that you can return to and reference at a later date.

The Samplers

We discussed this client type in the previous section. They are the ones who will immediately ask for samples. They will not care how many URLs or documents you send them—they want you to write something there and then on a topic of their choosing. Personally, I don't understand their reasoning. I was once asked to write a sample about a job on a historic comedian, even though my portfolio displayed previous biographies, historical texts, and even comedy pieces. They are of the belief that writers can only write about specific things and they need you to prove this to them. I usually ignore them, but if they offer to pay you for these samples, then go for it, using the method discussed in the previous section. If not, ignore them.

The Ghosts

Often businessmen and almost always new members, Ghosts are clients who will look at your proposal and then immediately make you an offer. You should never jump straight into a job like that, especially when the client has had no previous jobs and has not left feedback. There are some sites that complicate this process, including Freelancer, and that's one of the reasons I do not recommend it. However, on most sites you need to confirm acceptance before the job begins. When this is the case, don't do anything. Message the client first, thank them for the offer, and then politely tell them that you need more information before you can begin. If you're unsure how to approach the subject, a rewrite of the following will do:

Dear [Client Name]

Thanks for offering me the job. I'm glad you liked my proposal and I can't wait to get started.

Just to make sure we're on the same page, though, can I ask you a few questions about the job before we begin? I don't want to keep harassing you or sending you work that is incomplete or not as required, so I like to get as much info as possible before we start. If you want, I can even complete a short sample so that you know what you're getting and can decide if I am a good fit or not.

Regards,

[Your Name]

This has happened to me on a few occasions, all of which were on Upwork. The first client never responded and I later found out she had offered a job to everyone who had applied. I was the only one to refuse, and because she never got back to anyone, they all suffered as a result (nobody wants too many "Job Canceled" marks in their history). The second was very helpful and polite and actually became my first long-term client. The third wanted something I was unable to do and couldn't make sense of. This means that of the three occasions, two of them would have resulted in canceled jobs if I had accepted.

Headhunters

You don't need to be anyone special for clients to seek you out and ask for you specifically to work on their job. This will happen if you have a niche set of skills, if you have written a book they read and enjoyed, or if you happen to have a sample on your portfolio that is exactly what they are looking for. I will explain more about job invites later in this chapter, but you can often tell if they are addressed specifically to you or not. Are you the only applicant or are there dozens? Did they address you by name? If an invite is addressed to me directly, I like to give them the time of day, even if I am refusing the job. They took the time to find me and message me after all. If you are accepting the invite, then getting the job shouldn't be difficult. They are already primed to hire you and more often than not you don't need to lower your rate in order to get the job. Be polite, thank them for inviting you to submit a proposal, show an interest in their job (regardless of how dull it sounds), and provide them with a deadline in your proposal. More often than not, the job will be yours within two replies.

The Wary

If a client is wary with you, then be wary with them. Of course, don't show this, but if they are not sure about giving you the job or paying you what you ask, then it could lead to issues down the line. Half of them have been stung by poor freelancers before, and the other half are new to the site and do not trust it. You may have to offer to work cheaply, you'll probably have to sign NDAs **(see Section 5.10 on page 111)**, and you'll certainly have to reassure them. It may take many messages and even many days, but the good thing is that when the job finishes, more often than not they turn into very happy clients. This is because they are so used to shoddy work from half-assed freelancers that when they finally get something good, they will immediately give you every job they have going. This is why you need to stick at it with this client type, because in the future they could become your biggest employers.

The Excited

These are the polar opposite of the above group. These clients are excited by your proposal and/or portfolio. They believe they have found the perfect fit and are not afraid to show their delight. These clients are generally very easy to work with and you usually don't have to negotiate much. They won't ask for samples and will usually just ask how long the work will take you to complete and how much you would charge for "XYZ." Such clients can go on to become very valuable, long-term employers.

The Indifferent

This group covers editors from large companies, people that are often very busy and don't have much time to spare. They will not ask for samples; they will simply give you instructions and ask if you can follow them. There is an easy way to win them over. Once you have those instructions, quickly write a paragraph or two based on them and then send them it. More often than not, particularly if you're a good writer, they will be impressed by your ability, your speed, and your ingenuity and will give you the job there and then. Always submit work very early with these clients. They have strict deadlines to meet and are therefore more inclined to give good feedback and even pay bonuses for work that is submitted early. On the flip side, do not nag them when they delay payment, which they will do. They need to read and review your work, and they're busy, so this can take some time. I expect to wait about a week before I chase them up with another message. I find that on average, clients that fall into this category will pay two weeks after the work has been submitted. They also tend not to turn into huge long-term clients, but they do pay a lot more than any other clients, simply because the money is usually not theirs.

The Silent Type

If you get a response to a proposal and reply immediately, but have to wait several days before they respond again, then be wary. Such clients are just time wasters. I have had clients who took days to respond and dragged the process out over several weeks before disappearing altogether. They might give you excuses and apologize for the delay, they'll probably ask for your email address, and they'll almost certainly promise that the job will begin "soon" or on "XYZ" date, but it never does. I can spot these clients a mile away now and know that when such promises are made, they will not be fulfilled. Devote as little time to them as possible in the beginning, and as soon as you have established that they definitely belong to this group, then withdraw your proposal. I had someone do this to me in 2013. He emailed me a year later to apologize and say he was ready to go. He asked for samples both times and went silent both times, only to get back in touch in 2015 and repeat the process. I stuck by him simply because I didn't believe he would do it again, not when he seemed to have a job ready, but he did. I don't think he intended to waste my time. I think the issue is that many clients don't realize that a world exists outside of theirs, that there are other jobs to apply for, other clients to please, and a shitload of bills to pay. They think it's okay to keep freelancers hanging on, to ask stupid questions, and to make empty promises that only serve to waste the freelancer's time.

The Talkers

This is the most frustrating group, but they have good intentions. This group will take your politeness and your promptness to mean that you are ready and willing to talk to them regardless of what they have to say. They will keep you talking all day if they can, and they'll ask questions about anything and everything not relating to the job. They may make promises for far-fetched projects; they may tell you that they "plan" on doing this or that. They will compliment you and express gratitude, but they will never give you a job. Usually it's because you are too expensive and they have a small budget. They want a professional writer, but can't afford them, so instead they talk their ears off. My belief is that they know they won't hire you, but feel that they are doing you a disservice by ignoring you when you are clearly a good fit. So, they talk . . . and talk. Perhaps not realizing that they are doing more harm than good, and assuming that because you are so quick to respond you have nothing else going on. Give it a few messages and if they start to change the subject and have still not hired you, then slow down your responses. If they continue for a few more days and their messages are getting vaguer and vaguer, apologize to them, tell them something came up and you no longer have the time, and then withdraw your proposal. On some sites, this will stop them from being able to contact you.

The Friends

These are my favorites. These clients will treat you as a friend from the beginning, and if you return that attitude, you can win yourself a lot of brownie points. The clients that fall into this category tend not to be strictly professional, but that's not to say that they aren't intelligent and rich. They are typically just nice people enjoying life. The ones I have encountered included two different website owners whose websites went viral, making them rich and creating a need for content and writers. Always use their name when sending a message and always sign off with yours. But be sure to slip in some friendly questions. If they mention their day and/or their business, mention yours. If they talk about their success, congratulate them and slip a few exclamation marks in there. You would be amazed at how such an attitude can help. Not only will they be more inclined to hire you for longer and better jobs, but they also will be less inclined to demand edits or give you bad feedback. When these clients become long-term clients, the work will dry up on many occasions; but there is a way you can land more projects, one that never fails to work (**see Section 16.1 on page 249**).

3.6 — UPWORK QUESTIONS

On Upwork, as well as on a cover letter, you may be asked to answer some questions before you can submit a proposal. These questions don't always make sense and rarely relate to the job. For instance, it's not uncommon to see the question "What part of this project do you think will take the most time?" even though the job itself consists of just a handful of words, such as "I need a book edited."

Client Types

	The Sampler	The Ghost	The Headhunters	The Wary
	Businessmen New members No interview Little communication	Businessmen New members No interview Little communication	To the point High paying Personal invites	Quizzical Worried Always seeking reassurance Stung in the past
Pays well	★★★☆☆	★★★★☆	★★★★★	★★★★☆
Easy to work with	★★★☆☆	★★★★☆	★★★★★	★★★☆☆
Recommended	👍	👍	👍	👍

	The Excited	The Indifferent	The Silent Type	The Talkers	The Friends
	Excitable Complimentary Informal Friendly	Large Companies No samples Rigid instructions Big pay Little communication	Nonresponsive Time wasters Occasional promises.	Talkative. Vague. Full of promises. Rarely follow through.	Friendly. Responsive. Informal.
Pays well	★★★★★	★★★★★	★★★☆☆	★★☆☆☆	★★★★★
Easy to work with	★★★★★	★★★☆☆	★★★☆☆	★★★★★	★★★★★
Recommended	👍	👍	👍	👍	👍

This is because the question comes from Upwork and not from the client—well, kinda. When they create jobs, a client will be asked if they want to include any questions, and by default a couple of these will appear, which are taken at random from the Upwork bank of questions. When you see one of these questions you need to understand that the client probably does not give a shit whether you answer it or not. Therefore, don't waste your time on them. In the case of the above, I like to write, "I would need to know more about the project before I can answer this," which also works for many other questions.

Of course, if the client has deleted those questions and asked their own—which I do myself when creating a job as a client—then you should focus all of your efforts on answering these, using only a basic cover letter. Nine times out of ten, if there are two or more questions from the client, they will pay more attention to these than to the cover letter. In most cases they will uncheck the box that says, "Require a cover letter" when creating the job.

So how do you know which questions are which? Well, over time you will see the same questions repeated and will get a good idea of when you're looking at a default question and when you're looking at a client question. The default questions at the time of writing, and ones that have been used for at least the last two years, are:

Why did you apply to this particular job?
What part of this project do you think will take the most time?
What questions do you have about the project?
Why do you think you are a good fit for this particular project?
What part of this project most appeals to you?
What questions do you have about the project?
What challenging part of this job are you most experienced in?
Have you taken any Upwork tests and done well on them that you think are relevant to this job?
What of the required job skills do you feel you are strongest at?

If the question really does not make sense in the context of the job offer, then a simple "N/A" will do. I also occasionally just use a comma, because it's the least noticeable thing you can type that will still register and allow you to submit the application.

Conversely, questions that have come directly from the client tend to look something like this:

> *Would you be prepared to complete a paid sample so we can judge your skills?*
> *What is your overall price for something that is [XYZ] pages long?*
> *Have you published any books before?*
> *Do you have any writing samples directly related to [job content]?*

Generally, if there are spelling and/or grammar mistakes, if there are words that directly relate to that specific job, or if there are links or specific requests, then you're dealing with a client question; but as I said, you will figure this out for yourself in time.

3.7 — INVITES

Most freelancing platforms allow clients to pick their own freelancers and to invite them to the job. When you see your first invitation you'll get excited, and that's understandable. Someone wants you and you alone. Except, that's not really the case. While I hate to piss on your parade, your excitement is misplaced, because it has more to do with luck than your profile, your portfolio, or your skills as a freelancer.

When you create a job on Upwork, the system will throw up some random freelancers whose profiles and experience match keywords in that job. With a click of a button the client can then invite all of them to that job. The message that they send is generic, created by Upwork, and it looks something like this:

Hello [Name]!

I'd like to personally invite you to apply to my job. Please review the job post and apply if you're available.

[Client Name]

If you get this, you can guarantee that you have not been head-hunted and that you just happened to be on that list when that job was created. There are clients who send hundreds of invites, which is thanks to another automated process. As it happens, this is a terrible way to get people to apply for your job. The questions you ask in your job post are what tells you whether the freelancer is right for the job or not, and if you invite someone to your job, then you are allowing them to bypass all of those questions.

This is not restricted to Upwork either. There are similar systems on most other sites. The problem is that while invites like this are absolutely pointless and should be ignored (95 percent of spam invites will be for low-budget jobs from low-quality clients), the ones where you actually are headhunted, where the client has taken the time to find one or more freelancers who actually fit the role, are some of the best opportunities you will get.

There is an easy way to tell which is which. The first thing you should do when you get an invite notification from Upwork is to visit the job page. Simply click on the hyperlinked title as opposed to the "Accept" or "Decline" buttons. From here you need to look down the right side of the job post, below the client's stats and where it says "Activity for this Job." Here you can see how many other "Applicants" have been sent that message and have applied to the job, and you can also see those currently being interviewed under "Interviews."

If the first number is small (even jobs created just for you may have other applicants as they are still searchable on the system), and the second number is zero, then there's a good chance that the client took the time to find you and to send you a personal invite. You will also find that clients seeking you and you alone will often delete the default message shown above and will write something a little more personal—although this doesn't always apply, so don't dismiss invites just because they use that default message.

If you have a strong background, a stand-out portfolio, or a high ranking, you will get the occasional job created just for you. More likely, you will get invites to jobs for which the client wants someone specialized; the client will then contact you and another few freelancers. Either way, the rules of applying and going through the interview process remain, albeit with a few tweaks. The first of these is that you don't need to lower your price. Even if your price is beyond their quoted budget, feel free to quote your top rate and be strict with your negotiations. If they really want you, let them know they have to pay for you, because in many cases they will do just that.

There will be no questions to answer on such jobs, and unless the client asks you specific things in the "Message from Client" section, you'll just need to send them a short message expressing your availability and your interest in discussing things further. Avoid a copy-and-pasted cover letter; they have already seen what you can do and they already want to hire you. Be succinct and reply quickly. If you show them you have read the proposal, the job could be yours.

3.8 — WHEN TO RUN

There are some clients, ones who take the piss, who do not deserve negotiations and/or discussions. The trick is to not let these clients get to you, because as infuriating as they are, it's all part of the game. As an example, I once applied to a job asking for a "Bestselling Novel." Now, I'm sure I don't need to tell you that it takes a lot to make a book a bestseller. Even the best book in the world might not make the grade. I explained this in my proposal, said I would do my best, and offered a very reasonable price. I had also achieved bestseller status on Amazon with several of my novels and had worked with other authors and indie publishers to improve their sales figures, so I had a good idea of what was needed both as the author and the publisher. It was early on in my career, so I was focused on feedback and on establishing contacts. Also, at the time, I could write a novel flat out in just four weeks, so I was happy to do it for $7,000.

Not bad for a "bestselling novel," right? Wrong. The client demanded that I write the novel for $300. He didn't have a story fleshed out—didn't even know the genre he wanted. It was all down to me, and he wasn't going to pay me a cent more than $300. If he had left it there, I would have ignored him and moved on, but what he said next stayed with me:

"You are a writer and are supposed to love writing. It has nothing to do with money. You should do it because you love to write, otherwise you're just being greedy."

He wasn't trolling, he was being serious. In the end, I ignored him and a nonnative English speaker took him up on his proposal. I don't know how that one worked out, but when I checked at a later date, he had left horrible feedback. Apparently the $300 he paid for a novel written by someone who barely spoke English was not up to scratch.

Still, at least the guy had fun writing it.

This client deserved a lot of things that he didn't get. I'm sure half of the people reading this book right now would have slapped him, and the other half would have laughed in his face. Of course, there may be a few of you who agree with him; if so, please put down this book and go somewhere the world can't see you. This is a job, pure and simple. Whether you love it or not is irrelevant. You wouldn't ask a carpenter to build you a table for $0.50 and the added enjoyment of giving away his livelihood. For the same reason, you shouldn't ask a full-time writer to ignore high-paying positions, to disregard the fact that he could have published that very novel himself and made much more, and to work for pennies on the hour for a greedy, ignorant dickhead.

Of course, I could have said all of these things to the client, and I certainly felt like doing that. But I didn't. The best thing to do is just walk away. Getting involved in an argument and being bitter about these things is not going to get you anywhere and will only waste your time. You can't alter the understanding of an idiot just like you can't change the beliefs of a racist, a sexist, or a homophobe. These people are best ignored.

You might not encounter anyone so brazen, but you will meet clients who push their luck. I have already told the story of the client from Freelancer **(see Section 1.1 on page 3)** who tried to pay me pennies an hour on the basis that "I might as well," and these two are not the only ones I have encountered. There are imbeciles as far as the eye can see on these sites, so just turn tail and run as soon as they display any signs of such shameless stupidity. If you don't, they'll waste your time, and as a freelancer, time is your most valuable commodity.

3.9 — BROADEN YOUR HORIZONS

Mark Twain said that you should always "write what you know," which certainly applies to authors; but for freelancers, we can change this to "write what you can." Never limit yourself to a genre, a topic, or anything of the sort. It doesn't matter if you know nothing about the subject at hand—that's what Google's for. If you can use a search engine, you can research; and if you can successfully research, you can write about anything.

We'll look at the research process a little later **(see Section 19.1 on page 292)**, but for now, do not dismiss something just because you know nothing about it. There are limits of course—if you only speak one language and are a technophobe, then you're probably not ideally suited for multilingual translating or HTML coding jobs. But when it comes to nontranslating writing jobs, you shouldn't be placing many limitations on yourself. In fact, if the pay is right, if the client passes the tests discussed in this book, and if you are new, then jump at the chance. A little later on you can afford to be more selective based purely on preference, but never refuse jobs just because you know nothing about the subject.

Some of my best jobs, and the ones that paid the most, were on niche subjects I knew nothing about beforehand. I've already mentioned that a client will not expect to pay for research, but you will find that the average price per word is higher for niche subjects and academic subjects. A client knows that everyone and his dog can write about celebrities, current events, and films, but that it takes a writer of a different class to pen something about interior design or pet care. These are examples, but ones taken from real-life experience, and both are very easy topics to research.

Don't go overboard. Always do the bare minimum. This applies whether you are being paid to research or not. You might not be an expert on that particular subject, but there are experts out there, and a client will be very annoyed to discover that they paid you "ABC" to research plus "XYZ" to write when they could have paid a knowledgeable writer just the "XYZ."

However, you shouldn't take on something you think will be too complicated for you to understand or something that will require too much research (there are some subjects that require very hard-to-find answers). As you advance, you will spot the potentially complicated jobs immediately; but to begin with, as soon as the client shows an interest, do a little advanced research. If the information you need for the job is easily accessed, so much so that you're already mentally writing the article just by glancing at a Wikipedia page, then go for it. If not, and if the offer doesn't cover any extensive research, then politely refuse.

Chapter 3 Summary

- Always be professional and polite when dealing with a client.
- Do not treat all clients the same. Let them reveal their personalities and then react accordingly.
- Always send complete messages and use the client's name and your own.

- Be prepared to negotiate a job before it begins.
- Never work for less than you feel you are worth.
- Remember that an invite is not necessarily a sign that the client wants you and you alone.
- If an invite does single you out, tighten your negotiation and be prepared to walk away.
- Never accept a job without discussing it with the client first.
- Offer to write a free sample, but only on your terms, and only after they have offered to pay you for it.
- Remember that all clients are different and need to be dealt with in specific ways.
- Do not persist with rude clients or clients who try to exploit you.
- Remember that you can always back out of a job without suffering any consequences.
- Never refuse a job because you know little about the subject. Use Google.

See Also:

Chapter 4

THE RIGHT PRICE

I have always loved to write and it's always been a big part of my life. But as soon as I began to freelance, it became a job just like any other. And contrary to the beliefs of the dipshit client who wanted me to write him a bestselling novel because of my love of the craft **(see Section 3.8 on page 67)**, it's all about the money. Business plays as much of a part in your freelancing career as writing does. Limitations in your ability to negotiate, to set a competitive price, and to maintain a professional demeanor will be just as destructive to your career as limitations in your abilities as a writer.

Your price is part of the proposal, but it can have more of a bearing on a client's decision than anything you say. You can write a proposal that would charm the knickers off a nun, but if the price is nowhere near their budget, they're not going to hire you. You need to treat this process like a used car salesman would treat a sale. Basically, your goal is to get that client sitting down and talking to you, because as soon as that process begins, your chance of getting the job increases tenfold.

My lowest hourly rate is high. I know this, but I also know that long-term clients are willing to pay it. The same doesn't apply to many new clients, not unless they don't realize they're paying it. For instance, $100 an hour sounds like a big price, but I can write 2,500 words in that time and clients will not flinch if I quote them a fixed price of $70 for a 1,000-word article, even though that means I'm earning an average of over $150 an hour.

If you're also quick, then always focus on a fixed price and ignore the hourly rate. Many jobs will be quoted as hourly, particularly on Upwork, so be sure to tell the client your minimum hourly rate but remind them that you can give them a better deal on a fixed-price contract. (All jobs can be converted to fixed price from hourly, and vice versa, even after they have been accepted.) This might sound a little unfair on the client, but not all writers are that quick. I'm merely exploiting an ability I have that the client does not know about and that many other writers don't have. In the end, they get what they want while thinking I'm working cheaply; I get what I want while knowing I'm not.

As an example, let's imagine that you are applying for a job that pays by the hour. The job is to write ten 1,000-word articles. That client will be receiving a number of quotes for $15 and even $10. That's always the case, no matter which site you use. In the client's estimation, it will take a writer around two to three hours to finish one article; so if they see a price of $15 an hour, you can assume they are expecting a cost of $30 to $45 for a single article.

If you are a better writer than the ones making these offers, a writer that would usually command more than $0.05 per word, then this job will easily be yours for $0.06 per word, or $60 an article. This only works if you make the switch to a fixed-price contract. Because most clients want to know the full cost of a project from the outset, they are often prepared to make this switch. If you're as fast as or faster than I am, it means that while the client thinks they are paying you about $20 an hour, you're actually earning $150 an hour. The same goes whether you're a great writer or not. If you have any extensive experience as a writer, then you'll be able to write much quicker than the average client thinks you can, and this is something you need to use to your advantage.

On some sites, Upwork included, you can get a better idea of what the client will be prepared to pay by looking at their history and the average hourly rate they have paid in the past. There are very few clients that will negotiate with you, so don't aim high expecting to be knocked down. Give them your final price, your best price. For a better understanding of what this might be, read on.

4.1 — THE RIGHT PRICE

American author and journalist Irvin Cobb said, "If writers were good businessmen, they'd have too much sense to be writers." That certainly applies if you pay attention to the statistics, where annual figures of $10,000 and even $1,000 are quoted for the average writer's earnings. But this includes a wide spectrum of writers, from those who simply haven't tried, to those who work part time, and to those who lack the skills and the sense. Cobb was also writing in a different era, and if you're a writer in the modern era, with freelance sites, blogs, and so much more at your disposal, there is no excuse for such a small salary.

All writers are different. What's easy for me might not be easy for you, and what's easy for you might not be easy for me. If you don't really have any preferences to begin with, you will develop them in time. After my first few months, I refused to take on any jobs writing press releases. I also refused academic essays. This was my choice and it was based on how difficult I thought these jobs were compared to how much money I was getting for them.

You will have a set amount, a price per word that you want to work for. This will go up and it will go down, but it won't deviate a great deal, not in the beginning. If your price is $0.05 per word, you can hope for as high as $0.07 and you might also go as low as $0.03. The price that is right for you depends on your ability. If you underestimate yourself, you'll make much less money than you should, and if you overestimate yourself, you'll be hit with a lot of bad feedback and your career will be over before it begins.

Most clients will pay you based on a word count, and in most cases this is the best way. As I said earlier, many clients will not pay me $100 an hour, yet they won't bat an eyelid if I charge them $0.07 per word, even though I'll be earning upward of $150 per hour because of that. However, what if the job requires a lot of research, formatting, or technical writing? That $150 might be reduced to just $50 or even less, at which point the hourly rate begins to look more palatable. That's where press releases and academic essays come in, because for me it is much easier and much quicker to write a simple fluff piece for a content website. Because the fixed-price payment is the same for both, I am making less money from the former than I am from the latter.

To most clients, 1,000 words is 1,000 words, but this is not the case for a freelancer. Ask me to write an article on most sports, gambling, films, games, or history, and I'll do it off the top of my head and give you 1,000 words in twenty minutes. Ask for an article with the same tone, style, and length, but on hair care or golf (there is a line I refuse to cross), and it'll take me four or five times longer and therefore earn me four or five times less.

This is why it's important to select your jobs carefully, decide which jobs are better paid per word and which jobs are better per hour. If you're a slow writer taking on jobs that need a lot of research, then aim for the hourly jobs. If you're a fast writer taking on jobs that require little research, then apply for fixed-price jobs.

Regardless of what sort of writer you are, you will notice that creative jobs pay more. This is because it's thought of as a greater skill, a *rarer* skill. This is despite the fact that most writers can write a short story or a novel as quickly as they can write an article on a favored subject—with very little pause for thought. Alternatively, something like a press release or even a blog is considered less of a skill, so even though they may take you longer to write, even though you will need to research and may even need to post the finished product, you will earn much less than you will from the creative jobs. Strange, I know, but it simply means that you need to find your own favored jobs, your own niche. That way you can increase the money you make from every hour that you spend typing.

Of course, this only really applies further down the line when you can afford the luxury of cherry-picking the best jobs and refusing offers that come you way. If you're just starting out, you need to be less selective and more willing to take on anything in your price range.

It doesn't matter how good you are, you should never price yourself at more than $0.10 per word when you first begin. I made it to the very top of Elance and even then I didn't pass this price, yet I bumped into writers who couldn't spell their own name quoting more. The difference between me and them is that I got jobs and made money—they tried, failed, and then quit. No one will hire you for that price unless you have amazing credentials to back it up.*

If you have no credentials but you believe you can compete with the best of them, then start at $0.03 per word and work your way up. If you're not sure, bring yourself down to $0.01 per word. From then on, let your feedback and your clients dictate whether you increase your price or not. I knew of a freelancer who came to me for support and was absolutely terrible in every way. Not only did he have poor grammar, punctuation, and everything else, but he was rude, short with clients, and generally obnoxious. He knew how much I was making and he decided that he was worth at least half that. In the end, he priced himself at $0.05. He got one job at that price, and the client was so appalled at what he produced, he reported him and got his money back. In the end, he went down to $0.01 per word. While it's not a lot of money, clients still expect good grammar and decent content, so he couldn't compete there either.

If you don't think you can make a profit from $0.10 a word, then you're not writing quickly enough. At the very least, you should be doing 1,000 words an hour, which is $100 an hour. And there are writers that can do ten times this.

As it happens, he wasn't cut out for this writing game, but that doesn't apply to everyone. His writing skills were terrible, a long way from basic. If your ten-year-old son was writing that poorly, you would disown him and sue his school.

Not everyone has a price. If your writing skills are not even basic, then there is no price for you because professional writing is not for you. I genuinely believe that you don't need to be a writer to make it in this game, but you do need to understand basic English. It doesn't matter if you didn't go through high school and/or university—you don't need advanced language skills or a degree in creative writing. Writing is all about improving, and providing that you have the fundamentals on which to build, and that you don't set the bar too high, then you will have plenty of room to improve and advance your career.

I knew a very talented writer who worked for just $0.01 per word. She was a long way off what was needed for $0.03 per word, but she could have easily charged twice what she was charging. She was young with plenty of room to grow into what she was doing, to move from part time to full time, but in the end her lack of professionalism beat her. She missed many deadlines and got a lot of bad feedback.

Always err on the side of caution. You should never deviate too much from the price you set yourself, but that's assuming that the price you set is a fair reflection of your ability, and so often that is not the case. Of course, if you're reading this as a novelist making millions a year and looking for a few extras zeroes, you're in the wrong place. The most you can hope to make as a writer on these sites is $150,000 a year, and it takes a lot of work to get to that level.

4.2 — PRICING CHART

Contrary to what your mother may have told you, you're not priceless and you're not unique. Everyone has a price, and while setting that price is not easy, it is essential that you get it right. If you set the price too high, even if you get a job, the client might be upset that your work didn't match the payout, causing them to leave you bad feedback as a result. They might even refuse to pay you. If you undersell yourself, you could struggle to make a living. You shouldn't have just one price, but you want the client to believe that you do. I always give my clients a set price per word, and I let them know that from there it will go down if they order more, but it will never go up. They assume they are paying the same as everyone else, and if it does go down for bulk jobs, they then assume that they are paying less than everyone else. This keeps them quiet, but the truth is that the first price I give to a client changes all the time. I lower it if I don't think I will get the job otherwise; I increase it if the job looks difficult, if the client looks problematic, or if I think I can get away with it.

There are two occasions in which you should lower your price. The first is when you have just started out and are erring on the side of caution as you find your feet and build a reputation. The second is when you are struggling to find work. If you have sent dozens of applications, received nothing in reply, and have nothing to do with your time, then lower your price (not by much) and apply for more jobs. However, never edit proposals to lower your quote and never message active clients or those who previously interviewed you to tell them you are now willing to work for less. If you do that, you'll undermine your initial quote, and it will give the impression that you don't know what you're worth or that you tried to rip off the clients initially.

Once you have found a price that matches your abilities, then you can increase it at will. The best time for doing this is when you have plenty of jobs on the go and are receiving invites for more. You can afford to be turned down, and clearly the clients want you to work for them (unless the invite was a spam invite, as discussed previously [**see Section 3.7 on page 65**]), so you have nothing to lose. Never raise it with a long-term client though, as you'll only appear greedy and will damage a relationship you have worked hard to establish.

Those situations aside, experienced clients will have certain expectations when paying a certain amount of money. To give you an idea of this, take a look at the chart below.

Pricing Chart

PPW*/Hourly	$0.01 / $10	$0.03 / $30	$0.05 / $50	$0.07 / $70	$0.11 / $110	$0.15 / $150
Ability Level	**Basic** writers. Either a very poor writer or a non-native with basic understanding.	**Decent** writers. The first step for many freelancers with talent.	**Good** writers. The first step that demands an absolute understanding of the English language, with few to no mistakes made. Make a mistake here and it will cost you.	**Very good** writers with something to show for their talents.	**Exceptional** writers, typically with a history of publishing success. Also includes journalists who have worked for the biggest media outlets.	**Elite** writers. The best of the best. Experts in their field, able to handle any subject.
Experience	No experience needed for native speakers; some experience needed for nonnatives with a poor understanding of the language.	Limited experience. Those with less talent can remain here if they have more experience.	Standard experience. This is the highest level that many un-published writers and amateur writers can hope to achieve.	Published authors. Talented writers with extensive portfolios and work history.	Limited experience will not get you anything here, even if you have the talent to back it up. An extensive portfolio is a must, a full job history is often required.	Years of experience, or a bestselling book or two. Those with the best reputations both on the freelancing platforms and away from it.
Exceptions	Jobs that require no writing skill and basic English knowledge, such as game testers and product reviewers.	**Good** writers working on bulk jobs or simple jobs.	Jobs such as technical writing may allow **decent** writers into this level if they have the experience.	Copywriters with marketing experience can earn this much money even with only **decent** writing skills.	**Very good** writers who have made it to the very top of the freelance rankings can earn this amount on certain jobs, most of which come from invites.	Grant writers. Consultants, marketing experts and other specialized jobs may also be able to generate this sort of money for **exceptional** and even **very good** writers on occasion.

If $150 an hour does not sound like a lot of money, then this probably isn't the right job for you. It's true that you can earn more than this, and I have had a few jobs in which I have earned quite a bit more. But most of that is down to the speed at which I work, and if you don't work quickly and don't qualify as an "elite writer" or as one of the "exceptions," then you'll never make this kind of money.

There are those who think they are worth $300+ an hour. But you're competing on a site where bestselling authors are willing to work for much less, and they probably have more going for them.

In my time as a client, I have had two proposals from people quoting more than $0.20 a word. Not only were both of them new to the site, but I also spotted half a dozen mistakes in their proposals alone, and their samples were atrocious. Do not aim too high, because you'll get nowhere.

As an interesting aside, one of the clients who quoted me $0.20 per word was so bad that I messaged him back, genuinely thinking that he must have made a mistake and that he really meant to offer me $0.02 per word. After all, it's only a slight difference (although he wasn't even worth that), and from someone who struggled with basic English—as he did—it was an easy mistake to make. At least, that's what I thought. His reply?

"Your right, mr Paul, it was mistake. I mean to say $0.17 a word."

4.3 — NEGOTIATING

While often essential, negotiation can be a minefield when dealing with new clients and new jobs. It's something that requires a unique approach. My favored method of negotiation is not to negotiate at all. I am very strict. That works for me, and if you do it right, I don't see why it shouldn't work for you.

As an example, early on in my career I applied for a job and spoke to a lovely woman who offered me just $10 an hour. The job was quite taxing and skill-based, so this was not an acceptable amount by any standard. My lowest price at the time was $30 an hour, and I had no intention of lowering this. I could see that she was interested in hiring me. I was by far the most qualified of the applicants and she had already expressed her interest in my profile and my history. I didn't expect her to jump up in price, but I certainly didn't want to go down to $10.

Rather than negotiating, I apologized, telling her that I couldn't work for so little. I reiterated that my lowest price was $30 (a third of what I would later charge) and that I *really* couldn't go any lower, and then I wished her the best of luck with the project. This is always essential. It shows a degree of finality while ensuring you remain professional and polite. If you leave an opening that suggests you are negotiating, that you are hoping or pushing for more money, then the majority of clients will get angry with you. Not only is this a terrible way to start a relationship (assuming they do eventually hire you), but more often than not they'll want to get the upper hand by sending you something that expresses finality. Most of the time you're dealing with business-minded people, and they always like to think they have the upper hand. If you show them that you're not negotiating, that you're just refusing outright (in a professional manner), then you become unattainable, and people of that mind-set never like to give up on something they want. This is not just the mind-set of businessmen and businesswomen either—it is one shared by many clients. The woman I negotiated with was definitely not a businesswoman, and yet when I refused the offer, apologized, and wished her well, she replied with a big increase.

Her "maximum" offer of $10 an hour soon changed to $20. Still, it wasn't enough and I basically repeated my first refusal. I then received a message that said, and I quote, "I'm not letting you go that easily. $30 it is."

This is not just about getting a good price, though; it's about ensuring the client is not annoyed with you before the job begins. This is a relationship that will rely on the client finding you professional and polite, a relationship in which the client has to actually like you. If they don't, they can destroy you, especially early on in your career. If you try to squeeze every penny out of them, if you start making demands or sounding like a used car dealer, they'll get frustrated with you. It's a perfectly natural reaction, but if they eventually accept, that frustration will remain in part and it might have a negative impact on your feedback.

If, however, you are nothing but polite—if you have wished them well, shown an interest in their project, and even left some tips and advice in your wake—when they eventually relent and hire you, they'll consider you to be a friend (or a very nice person at the least). As it happens, that's exactly what happened with the woman above. These days I actually get postcards and boxes of treats from her, and she has never stopped showing her appreciation for the help I gave her.

Of course, this was a long shot. I was very indifferent about the job to begin with, and our quotes were miles apart. All of that meant that I didn't really care whether she met my price or not. If I had been offered a job I didn't mind doing and the initial offer was within 20 percent of my quote, I would have accepted and suggest you do the same. No quarrels, no negotiation. Take the offer, do the job, make a deal for another. Don't complicate things when the margins are so low.

4.4 — NEGOTIATING BULK JOBS

Let's imagine that you submit a proposal for a job that, in vague terms, is asking for some gambling articles. You get a reply asking you if you can complete a paid sample article, which you agree to. They love your work and they pay you for another ten articles. Once those articles are finished and they ask for more, it is time to make them an offer they cannot refuse. Timing is important. Don't do it after the sample, because with only one article, they don't have enough to go on and will be unwilling to order anything in bulk.

You could take your chances, assuming that the worst thing they can do is say no. But not quite. They may be less willing to order any bulk jobs in the future and may have already perceived you as pushy or forward. On the off chance they say yes, then the apprehension they feel at not having received a full batch from you will cause them to limit their offer, to tighten the reins a little. Biding your time with an offer like this will drastically increase the amount of articles they give you.

Also, the longer you leave it, the more time you will have had to work out the client's personality and his or her likely reactions to such an offer. You should have also worked out if the client is going to be easy to work for or not and, therefore, if you actually want to give them a good price or not.

The approach needs to be carefully measured. If you completed those ten articles at $50 each, for a total of $500, and they are asking for another ten, then politely ask them if they would like any more with a message like this:

Hey [Client Name],

Thanks for your message, I'm glad you liked my work.

I would love to complete some more articles for you. I actually really enjoyed the first batch. If you want another ten, we can go with the same price as the last ten. I can also come down in price if you wanted more. Rather than doing lots of ten at a time, I can offer to do fifty for you at $40 a piece, or 100+ at $30 a piece. I don't usually do this, but I enjoy the work and I have some free time, so I don't see why not.

Best regards,

[Your Name]

How much of a discount you give them is up to you. However, bear in mind that clients who order bulk articles may need hundreds or thousands over the course of just a few months, so as soon as you start dropping your price, there is no turning back. Work in fine margins, and let them know that you can't offer much for just twenty or thirty articles but can provide more of a discount if they order in the fifties or hundreds.

Sample Discounts for Article Writing
Full Price = $50 per 1,000-word article
10 articles = $500 (no discount)
30 articles = $1,200 ($0.01 per word / 20% discount)
50 articles = $1,750 ($0.015 per word / 30% discount)
100 articles = $3,000 ($0.02 per word / 40% discount)
200 articles = $5,000 ($0.025 per word / 50% discount)

Thirty dollars might seem like a big drop, but unless you were massively underselling yourself with your initial price, then a reduction of 40 percent is not going to effect you. Having so many articles to complete in one go, and removing the need to constantly apply for more jobs and to go through the stages of getting a job, which in itself is basically unpaid work, is a godsend and one that is definitely worth the reduction.

Never offer such a big reduction for a small batch of articles and never lower your price too far. If your initial price is $50 and you then offer $15 or so, what happens when the client asks you to complete a small batch of articles? You'll want to keep on his or her good side, so you can't quote the full price again. If you did, they will have become so used to paying $15 that they won't want to pay $50 again. Many clients will always seek to pay less for more work, so when you offer deals like this, you need to make sure you are profiting as much as the client is. Otherwise it will work against you in the future.

It is natural to increase your price, charging more and more as you go on. In fact, I have recommended that you do just that in this book. However, you should never do this with a single client. I have had this done to me as a client, and I have seen other freelancers do it as well. It annoys the client, and if you have an open job, it is a surefire way to get that job closed and to get bad feedback. After all, if you have hired someone for $50 an hour for many months, and all of a sudden they tell you their price is $100 an hour, you're not going to be happy. It might seem natural to you as a freelancer, and that certainly seems to be the case with many freelancers I have encountered, but if you hire a contractor to fit a new bathroom and he quotes $50 an hour, you're not going to be very happy with him when he doubles his price halfway through.

Keep your long-term clients happy by offering them the same rate that you have always offered. Always look to lower your price when dealing with the same client, never increase it. In this business, that's how you make friends, get the best connections, and land the best jobs. And if you set an acceptable price in the beginning, then this will still be enough.

I lowered my price in the beginning as well, and yet today I still work with several long-term clients that pay me the same price. Those same clients have given me endless work, helping me out during times when the jobs have been hard to come by and constantly feeding cash into my bank account. They have also put me in touch with other clients, including one client who went on to become a long-term client himself.

If at any point I had told these clients my price had increased, they would have found someone else and I would have lost tens of thousands of dollars, not to mention huge jobs that helped to inflate my portfolio and take me to the top.

As a freelance writer you will be tasked to write content you know little about, content that is incredibly tedious. I had one job where I was essentially tasked with writing the same description more than 1,000 times, and another where I rewrote thousands of descriptions on the same product.

You can't turn these jobs down, because there are not enough of the good jobs to cover you if you do. You can, however, make them easier for yourself. Many clients are not entirely committed to the content. They *think* they want something *like* this and something *like* that. These clients are open to suggestions from writers, because in many instances those writers know more about the content than they do.

I can use another one of my own experiences as an example here. I once took on a small job for a client who needed articles written about poker and other forms of gambling, which just so happens to be a big interest of mine. I was very happy to do the work, even though I was working for my minimum rate and even though he only needed ten articles. The job took a little longer than I had anticipated, but it went fairly smoothly.

Afterward, the client came back to me with more work. He wanted one or two articles of a nature that was very difficult for me to complete. Simply put, they would have required a lot of research, turning a thirty-minute writing job into a three-hour researching and writing job. I was honest with him, telling him that the job wasn't for me and that it would be difficult to complete. I also noted how unsure he was of the job, and I suggested an alternative. He agreed to this alternative, and as well as being an easier job, it was also ten times bigger and paid ten times more.

This is a particularly poignant story for me, because that client would go on to become my biggest client and one of the ones I enjoy working with the most. He has always appreciated the fact that I am upfront, and that I am always willing to negotiate and give him a good deal. I was lucky enough to find him early on in my career, and in the two years that followed, he gave me enough work and enough money to constitute full-time employment. If in the beginning I had agreed to do a job I didn't really want to do, none of that would have happened.

Of course, these tactics don't work with everyone. There are some clients who will want to treat you like a submissive automaton. You are there to listen, to follow orders, and to deliver. You are not there to speak out of turn. But, as discussed already, you should ignore clients like this because they will only cause you trouble in the long run **(see Section 3.5 on page 57)**.

4.5 — THINGS TO LOOK OUT FOR

Time-wasting clients are best avoided, because your time is limited and it definitely isn't free. On Elance, this was a very easy thing to do, but the same doesn't apply to Upwork and other sites. To give you a better idea of what I am talking about, here are two examples from my own experiences. The first happened on Elance, where it wasn't a problem. The second happened on Upwork, where a flaw in the system allowed it to be a problem.

1. An LA-based client wanted someone to write and publish books, and because of my experience, I applied for the job and had a good feeling about it. He messaged me and expressed his interest. The truth is that he had no intention of hiring me, and as I would later discover, he just wanted to get free advice from me. He wasted a lot of my time and then hired someone else, someone much cheaper, when he realized I didn't work for free. When that freelancer messed up, gave him a book that was terrible, and gave him advice that didn't sell a single copy, he came back and continued to ask for free advice. I ignored him, but he invited me to more jobs and he continued to create more jobs, ones I might have applied for if I hadn't been able to see they had been created by him.

2. I received a message from a client who needed a batch of articles written. He showed interest and asked me for samples, but he took a week or two to reply, apologizing for his delay all the time. After six weeks, he apologized again and asked for samples again. He then said he was getting ready to hire me, but I never heard from him. I accidentally applied for another job he posted a year later and went through the same routine. He had no idea it was me, because it seems he had been doing the same to many others. I gave him the benefit of the doubt and jumped through more hoops, but he dragged me through the same bullshit and then disappeared just when he was "ready to give me the job." Two weeks later, I applied for another one of

his jobs and received a message from him immediately, asking me for samples of my work.

Whatever the motives of the client in number two, this is a huge flaw in the Upwork system, one that has crossed over from oDesk. There is no way of telling who you are dealing with when you are applying for a job, because their name doesn't show until they message you. By that time, you've already wasted a few Connects and several valuable minutes. The same happens on other freelancing sites. It's not isolated to Upwork.

The reasoning behind it is sound. In the eyes of these sites, all jobs should be treated as separate; just because a client rejected you the first few times (which might stop a freelancer from applying again) doesn't mean they will always reject you. On Elance, not only could you see more of a client and therefore get a better idea of who they were, allowing you to recognize them again, but it actually let you know if you had previously messaged them or applied to one of their jobs. In fact, it did that as soon as you clicked onto the job page.

There is currently no way around this, and it is not possible to memorize enough information about a client's visible profile in order to avoid them in the future. But you will see their names when they message you. So, if you ever run into a number two (an apt description in more ways than one), as soon as they send you that message, simply withdraw your application.

When you do this, you will be faced with an option that allows you to "Block this client from sending you future invites." This will not stop their jobs from showing and you from applying to them, but it will limit the ways in which they can annoy you. If you encounter someone who sends you an invite to every job, despite you not showing an interest in any of them (and this will happen), then be sure to check this box. I like to check it whenever I get a job offer for stupid money, thereby limiting the number of clients contacting me who think it's acceptable to pay a freelance writer less than $2 an hour.

Chapter 4 Summary

- Set your price based on your abilities; never aim too high.
- Once they know you are a good writer and a hard worker, let them know you offer bigger discounts for bulk work, and don't be afraid to tell them these offers. You are a businessperson as much as a writer.
- Give up on clients who refuse to come close to your rate; they'll only waste your time.
- Don't be afraid to make suggestions to long-term clients about content you can provide.
- Be wary of time wasters and clients who only want free information or work.

See Also:

Part 2

YOUR FIRST STEPS AS A PROFESSIONAL

". . . the moment you know you've made it as a writer is the moment you stop caring about reactions to your work."

Chapter 5

YOUR FIRST JOBS

Once you create your profile, setup a portfolio, start applying for jobs, and hustle your way through the negotiation process, the actual act of working will probably come as a relief. But keeping a client happy is one of the hardest things about this job and also one of the most stressful. There are two moments in a writer's life that trump all others in terms of stress and anxiety. The first is the moment you first put your work out there and the reviews start coming in. The second is the moment you start completing jobs for clients and worrying about whether they like your work or not, whether the past days or hours you spent working will result in a prompt payment and a good review, or whether you will be subjected to a list of demands, a negative reaction, and a refusal to pay.

I can't make you feel less anxious about those moments, but I can promise that once you settle in, once this becomes a daily occurrence, you'll simply stop caring. As far as I'm concerned, the moment you know you've made it as a writer is the moment you stop caring about reactions to your work. Eventually, whether the client likes your work or not won't matter to you; rather, what will matter is when you're going to get paid. Hopefully, this chapter can also help to ensure that the relationship you have with your client is a positive one.

Not all of this is difficult, and some of it is common sense and common decency. I could have written a book titled "How Not to

Be a Dick," which I'm sure would have improved the careers of many freelancers. There are some unbelievable attitudes out there. While your main goal may not be to be the perfect person, you should be trying to be less of a prick than everyone else.

Don't Be a Dick: Crash Course
- Never insultingly point out a client's flaws.
- A client is always right (even though they rarely are), and unless it has a hugely negative impact on your time or finances, this point remains.
- Don't be forward or friendly with a client who has not expressed a similar attitude to you.
- "You can't expect me to work for that" and "You're kidding, right?" are not acceptable responses to a weak offer.
- If you're going to miss a deadline, let them know in advance. Don't wait for them to contact you after the deadline has passed.
- Always respond to their messages immediately; apologize if you delay by more than twenty-four hours.

5.1 — SUBMITTING FINISHED WORK

There is no need to go into detail here. I'll only end up repeating half of what I've already said. Basically, when submitting your work through any platform, try to be as casual as possible. I noticed early on that clients don't always appreciate status reports, marked milestones, and job closure requests. Going through whatever system is in place is not only very formal, but on many sites—Upwork included—the clients are not used to it and often miss the notifications.

Rather than submitting the work through the proper methods, simply send them a message to tell them you have completed it, and then attach the document to that message. This is an informal approach, but it will benefit you in the long run. During your first exchanges you can also tell the client something to the effect of, "I have not marked the milestones as complete, so please do so if you're happy with the work, or let me know and I'll do it for you." You should always be prepared to make changes and should have mentioned this prior to the beginning of the job, but once you have finished, don't mention it. A simple and vague "Let me know what you think," will suffice. If you start mentioning changes, telling them that you'll be on hand to make them and will do additional work until it is perfect, then before they've even read the work they'll be thinking of how they can give you something extra to do. A lot of clients think you are there to work for them and them only, that your sole purpose in life is to make them happy. While it's okay to let them think this, it couldn't be further from the truth. Talk a good game before and even during the job, but keep it short, even vague, at the end—do not give them an opening, because they will exploit it.

Never close a job and never submit milestones officially. Leave that all to the client; they'll appreciate the control and the informality.

5.2 — PAYMENT

The issue of nonpayment is not one that really needs addressing, because it is very rare. Much more so than the majority of first-time freelancers seem to think. I was just as paranoid when I first began, believing that every client was going to rip me off until they actually paid me and finalized the job. This is a job that has, historically, lacked a certain degree of stability. Robert Benchley famously said that a freelancer is someone who is "paid per piece or per word or perhaps." Unfortunately, to some extent, especially in the case of offline freelancing **(see Section 17.2 on page 272)**, that continues to be the case.

Sites like Upwork and Guru counteract this though. There are systems in place to stop freelancers from being ripped off. While it is possible for clients to work around that, if you stay vigilant and don't do anything stupid, you should be okay. If you do have any issues and you are worried about nonpayment, refer to the relevant section in the troubleshooting chapter **(see Section 13.9 on page 209)**.

Elance had the best payment system I have ever used. As soon as the money was deposited by the client, it took five days to clear. That rarely affected you as a freelancer, and by the time the job was over, it had already cleared in the system and would be waiting for you. From there you could initiate a PayPal payment, which would take less than an hour to clear, or a bank transfer, which would take twenty-four hours.

Upwork is not as quick. You can expect to wait ten to fifteen days from the moment a client pays you until the moment that money clears in your bank account. There is a $2 charge for all withdrawals, which is not too bad, and there are two stages to each payment. The first is when you are paid and are waiting for that money to clear into your Upwork account, taking around a week; the second is when you initiate a withdrawal and wait for it to clear in your bank, which again can take up to a week.

Platforms and Their Payment Methods

Upwork: Local Funds Transfer; Wire Transfer; Skrill; PayPal; Payoneer; ACH (US only)

Guru: PayPal; Prepaid MasterCard; Wire Transfer; Direct Deposit (US Only)

Freelancer: PayPal; Skrill; Wire Transfer; Payoneer

Fiverr: PayPal; Fiverr Revenue Card; Bank Transfer (Non-US); Direct Deposit (US Only)

Guru mainly uses PayPal, and in most cases you will be paid within a few days. PayPal is also the main method on Freelancer, and for many years this was the only method for Non-Australian members (they are based in Australia), but that changed. On Freelancer, they will put a block on your first withdrawal and force you to wait fifteen days before they even begin to process it. They say this is to stop fraud, but there must be a better way; otherwise they wouldn't be the only ones with this system in place.

On Fiverr, PayPal is also the main method, and one of the few that makes sense. Fiverr take a large cut from every $5 "gig" that you sell, which means your margins are very slight to begin with. Add a minimum $3 withdrawal charge for bank transfers and a fourteen-day wait before you can even begin to make a withdrawal, and you begin to understand just why it is so difficult to make a living from this site.

Many other platforms also use PayPal, and if you have a verified PayPal account there is nothing wrong with this. Always be aware of payment processing times, though; if you're relying on this money to pay your bills, you need to know when you will have access to it. In many cases your location and your payment method will dictate how fast things go, so take everything I have mentioned regarding dates with a pinch of salt.

5.3 — WAITING FOR FEEDBACK

The feedback system needs to be discussed in more detail, which is why the next chapter is devoted to it. Your first taste of this will be when you have submitted the work and received payment. This is a big part of your career, so you're entitled to shit your pants a little. Whatever you do, don't push the client to leave you feedback unless you have worked with them for a long time and know for a fact they will leave good feedback. If a client is abstaining from leaving you feedback, it might be because they don't feel they can leave you anything positive and, in their eyes, saying nothing at all is better than saying something horrible.

It's not the end of the world if they don't leave you feedback, and while it can be frustrating early on in your career, your need to ignore it and move on. Eventually people will leave feedback.

On both Guru and Upwork you can leave the client feedback, but unless you have genuinely had the worst experience, then don't leave anything but positive feedback. When a client looks at your history, they won't just look at the feedback that other clients have left you— they will also look at the feedback you left those clients. Always be the bigger person, always focus on the positives of a job. No client wants to read unprofessional remarks from a freelancer who has received bad feedback. They don't want to see you attacking the client, calling them a liar, or—in the case of so many freelancers—saying, "As you can see from my profile, I have had nothing but five-star feedback. No one else has had an issue with me, so this client must be lying." I see this a lot. As a freelancer it's amusing; as a client it's worthy of an eye-roll or two. Who cares about the rest of your profile? Just because you were a good boy six days of the week doesn't mean you weren't a dickhead on Saturday night. Past positives do not discount bad feedback, nothing does. So, if you do get bad feedback, respond by apologizing, saying you did your best, and focusing on the positives.

It will kill you inside to do that. I know that from personal experience. I had an encounter with a minion from the bowels of hell, a man to whom lies, manipulation, and even blackmail were second nature. But I knew that in the long run a simple apology and some home truths would work better than a scathing reply.

5.4 — TIME TRACKERS

Unsurprisingly, the platforms and the clients don't trust you enough to let you submit your own time sheets. On all sites that offer hourly setups, you will find a time-tracking app. This is known simply as the Time Tracker on Upwork, and it goes by different names elsewhere. You should install this early on just to make sure it works, as I have had issues getting some of these apps to work.

They are not essential to all jobs and they are certainly not essential to your success as a freelancer, so don't worry if they don't work. Most of the jobs I do, and most of the jobs many other freelancers do, are fixed price. On the occasions where the client has asked me to work on an hourly basis, I have simply informed them that I can give them a more exact quote if they work on a fixed-price contract. This is incredibly important to all clients, because they want to know how much a job will cost before it begins, so this is usually enough to convince them to switch.

Despite completing jobs for more than 100 clients, many of which I worked with on dozens of jobs, I have only used the tracker half a dozen times and for fewer than half a dozen clients. When Elance began to switch over to Upwork, the tracker stopped working, but I simply informed the client and they were understanding. In such cases, the hours can be added as "Offline" or "Manual" hours. Basically, you tell the system how long you worked and they bill the client for it. On Upwork the client needs to agree to this option before you can do anything. If they do not, they are not liable to pay you anything, no matter how many hours you clock. They can also set a weekly limit, so you should always be aware of this before you do any work.

The apps are easy to use, although the Upwork one has gotten a little too complicated for my liking. They have introduced a live chat facility that shows all clients when you are online and lets them speak to you. I avoid using Skype so that people don't pester me all day, and I stay clear of Facebook for the same reason. The last thing I want is people pissing me off when I'm busy. Luckily, there is an option to go "offline," although you can't really do this with the client who you are working for, as they will see the work you do and will know when you did it.

The app will take screenshots as well as monitoring the time you spend working. Some apps will also monitor your clicks and your keystrokes. This is great in theory, as it tells the client whether you have been working or whether you have just been flicking through Facebook in-between screenshots. In practice it is not so good though. Some jobs simply don't require a lot of typing or clicks, and in such cases the system will essentially inform the client that you have been twiddling your thumbs all day.

If you do decide to work an hourly job (bear in mind that you can probably earn a lot more money by going with the fixed-price option, as discussed in **Chapter 4.0: The Right Price**), make sure you are working with an experienced client, someone who has worked many similar jobs in the past. Otherwise you'll find yourself trying to explain your actions, and why there were no constant clicks or keystrokes, even if you were only tasked with reading and reviewing a book. Believe it or not, those people do exist, and they will find you.

5.5 — WHAT NOT TO DO

To be honest, I didn't think this section would be needed. When I began work as a freelancer, I didn't think I was doing anything special. I was working hard, being professional and friendly, and using common sense where needed. I had no idea why clients valued me so highly when there were hundreds of thousands of writers out there who were surely doing the same thing.

Then I created a client account and began to hire people myself, at which point I realized that for a lot of freelancers, common sense is a luxury that they just can't afford. Of course, a lot of what it takes to make it as a freelancer is not just common sense—this book wouldn't exist if that were true—but you can go a long way with a little sense on your side. And if you let it slip, you can end your career before it begins.

Below is a list of things you should always refrain from doing. Some of these will seem obvious and you might question my reasoning for including them, but the truth is that every fuck-up on this list has been committed by more than one freelancer I have either hired, worked with, helped, or spoken to. These are the ten commandments of fuckery, and in this religion there is no forgiveness and no second chances if you break any of them. Most of these rules concern waiting for feedback, because what you should actually do is wait patiently and cross your fingers. Still, just so I can be clear:

Do NOT

- **Retaliate:** If a client is a dick in response to a message or a proposal, do not respond in kind. Be the bigger person. Ignore them and withdraw from the job so they can't contact you again.
- **Use Text Talk:** In a professional environment such as this, there is no call for "thx 4 the job, I wont let u down." On the plus side, the three seconds you saved by writing like an imbecile will come in handy when they cancel the job and you're forced to look for a new one.
- **Be Pushy:** If a long-term client promises a job they don't deliver, message them and inquire. Do not send repeat messages, and do not persist like this with a client you have only just met, because they were either using it as an excuse or have changed their minds.

- **Nag:** Do not persist if a client is delaying a payment. One message is okay after a few days, but sending the same message every twelve hours is only going to frustrate the client and increase your chances of getting bad feedback. These are professional people with shit to do—they'll pay you eventually.
- **Be Weird:** I once dealt with a female client in Italy who seemed to think she could use the fact that she was young and attractive to offset work that looked like it had been written by my cat. She even volunteered to deliver it in person, despite the thousand miles between us. Don't be too forward, don't be clingy . . . basically just don't be weird.
- **Blindly Outsource:** While outsourcing is okay, I would not recommend it unless the client knows about it (this is up to you though), and even then, you need to outsource to someone who you know is competent and capable. There are many unprofessional writers out there, and if you call on one at short notice and rely on them, you might live to regret it. Build a team in advance and understand their schedule and ability. More on this in **Chapter 11.0: Outsourcing**.
- **Delay a Response:** Always prioritize responses to potential clients; otherwise they'll never become actual clients. Do not hang up on a client if you're talking to them, but if you're doing a job and a potential client messages you, then pause and respond. They are usually so impressed by quick responses that they'll put you first on their shortlist.
- **Act Like You Know More:** I once paid someone to write a personal "review" of an affiliate site, and he gave me an article full of quotes. When I quizzed him on it, his response was, "Well, I never used the product, but these people did." He then changed the subject and out of context claimed to be the most experienced freelancer on the site, all in an effort to show he knew my work better than I did, because I was just a humble client who didn't know what he wanted and certainly knew nothing about freelancing. He had no

common sense, no talent, and no redeeming qualities. Even if you tick these boxes, you should never belittle a client and go into a highly strung defensive mode when they critique your work.

- **Ask to Use PayPal Instead:** Many freelancers don't like the idea that these platforms take a share of the money. Personally, I don't care, and nor should you. They provide a service, they connect you to the client, and they ensure all transactions are safe and fair. However, you could work for someone through PayPal only for them to refuse to pay you. Then what do you do? Even if they do pay you, they can do a chargeback at a later date and you won't have a leg to stand on. Security aside, most sites will also ban you if they catch you soliciting clients to work outside of their system. **(see Section 9.1 on page 150).**
- **Use Excuses:** If you fuck up, be honest. Apologize sincerely, and for the love of God, do not give an excuse, no matter how original you think it is. Clients have heard them all before, and even if you're telling the truth, they won't believe you.

5.6 — EXCUSES

In the beginning, as a client on Elance and oDesk, I hired a number of writers who missed deadlines and then blamed a wedding, either their own or a friend's. At the same time, I also heard this excuse from an eBay retailer who was two months late with an order. Weddings are not the sort of thing to take you by surprise, so I have no idea why they thought this was a valid or believable excuse. Maybe they thought I would be so happy for them that I couldn't possibly call them out on their nonsense. Maybe they were all going to the same wedding, an impromptu event that was arranged at the last minute and had to happen there and then. Either way, for those two months I was one pissed off Cupid, because everyone around me was arranging surprise weddings and none of the work I paid for was getting done.

Terrible Excuses Clients Hear Too Much

These are so common it is ridiculous, and I've heard them all myself more than once. None of these explain why you can't message the client for days or weeks, why you can't forewarn the client, or why you can't access another computer/device or another connection for a prolonged period.

- "My wife/child/mother had an accident and I couldn't get online for a week."
- "My Wi-Fi was down."
- "My computer was stolen."
- "My sister/brother/self recently got married."
- "I was in a car crash/accident, and the doctors wouldn't let me use the Internet."

There are few things that annoy me more as a client than a freelancer who reels off the excuses like one-liners from a shit comedian. I have heard them all, from "my dog died" to "I had to rush my mother to hospital." The problem is, these excuses are designed to play on your empathy, and because I'm not a complete bastard (just a partial one), I couldn't call them on their nonsense. I had to accept it. In that sense, the excuse worked, but I thought significantly less of every freelancer who sent me one. On many occasions, I found out they were lying and stopped being so empathetic.

Of the thirty-plus excuses I have heard, I am confident that none were honest. Not only were all of them dramatic, but many of the freelancers went on to give more and more. I had one repeat offender tell me that his mother was seriously ill, which made sense, considering she was supposed to have died six weeks earlier. Another killed off so many of his pets that I contemplated phoning the RSPCA, and another had a habit of landing himself in hospital, where he had access to the Internet, but on advice from his doctor was not allowed to do anything but email people.

Any client who has hired more than five freelancers will be sick of excuses, because you can guarantee they will have heard at least four of them. If you have a genuine excuse, then don't tell them. Apologize and say something a little more believable and simple.

Don't tell them your computer was hacked or stolen, don't tell them someone close to you died or fell ill. Tell them things got on top of you, that you kept rewriting the same passages because you weren't happy with what you produced and you wanted it to be perfect.

The one thing that bugs a client more than an excuse is an excuse that only comes after the deadline when the client chases the freelancer down. This has happened to me many times, and I have no idea why freelancers do it. It's as if they think things will just blow over or disappear or they can hide their head in the sand, and when they pull it out, everything will be fine. It won't be, trust me. If you're going to be late, tell the client in advance. Failure to do so will not only piss them off, but it may cost them money or their reputation, and that will be bad news for you.

You should also give something a little extra to make up for it, or offer a discount. After all, you're here to build a reputation. Telling a client that your dog died will not pull their heart strings— most will assume you're lying, and because they think you're lying, they'll also think you're horrible. After all, what kind of monster lies about stuff like that? On the other hand, an offer of a slight refund, or a little extra effort on your part, will quell their anger and get you back on track.

There are other ways around this problem as well, as discussed a little later **(see Section 16.6 on page 258)**.

5.7 — COMMUNICATING METHODS

I like to keep all communication on the freelance platform. This means no Skype, no emails, and certainly no phone calls. I have had issues with clients/stalkers who have gotten my number through an Upwork invoice, which means I didn't give them my number and certainly didn't give them permission to phone me. This led to them ringing me several times in the middle of the night and leaving me a bunny-boiling string of messages, purely because they wanted me to give them some advice about HTML, which I know precisely jackshit about. I have also had issues with clients wasting my time on

Skype, insisting on drawn-out conversations that eventually lead to small jobs or no jobs.

You will lose some jobs if you refuse to communicate through Skype. I know because I have lost a couple of jobs this way. Still, in the grand scheme of things, it will save you so much time. For every job that passes you by because you refused to go on Skype, you're saving yourself twenty or more hours of interviews, conversations, and even "friendly" chats that go nowhere and earn you nothing.

Be polite about it. Tell the client that you don't have Skype because being a freelancer means you follow an erratic schedule and can never make promises to be available at certain times. Tell them that you are still available through messages if they want to contact you. If a client asks for your email address, give it to them. They will ask for this to send you attachments or even just to make conversing easier. It's not easier of course, but if they think it is, then who's to argue? Give them your email, talk to them, and be sure to bring any jobs you agree upon back to the freelancing site.

There are exceptions to the rules mentioned above, as there always are. If you are talking with a major company who is looking for a long-term employee, then you will need to go through the phone or through Skype. That's how these things are handled for businesses like that, and I did the same thing with a writing college who wanted to hire me as a tutor. In those situations, you are dealing with a professional who genuinely wants to hire you, someone who will ask a few questions quickly, talk some details over with you, and then get back to their busy day. You are not dealing with someone who will talk your ear off, waste your time, and then do the same to another dozen freelancers before hiring no one.

Primary Communication Methods for Clients (figures based on personal experience)

- 60%: Freelancing platform
- 20%: Skype
- 15%: Email
- 5%: Phone

Your time is money, and as you advance you will have less and less of it to spare. There are a lot of clients out there who either don't realize this or don't care. From their point of view, it is sometimes understandable. Let's take a scenario that actually happened to me. You have a start-up company that needs a small press release completed. This is thirty minutes of work for a professional writer, so while they're not willing to pay more than $40, you're happy with that fee.

That person wants you to look at their site to get a feel for their business. They want you to look at their new products, their staff pages, rival press releases, and everything else they can think of. They then expect you to meet them on Skype for an interview. During this they will tell you everything you have just learned, they will repeat everything they already mentioned on the job proposal, and then they'll ask for your credentials, which, of course, they have already seen on your proposal and your profile.

At the end, you'll have spent three hours prepping for a job, and if you're lucky enough to get it, you will earn the princely sum of $40—but only after you have done the actual job. In the client's eyes, they were just doing what they deemed necessary; in the freelancer's eyes, you've just wasted half a day and now despise that prick and his company. Of course, you could have produced exactly the same work without all of that nonsense, but some clients think that nonsense is an absolute necessity, as if you don't know how research and writing works.

These days I only work with clients who understand that this is unnecessary. I have written more than three hundred About Us pages, FAQs, home pages, and more, and the only thing I ask from the client is the name, the purpose, and whether they want informal or formal. The job gets done, they're happy, I'm happy, and I didn't waste hours doing nothing.

I probably sound bitterer than I am. The truth is that this doesn't bother me anymore, but only because I don't let them drag me in anymore. If you refuse their Skype demands early on, if you refuse to jump through their hoops for insignificant jobs, then you can avoid this frustrating aspect of freelancing completely.

Luckily, it's fairly easy to spot these clients. Just look for the word "Skype Interview" and then run a mile.

5.8 — TIPS FOR OTHER FREELANCERS

This book was created with writers in mind, but it can be used by all freelancers. As long as you're using sites like Upwork and the others mentioned in this book, then all of the advice here can help you. To make sure we cover everything, here are some tips for graphic designers, web developers, coders, voice-over experts, musicians, and other freelancers:

Professions Suitable for Freelancing Platforms
- **Writers** – all types
- **Designers** – all types
- **Developers** – all types
- **IT** – coders, tech support, etc.
- **Musicians** – mainly songwriters and producers, also voice-overs
- **Teachers** – mainly language, also music and key skills
- **Admin** – VA, data entry, analytics, customer support
- **Legal** – lawyers, legal writers
- **Accountancy** – tax forms, personal accountants, etc.
- **Consultancy** – publishing, marketing, etc.
- **Marketing** – mainly SEO and PR
- **Unskilled** – game testers, eBay/Amazon posters, researchers, telemarketing

Portfolio

Always focus on your strengths here. I have mentioned that even for writers it is important to be visual, which means that designers have it easy here. Showcase your best designs. If they are not yours, ask for permission; if you don't have any, then draw something from popular culture and use that. For website designers, take screenshots of your creations. Voice-overs, coders, and others will struggle here. In the case of voice-overs, post some videos of yourself exploring your range of voices, or create/find an animation and voice-over that. For coders, post pictures of the end product. If you have designed the code for an app, show a screenshot of that app. If you did anything for a video, post the video.

Time and Tweaks

Considering the minor tweaks needed, it's not always best to work on fixed-price contracts. Coders and developers should seek to work on hourly contracts, and while designers and others can focus on fixed price, you should always set out everything in advance so the clients know what they are getting. Alternatively, show them stages of the work. One of the worst feelings you can have in this business is to create something from scratch and then find out they hate it and want you to start again. I can tweak my writing easily; the same might not apply to your designs.

Platform

Regardless of what you do, Upwork should work best for you. However, those doing voice-over work may actually get a lot of use out of Fiverr and People Per Hour, while designers should also sign up to Guru and even to Freelancer, using the latter for contests as discussed earlier in the book (**see Section 1.1 on page 3**).

Rights

Understand the copyright situation where you live. In the United States, you need to apply for copyright. In the United Kingdom and other countries, you own the work as soon as you create it and it is up to anyone else to prove otherwise. If you give a design to someone and they refuse to pay but still use it, threaten to take legal action. Obviously, your end goal is not for them to pay, otherwise they will be allowed to leave feedback and it won't be pleasant. Your goal is to get your work back and to ensure they don't get away with blatant theft. Coders, like writers, may struggle in this area, so extra caution is needed.

Understanding

Always make sure you know exactly what the client wants before you begin. Show them sample websites, designs, or whatever matches the job, and ask them if this is what they are looking for. If not, ask them to submit samples. Once you begin, drip-feed them the work to make sure you're on the same page. If they are vague, leave that job alone.

Book Covers

If you have the skills in design, there are many easy ways to make a living. I have seen so many designers make a killing through this method, and many of them are outsourcing the work. Do it yourself and you're set. You need to create a simple website and a Facebook page linking to it. Create a number of book covers replacing the name and title with "Your Info Here." Offer several different types, from basic to complex, and be sure to link to a "Custom" cover where they send you the details. Also, include details of your freelancing account. From then on, you should focus on Facebook ads, targeting "Indie Writers," "Self-Published Writers," "Kindle Writers," and similar groups, and spending as little as £50 a month. This will drip-feed you regular work, and if you spend the earnings from your first few books on more advertising, you should have regular work from then on. Then, whenever you have some spare time, you can focus on expanding the covers you have for sale. Of course, with so many people looking at your work, buying your covers and contracting you for other work through freelancing websites, free time will be hard to come by.

5.9 — CONNECTS

The Connect system, which was first used on Elance, is also used on Upwork. Prior to this, Upwork had a system in place whereby you could apply for up to twenty jobs a week free of charge, waiting for one application to end before you could free up another space. Connects work better on platforms that you intend to use full time, and this system is considerably better for writers with high minimum rates who are just starting out, as there will be a lot of rejected proposals.

How many Connects you get depends on whether you're a free member or a paid member. It is not essential that you pay for your membership on Upwork straight away, but you may need to do so as you progress. A Connect is essentially a credit, which allows you to apply for jobs. Job applications will cost anywhere from one Connect to five Connects, but the average is closer to two. You will be given a set amount every month, which at the time of writing is sixty for free members. If you pay for your membership you will get slightly more, but more important you will also be allowed to purchase more.

All first-time members should stick to free memberships. Apply for jobs, use Connects, and see how things go. If you run out and are still not working full time, then sign up for a paid membership, buy another batch, and keep going.

Don't worry if this happens. I often hear from writers and artists who tried to get started on Upwork and struggled to get any jobs for their going rate, only to give up when they had used all of their Connects. This happened to me as well, and at one point I had to buy several lots of extra Connects—around two hundred in total—before I got things going. This means that I blew $200 on nothing, but it all worked out in the end, and the clients that came as a result of that $200 included one who would later give me a total of $40,000.

You will eventually get to a point where you barely use any of your Connects. In fact, in the last year I have used less than fifty. Also, because the Connect system came into play when I was still using Elance and when I was working on many full-time jobs, I am still on a free membership as I write this. That's not because I'm cheap (my cheapness is unrelated) but because my account has rolled over from the days when this system wasn't in place, and paid membership has yet to become a necessity.

Of course, if you charge very little for your services and work toward the lower end of the pricing chart (**see Section 4.2 on page 78**), extra Connects are only going to eat into your profits. In this case, try to avoid them, use your monthly allotted Connects carefully, and try to stay on a free membership. If you find that you can only work part time this way, then simply sign up to other sites and spread your services around.

5.10 — NDAS AND OTHER AGREEMENTS

You will come across something called a non-disclosure agreement, or an NDA, very early on in your career. This is a simple contract that you will need to sign before you can begin a job, before you'll be hired, or even before you can finalize the job. The timing is down to the client, but the reason is always the same. The purpose of this contract is to ensure that you don't tell anyone about the project and that you don't steal the idea for your own projects. If you do, then the client might sue you.

Nothing will come of this, so don't worry. The client just wants to make sure that you don't go giving their idea away or releasing information about something that needs to be kept under wraps. These are very simple documents, often no more than a page. You can sign them electronically, you can scan in your signature, or you can use an online e-signing website or app.

Whatever you do, don't panic and refuse to sign this document. I have spoken with several freelancers who did just that, refusing to "get involved" with something they knew nothing about. One of them even insisted that he needed a solicitor to look it over first. Not necessary. Sign it. Send it. Start the job.

An NDA may also be listed be a confidentiality agreement or CA. And on sites like Freelancer they are programmed into the system, which makes them much more common but much easier to deal with at the same time.

You may also be asked to sign permission forms, which I have handed out myself. These essentially allow the client to publish someone else's work or story and should be used even if he or she is just publishing excerpts or short narratives, such as the ones used under "Horror Stories" in the final part of this book **(see Chapter**

14.0: Horror Stories). Agreements for ghostwritten projects are also common if you take on those type of jobs. These ask you to relinquish all ownership of the book you wrote and promise never to ask for royalties and never to claim that you wrote it.

You should always read anything you sign, but most of the time it's just a formality and the client will make no attempt to verify your signature—or even your name.

Chapter 5 Summary

- Don't submit milestones and completed projects through the standard methods. Instead, send a professional and polite message and attach the work to that, putting everything else in the hands of the client.
- Download the Time Tracker in preparation.
- Be careful when using excuses. Honesty is best, unless the truth is hard to believe.
- Be careful of time wasters on Skype.
- Weigh up the pros and cons of a paid membership on Upwork.
- Don't fuss or worry about NDAs and other contracts.

See Also

Chapter 6

DEADLINES, DEAD PROPOSALS, AND MISTAKES

Unless you're reading this book through in one sitting before you begin you career, then hopefully by now you will have won a few proposals, completed a few jobs, and gotten the ball rolling. That's the hardest part, but it's not exactly easy from here on out. The life of a successful freelancer is one of never-ending work. I spent my second year sitting on my ass with my computer on my lap, working endlessly while my cat vied for attention and poked his ass in my face.

There is a lot to learn from this point onward—not least of which is the fact that if you feed your cat when he annoys you, he may leave you alone, but in a few months that cat is going to be a lot fatter, a lot heavier, and therefore much more likely to get in your way.

6.1 — OLD PROPOSALS

One of the hardest things to wrap your header around in the beginning is just when a proposal has been rejected or ignored and when there is still a chance you will be given the job. You might send out dozens of proposals and panic when you get interviews for more than you can handle. The truth is that even if all of those clients are expressing an interest in hiring you, they might not hire you. In fact, many of them will certainly not.

The reason for this has always baffled me, but I can now sense exactly when a client is not going to hire me, even if they have said they will. Conversely, I can also sense when a client will hire me. As I worked on this book I received interest from a client who wanted me to write an ebook. I gave him some suggestions and he loved them. We talked a little, he agreed to my price, and I mentioned more than once that as soon as he gave me the job, I would make a start.

When a few days went by with those talks continuing, it was clear that he wasn't going to give me the job. At the same time, a client got in touch regarding a proposal I had sent six weeks earlier. He had dismissed me as being too expensive and had hired someone cheaper. That person had messed up, produced poor work, and then disappeared, so he wanted me to pick up the pieces. The immediacy of this, the fact that he was discussing prices there and then and was willing to offer me terms, made it obvious that I was going to get that job.

In the end, that's what happened. I got the second job and didn't hear from the first one until three months later. At this point he had given up on the previous project and wanted to discuss an "exciting new" project with me. He invited me, and I politely refused the invitation.

In my early days, this would have surprised me. If you had asked me which client was more likely to hire me, I would have said the first guy. You will learn yourself when someone wants to hire you and when someone wants to piss you about. But even when you do, there's very little you can do about it. You can't ignore the first guy, not when you're already conversing with him. That's unprofessional, and even if there is only a slim chance, you need to go with it. What you can do, however, is not invest too much time or hope in the first guy and focus on the second one instead.

The second client brings us back to old proposals and the cutoff point of when these should be ignored. If you're more expensive, then a lot of the time a cheaper writer will be hired ahead of you.

There is an entire community of cheap and cheerful writers on these sites, and they all share basic things in common: they are often non-native speakers, they are certainly not experienced writers (they usually come from IT backgrounds), and they work cheaply. If someone wants a writer for a serious project, one where the language needs to be impeccable, it is inevitable they will fail. This is not their fault—you can't expect perfection from someone who doesn't write professionally and doesn't understand the language.

When those writers fail, then the clients turn to professional and competent writers. Even if the proposal was sent months ago, even if they never spoke to you or interviewed you. The chances are they will have noticed you and will come back for you, asking you to pick up the pieces. When they do, charge them more. It serves them right for ignoring you in the first place. If you want a job done well, you need to pay for it. It annoys me when they ignore this fact, try to get it done cheaply, and then unleash hell on the poor, inexperienced writer who they expected the world of. The same goes for the clients who talk to you initially, discuss your price, and then hire someone cheaper, before knocking back on your door when that cheaper writer messes up.

I took time out of my day to give them a reasonable quote, to propose some suggestions, and to generally be there while they hummed and harred over my price and then pissed off with someone else. If you're willing to take the piss, then so am I, and when you inevitably come crying back to me, guest what? My price just doubled.

If I'm not a bastard, then they'll never learn.

You should never assume a job will not come your way just because the application process has finished, just as you should not assume you have failed just because it has been a few days or weeks and you've heard nothing. Sometimes people are just slow. However, if you have spent a few days speaking to them with no results, you can then safely assume it's not going to happen. You can also take the words, "I'll get back to you in a few days/weeks/months; I just need to sort some things out first," or any variation of them, as a sign that you will never hear from that client again. The more experienced you are, the higher your quote is, and the more credentials you have, the more you will hear these promises. They know you are perfect for the job, they think they are doing a disservice by refusing you outright, and they don't want to admit they are cheap, so instead they waste your time with empty promises.

6.2 — SOFTWARE (MS WORD, EXCEL, FINAL DRAFT)

In many freelancing guides, you'll see checklists for software that you should download before you get started. The reason I didn't include this and the reason I haven't mentioned it until now is because it's nonsense. You don't need specific software, and while clients will tell you they want the work sent in "XYZ" format, there are always ways around this regardless of what you use.

I use a MacBook and all of the proprietary software. This was not really by choice; it's just something I got used to using many years ago and something I have stuck with. This means that I am in a very small minority when it comes to my word processor, spreadsheet software, and presentation software. To make matters even more complicated, I don't use Final Draft to write or edit scripts; I have always used Movie Magic Screenwriter instead. I have considered making the switch, but I have been able to complete all jobs using my current software, so there has been no call for it.

Use whatever software you want, but don't force it upon your client. There is an unwritten code in freelancing that states that whenever a client asks for a document and doesn't specify a file type, you should send in .doc (the MS Word extension). The same goes for spreadsheets, which should be sent as Excel files, and presentations, which should be sent as PowerPoint. Scripts are different, as the client will often specify Final Draft, RTF, or PDF.

Always convert to the standard before sending. Most word processors can convert to .doc or .docx, and most spreadsheets can convert to .xls or .xlsx, so you shouldn't have an issue there. If your software can't convert, then it is time to change.

I can't really make any recommendations in this regard, but I do have a personal dislike for Open Office. I have worked with a couple of freelancers who used nothing else and insisted on sending me files with the .ODT extension. I had issues opening these and could only open them in a basic format when I eventually did. When I asked them to convert, they gave me the virtual equivalent of a shrug, a grunt, and a suggestion that they thought everyone used Open Office.

Most computers come bundled with word processors and basic software, but if for some reason (like the freelancers mentioned above) you don't have access to these, then that needs to be your main goal before you start. Save up, take out a loan, do whatever it takes to get a decent software suite. You wouldn't expect a carpenter to succeed without access to wood, and you can't expect to succeed as a writer if you don't have the basic software.

6.3 — MAKING MISTAKES

Dealing with so many new people and discussing high-pressure jobs is not an easy task, but you have to ignore all of that. Simplify it. Focus on the tax and the money, nothing else. If you mess up, it's not the end of the world. I've said it before, and in this chapter I'll say it again, bad feedback early on can be the death of you. Still, everyone messes up. The trick is not to linger on it. Don't let it consume you.

If in messing up you have disappointed a client, then it's not as easy to ignore, but there are ways you can make it up to them. Offer to do some extra work for free or write off the cost of the project if it is small enough. If you submit substandard work, then don't just apologize and expect payment. Half an hour or an hour of your time spent fixing jobs like this and repairing relationships with clients will not only ensure you get better feedback, but it will also ensure that that client returns to you when they need more work.

Also, if you do offer to do work for free, they might not accept it. Personally, I have done this on my two biggest mistakes. Both were minimal really, but for me they were disasters. I offered to write off the cost of part of the job, but on both occasions the clients refused. If your client appreciates your work and everything you have done in the past, they won't care and they will refuse to let you write off your work like that. However, the fact that you offered will go a long way.

If you make a huge mistake and the client is refusing to pay you until you fix it, then remember that you can just cancel the job. If it's going to be easier and quicker for you to just drop everything and run, and if the client has yet to pay you a dime, then by all means do so. These things happen, and they won't be able to leave you bad feedback.

If you have a short temper and are prone to react badly, do not respond to the client immediately after they request changes. I once asked for a very small change from a freelancer who reacted terribly, taking a small request as a personal insult and reacting aggressively to it. If this sounds like something you might do, just bide your time. Make sure you are calm before you respond.

6.4 — DEADLINES

One of the most famous quotes on writing came from one of my favorite authors, Hitchhiker's Guide writer Douglas Adams. He joked that he "loves" deadlines, and in particular the "whooshing sound they make as they go by." Adams was a funny guy, and probably talented and successful enough to make light of a few missed deadlines; but if you make this your mantra as a freelancer, your career will be short lived.

There is no such thing as writers' block to a freelance writer, simply because we can't afford the luxury of nothingness. We can't afford to spend days stressing over plots and paragraphs; we can't afford to do nothing but moan about our struggle. An author will banish writers' block when a contractual deadline arises; a freelance writer will never experience writers' block, because such deadlines are always just around the corner.

There is a trend among amateur writers for setting deadlines that will impress the client but will strain the freelancer. I write quickly, most writers do, and I can generally complete a 2,000-word article within one hour, with considerable ease. However, you will never catch me telling a client this. Some clients are of the belief that such an article will take a full day, most seem to think that it will take at least half a day. They're not writers themselves, and for many of them writing an article is a process that takes a long time. That may be the case for them, but it's not the case for an experienced writer who does that day in, day out.

A client will almost always expect you to be slower than you are. If you have ten 1,000-word articles to complete, you could probably finish that job in a day. However, the client will not flinch if you ask for a week, and many times you can get away with two weeks. It doesn't matter if you have nothing else to do, you should always stretch the deadline. You don't know what's around the corner. A long-term client might give you a rush job as soon as you sign up, or you might not be feeling up to a full day of writing articles. Also, if you tell a client you can deliver in a day and you do deliver in a day, so what? You met the deadline. Well done. No one is impressed. However, if you tell them you can deliver in two weeks and you deliver in a week, they'll be impressed. You still took your time, but in their eyes that project has been your sole concern for the last seven days. You've toiled over it day and night to deliver before the deadline.

Don't be too quick, though, because many clients will think you rushed the job. Rather than being impressed, they'll be suspicious and more inclined to ask for edits and changes, having developed a negative opinion even before their first read.

As a freelancer you will constantly be juggling half a dozen jobs and half a dozen clients, and at the same time you will also need to apply for more jobs, respond to invites, and negotiate with other clients.

Every client you have should know none of this, because every client you have needs to think that you are 100 percent dedicated to their project. It should be obvious that you are not, but you'd be surprised how many clients get annoyed when they discover they are not the only one I'm working for. One of them actually offered me $100 a day in the hope that would entice me away from everyone else. He didn't need me for more than three hours a day, but in his eyes it was more than that. Of course, I accepted it and I worked those three hours for him, but at the same time I continued to work for my other clients, making five times what he was paying me.

Call it narcissism, call it stupidity, but most of them want to be the center of attention at all times, as if by working on another project you will somehow be too tired to work on theirs. Not all clients are like this, but you can't take chances and just have to assume.

In the end, the schedule for a freelance writer should not be one of quickly completed jobs and constant negotiation with long-term clients. It should be a constant revolving door of new jobs and old money. If you prolong all jobs like I recommended above, then in any given day you will be working a handful of jobs for a handful of clients, keeping yourself busy and, most important, keeping yourself fresh. There are few things worse in this job than doing the same shit day after day.

6.5 — "OFFLINE" CLIENTS

I have already discussed how you should never solicit a client to work outside of a freelance platform, and how you should be wary of clients that do this to you. Freelancing platforms look down on this, more so than anything else. It seems that clients can get away with screwing freelancers left, right, and center, but as soon as they try to avoid paying those sites a cut, the sites go apeshit. It's not just about the fear of being banned either, because these sites also give you security that you just can't get through PayPal, a service that makes it possible for someone to pay you and then reverse that payment at a later date if they feel like it.

As a freelancer with an active online presence, you will be contacted by clients who do not use these sites. You will also be contacted by clients who post jobs, do not like the setup, and then leave, taking a freelancer or two with them. There is no harm in this. You're not taking work away from the platform, because those clients had no intention of working on those platforms. After all, if someone gets in touch with you through Facebook and asks you to do a job for them, you're under no obligation to go through a freelancing site. They are not your agents and do not own a cut of every job you do.

Although such offers are more common with published authors, those who have a wider presence, they are also common with established freelancers who have something special to offer, freelancers who stand out from the crowd. Clients who contact you through Facebook, Twitter, and other social media sites should be given the same treatment as clients on freelancing platforms. These days, my first step is to ask them to sign up to freelancing sites and to get in touch through there, assuming the job is big enough and is actually worth my time. In the early days, however, this posed a problem. I didn't want to work with clients who had no feedback and therefore no track record of leaving it. Therefore, I simply refused all jobs offered to me away from freelancing platforms.

If you want to give these clients the time of day, and they refuse to sign up to a freelancing site, then there are some simple rules to follow. First, just talk to them, get an idea of who they are and how likely they are to rip you off. You can also Google them or checkout their Facebook profiles. You can usually spot an honest person from a dickhead, but there are many gray areas.

If you're suspicious and the job is big, go through a site like Escrow. There is a fee, and a big one at that, but the client and the freelancer can split the costs. You can also request a bank transfer. If the client is desperate to hire you, they will likely pay all of the money upfront. If not, they should pay half upfront and half on completion. Of course, you might never see the second half, which is why it is important to judge the client based on the job and their personality.

For instance, if they want you to write a book, or even an article, then that work is yours, and only when you agree to relinquish control does it transfer to them. Copyright laws change from country to country, but this applies to most. In the United Kingdom, as mentioned earlier, everything you create is yours. There is no copyright office, no need to register; as long as you can prove you wrote it (send copies to yourself, keep original documents), you're good. In these cases, clients will not try to rip you off because they know they won't get the work if they do. However, it's different where editing is concerned. You're fixing their book, and you don't own the rights to some corrected spelling mistakes.

Of the ten or more clients who have contacted me to edit/rewrite away from freelancing sites, I took on one job. It was a Korean woman who was incredibly honest, kind, and generous. I had no doubt she would be fair, and she was. In that case, it was a small job and we went through PayPal. This is not advised unless you're 100 percent confident you are dealing with an honest person. The same goes for editing jobs. If you're desperate, then you might as well take it on. It's better to work for the potential of receiving a payment than to not work for the guarantee of getting nothing.

There is another type of offline job. This one will come from clients who were quickly disillusioned with the freelancing platforms for whatever reason. Strangely enough, of the four times this has happened to me, one of them was a billion-dollar company, another was a big international writing school, and the other two were fairly substantial clients as well. They canceled their accounts and had no intention of going back, so it was either a case of working outside of the freelancing platform or not working at all. Luckily, this was an easy choice, as they were big enough for me to trust them. If they have dozens of staff, payrolls, and a professional setup, you don't need to worry.

These clients will become crucial to providing some stability in your career, because it's not a comfortable feeling to know that whether you pay the bills or not, and whether you eat or not, is reliant on one or two websites. Elsewhere in this book **(see Chapter 17.0: Branching Out and Other Options)** we will discuss stability a little more, as there are some steps you can take to ensure your career looks less like the spin of a roulette wheel.

Chapter 6 Summary

- Give up on clients who only want to talk and make promises.
- Old proposals might generate future work.
- Don't fuss over the software you use, but make sure you can convert to standard forms.
- Let clients think that they and their work are your primary concern.
- Always be prepared to offer the client an apology and some free work when you miss a deadline.
- Prepare a payment method for clients that find you away from the freelancing sites.

See Also

- *Understanding Clients* **(page 57 – 3.5)**
- *Plan Ahead, Keep Earning* **(page 194 – 12.3)**
- *Horror Stories* **(Chapter 14.0)**
- *Branching Out and Other Options* **(Chapter 17.0)**
- *Resources for Freelancers* **(page 297 – 19.2)**

Chapter 7
FEEDBACK

The vast majority of the stress you will feel as a freelancer is because of the feedback system. Not only can a bad job or two end your burgeoning career, but it can also trip up even experienced freelancers. Fortunately, it is very easy to play the system. The only bad feedback I have ever received came as a result of me taking a risk when the jobs weren't coming in and working for some very bad people who I had doubts about from the beginning. This is why it is important to follow the guidelines in this book and to always ensure you work with good and honest people. In this section we'll look a little more at the feedback system, focusing on how to get good feedback and, most important, how to avoid bad feedback.

7.1 — AVOIDING BAD FEEDBACK

I have covered this already, but avoiding bad feedback is crucial to your success as a freelancer, particularly in the beginning. If I had received bad feedback on any of my first few jobs, I'm confident none of this would have happened and my life would look completely different. I'd probably be happier without all of this work, but I'd be decidedly poorer as well.

I have seen a lot of freelancers get bad feedback that they could have easily avoided, even if that feedback had already been left.

The first thing you need to know is how the feedback system works. Believe it or not, it took me a few months to figure this out, and while I didn't get any bad feedback in that time, I could have saved myself a lot of effort.

On sites like Upwork, a client can only leave you feedback if they have paid you for the job. They cannot retract any previous feedback and leave you a lower rating for jobs that have continued beyond that point, and they also cannot leave you bad feedback for a job that ended more than three months ago, even if they paid you for it. Obviously, they could just pay you $0.50 and leave you bad feedback. Except that feedback will vanish as soon as you initiate a refund. So, if you can afford to give the money back, then do it. If the client has left you bad feedback in the hope that you will initiate a refund, which unfortunately does happen, then you're fucked. It's hard to hear, but freelancing sites do not care about such predicaments. Of course, such evil clients tend to be very easy to spot, so unless you've taken some unnecessary risks and haven't followed the guidelines mentioned in **Chapter 3.0: Applying for Jobs,** you should be okay.

Here are some tips to avoid getting that bad feedback in the first place:

- Cancel a job and leave as soon as the client displays warning signs. Unless you're on Freelancer, it won't harm your status if you do so.
- Always get clear instructions and make sure you follow them.
- Write a sample first, and offer to do it for free if need be. That way the client knows what to expect and you can set a benchmark.
- Always be polite and professional, and never delay a response for more than twelve hours without prior warning.
- Do not request feedback, even if they do not leave it initially.
- Do not offer to work for less in exchange for good feedback (this is a banning offense).
- If you make a mistake, cover for it. Kiss their arse until your lips are blue. Treat small mistakes like it's the end of the world and you're sorry for dropping the bomb.

- Always check a client's history.
- Never jump into a job. If your application is accepted without any sort of interview, then be the one to initiate that interview. The more you talk to a client, the higher the chance they will expose their dickish side if they have one.
- Do not make demands. Always be patient with payment and replies. They will come.*
- Do not take risks early on. Never work with clients who have no working history or a poor working history. You can afford to take a few risks later on for bigger jobs.
- Do not argue with a client. If their ineptitude affects your work or your payment, point it out to them, but do so in a friendly and almost apologetic manner.

7.2 — THE FOURTEEN-DAY WAIT

Upwork has a unique system in place when it comes to feedback. The client and freelancer can leave feedback for each other when a job has been finalized. If they leave feedback for you, you won't be able to see it until you leave feedback for them or until you wait two weeks, at which point you can no longer leave feedback. This is not eBay. You can't wait to see if they leave you good feedback before replying in kind. It's actually ingenious, and it stops people from playing games.

As a freelancer you should always be the bigger person and leave good feedback for a client. Look at the positives of a job and mention those. Don't ignore the negatives if there were some, but remember that when a client looks at your history, they will spend as much time reading the feedback previous clients left for you as they will reading the feedback you left for them. They don't want to

---

I can't stress this enough. As a client I have seen this a lot and it infuriates me. It is very rare you will work with a client who refuses to pay, especially if you choose your clients carefully.

hire someone who has a habit of leaving nasty feedback just as much as you don't want to work for someone who has a habit of leaving nasty feedback.

If you suspect bad feedback is coming your way and can live with yourself if you don't reply (if you're anything like me, this will be difficult), then just ignore it. You will have fourteen days before it shows, which means that if y ou work your ass off for two weeks, you might be able to get enough positive feedback to offset it. Who knows, you might then discover that they didn't leave you any negative feedback after all.

7.3 — RECOMMENDED

Most platforms have a "recommended" score, which can be left by the client and will stay on your profile. On Upwork, this is more important than it is elsewhere, as it replaced the average feedback score (in terms of importance) after the merger of oDesk and Elance.

When a client signs off on a job, they will be asked to leave private comments and private information regarding your fluency of the English language. They will also be asked to rate you from one to ten based on whether they would "recommend" you as a freelancer. The score they give is added to your total score to get an overall percentage, which is displayed on your profile.

I tried my best to get this as high as possible in the days of Elance, but there was a flaw in the system whereby the "recommended" score was set to five (out of ten) by default. Clients are busy and usually rush through this process. This meant that even though I had 100 percent five-star feedback, I had two scores of five on my recommended, which lowered my overall score. This crossed over to Upwork (where there is no default score), and it remains as a blip on my profile, frustratingly shy of 100 percent.

Still, I did okay for myself. So if you do have a few clients who score you less than ten, don't fret about it. If you can keep this score at 100 percent throughout your first year, it will make things easier for you; but as long as it remains on a respectable amount (above 90 percent) you'll be okay.

I know of a few clients who use this score to say something they didn't want to say in the feedback section. Simply put, many of the clients who rely on these sites to get work done understand that if they leave a lot of bad feedback, freelancers will not apply for their jobs in the future. So they tend to be very forgiving when it comes to feedback. But if they've had a bad experience, they can be less forgiving when it comes to personal comments, fluency marks, and everything else they can leave when a job is finalized. This is why you should give a client your best at all times. Even if you know they leave five-star feedback whatever happens, even if you think they are a pushover and that you can piss about and still get full marks (never the right attitude), remember that they can still do a lot of unseen damage.

The other comments and notes a client can leave, and the impact they have, are discussed in greater detail a little later on **(see Section 9.1 on page 150)**.

7.4 — BAD CLIENTS

The majority of clients on freelancing sites are great, but there are a few bad apples that threaten to spoil the whole bunch. I have encountered a few of these in my time and I can usually spot them in advance. Basically, as we heave learned in the previous chapters, applying for a job and getting that job involve some level of communication with the client. You should also be looking at their history and their previous feedback. All of this means that you should be able to sense the clients that have the potential to turn bad.

As a freelancer you are always in a submissive position—always trying to please, always apologizing when the client is angry, even when they are also wrong. This is not a stance that I enjoy being in, but it is a professional one and one that has helped my career. Unfortunately, there are clients who will abuse this, clients who see it as a weakness and use it to bully you.

Immediate Signs of a Potential Bad Client

- Short, abrupt, cold, or overly formal.
- Demanding.
- Persistence or pleading with regards to the price.
- Makes promises ("I'll hire tomorrow") that are not kept.
- Sends a glut of messages before even giving you the job.
- Insists on free sample or Skype interview for small job.
- 50% or more jobs ended in three or less stars for freelancers.
- 20% or more jobs ended in four or less stars for freelancers.
- Average rating from freelancers is less than four star (freelancers score higher than clients)
- Paid an average hourly wage of less than $5 per hour (on Upwork profile page).

I have had several bad experiences, but only one that truly disturbed me and made me question my career choice. It was a bad experience that I would not wish on anyone. The client had issues, but I will not go in depth on these. He wanted me to write a bulk batch of articles, which included a lot of his opinions. Needless to say, it should have been apparent early on that he would be a problem, as a lot of his emails read like the ramblings of a madman. They were full of bile, of deep-seated hatred and paranoia. Here was a man who realized that the world basically hated him. A man who had been the outcast at work, at school, and even at home. However, rather than realizing that this was because he was narcissistic, bigoted, and downright rude (which I experienced myself many times), he took it to mean that everyone else was either racist or xenophobic (depending on their own race and origins). In the instances when it was not possible to be either, he decided that they must have mental problems.

Never in my life have I met a person like him, and it concerned me greatly that this didn't come out until we were deep into the project. The project also had many issues. I would write an article, he would ask for edits, and he would give me it back. He would pay me and we would move on. Two weeks later, he would remember something else and insist I included it in that "finished" article. Two weeks after that, he would remember something else, or decide he wanted a change. All clients are entitled to this and it's usually good practice to do it for free, but it got to the point where I was still getting emails about the initial article eighteen months and ten-plus articles down the line.

"My friend read it and thinks you could have mentioned this." *"Based on recent political events* [the articles were never political and the "events" were never relevant], *I think you should include this."* I should have charged him for these edits, but I did not.

There was also an issue with understanding. I would say one thing, he would take it to mean something else, and he would lose his shit. In the end, when I decided I needed to quit and when he began actively insulting me, I referenced a time when he showed his friends one of my chapters and then, eighteen months after completion and payment, demanded I change it. He somehow misread this to mean that I had been showing *my* friends, and went off on a tirade, threatening to sue me and reporting me to Upwork for breaking the terms of an NDA (not only did I not break any terms, but no NDA was sent or signed). Luckily, they had spoken to him before and knew exactly what to expect, so they didn't pay much attention to him, but it still hurt me to think that he would do this when I had been nothing but helpful to him.

I had done dozens of hours of unpaid work and, in the end, had scrapped over $1,000 of fees that he owed me, all in an effort to end his anger and psychosis. I had been polite and sympathetic. I had acted as a friend and a counselor. I had ignored all of the moments he had lashed out for no reason, all of the moments he took my friendly and submissive nature for granted and essentially treated me like shit. I am of the belief that maintaining an air of dignity in such situations will ensure you always come off as the better man in the end, but on this occasion, nothing I could have said or done would have stopped the abuse and led to a pleasant experience.

Not only do these clients exist, but when they bite, there is nothing you can do about it. I was already in deep when I realized how bad he was and there was nothing I could do. I would have left earlier, but I was worried about angering him and getting bad feedback. I wasted thousands and thousands of dollars, because I turned down paid jobs just so I could do things for him that he wasn't paying me for. To cap it off, he tried to get me suspended. You might think this is an injustice and one that deserves to be righted, but that's not the way these sites work. They categorically state that if a client pays you, they essentially have the right to do as they please. It doesn't matter if they leave feedback that is insulting and even libelous, or if they lie in order to get you suspended; what matters is that they have the right.

I may have not "won," but neither did the client. You see, I was not the first writer on his project. Many more had started and quit before me. I just happened to be the only idiot who stuck with him, hoping there was a modicum of humility in him and that he would prove to be human in the end, rather than just a fleshy ball of bitter anger.

You will bump into clients like this, and you should never stick it through. I had enough warning signs, and I ignored them all. Of course, it depends on what those signs were. I once had a polite chat with a client who wanted me to write a biography of a film producer. He was nice and it was amicable. However, as soon as he gave me the job, he changed his tune. With nothing to set it off, he became very demanding and very rude. My guess is that he had worked with writers who had let him down in the past, and that as soon as money was exchanged, he began to worry that I would do the same. I went back on my word and got out before I did anything, before he paid me, and long before that attitude of his could affect me.

It's best to avoid any clients that display any sort of rudeness or narcissism. A freelance project should be a friendly one. There should be no superior and inferior—this is not a workplace. The client needs something done, the freelancer is the skilled contractor who can do it, and they will part ways afterward. In many instances the freelancer is more skilled, more qualified, and earns more money than the client. If a client begins to treat you like a lowly employee, ignore them. Politely refuse the job and move on.

This usually only applies to the beginning of your career, when bad feedback can have a hugely negative impact, and to those who take all bad feedback as a personal affront and want to build a freelancing career on nothing but positivity, like me. When you have been freelancing for a long time and have worked a lot of jobs with a lot of good feedback, you can afford to take more risks; but even then, it is never worth it to work with such a client. Even if you ignore the bad feedback, you can't ignore the fact that you could lose a fortune. I personally lost thousands of dollars working for the aforementioned client, not to mention all of those sleepless nights because he wanted a hurried rewrite based on a dream or a random encounter with an errant cockroach. This was a job where I earned no more than $3,000, despite doing in excess of $20,000 worth of work.

There are some ways to delete feedback, depending on which portal you use. On Guru, you can basically remove your bad feedback if you have enough good feedback. You are rewarded points, and when you get enough of these, you can use them to block bad feedback. On Freelancer there is a similar system in place that lets you ignore bad feedback. On the biggest portal, Upwork, there is no such system in place. You can, however, simply refund the client, after which the feedback will disappear. Basically, feedback can only be left on this site once the client has paid. That means that if they do not pay or if you initiate a refund, they can't leave you feedback, and if they already have, it will disappear.

7.5 — GOOD CLIENTS

You will know when you have found a good client, and from that moment on, you need to do everything you can to ensure the work keeps on coming. A good client is not necessarily someone who is always on hand to answer your questions, to clarify the job, or to pay you instantly (although that certainly helps). Money is not the issue here. If you readily dismiss a client just because they were slightly late with payment, you'll be doing yourself a disservice.

Except for two or three, the very best clients that I have worked with have all been a little late with payments and with responding to messages. They're busy people, and that plays in your favor more than late payments take away. Not only will clients like this be less likely to check your work and ask for the tiniest, time-consuming changes (although that is no excuse for being sloppy), but they will also rely more on you when they have work to complete.

One such client of mine ended up putting me on a retainer, giving me the login details of twelve different sites, and paying me to fill them. I wrote the content, I posted the content, and he paid me. I don't think he checked it, but I always did my best and it was a very easy job. There were delays at times—on his part—but nothing major and certainly nothing that would turn that fantastic opportunity into a negative one.

Immediate Signs of a Potentially Good Client

- Very friendly, warm, happy.
- Flawless five-star feedback on more than five jobs.
- Excited about your samples/profile/application.
- Limited negotiation. Pays you what you ask.
- Is ready to start the job immediately.
- Is very responsive.
- Lets you know they are there if you have questions about the job.

If you do well by a good client, they will put more responsibility on your shoulders, and while this is tricky at first, in the long run it makes things much easier. Good clients will also treat you more like a friend, which makes things even easier for you. Not only can you get away with more (again, no excuse for sloppiness), but they will also offer you more work, they will be less inclined to ask you to reduce your price, and they will even refer you to their friends.

The client I mentioned above hired me in my first year as a freelancer. In the twelve months that followed, I made a decent wage from him alone, all of which was for what amounted to transient, part-time work. A year into our working relationship, he put me in touch with a close friend of his who was in the same business, and that friend ended up hiring me to do just as much work. I also worked with that friend on a number of projects and he even helped me to set up a profitable affiliate website. As I write this, even though my work with the initial client has momentarily dried up due to personal obligations on his part, I am still working for his friend.

Simply put, you should never underestimate what a single client can do for you and where a good experience can lead in this industry. Later in the book I'll discuss a friendly way you can ensure these clients keep giving you work, even when they have taken a hiatus **(see Section 16.1 on page 249)**.

7.6 — SENDING PROPOSALS AND COMMUNICATING WITH CLIENTS

I have worked both as a freelancer and as a client. This is mainly because I outsource some of my work, but also because I run several websites myself and don't have the time to write for them. In my time as a client, I have learned more about this business than I have as a freelancer. Most important, I have learned just why clients value me and people like me.

A lot of freelancers are not very good. In one day, I hired twenty different freelancers to write paid test articles for a long-term project. Eighteen of them missed the deadline, ten of them gave me excuses (three of those had weddings to attend **[see Section 5.6 on page 102]**), and nineteen of them were just very poor writers. This is what you are competing against, and this is why quality is always appreciated. And by "quality" I mean passable, high school–level English. A professional and polite attitude is equally rare.

I have been nothing but polite as a client, and while many of the freelancers have been equally polite, two of them were very rude. I looked back at their profiles and found a lot of bad feedback from clients saying the same thing. This rudeness is unnecessary and gets you nowhere. It does, however, get you bad feedback and bad reports, which can ultimately lead to a suspended account.

Most of the issues I have had have been with unprofessional freelancers getting the small things wrong. Some of them didn't respond when I sent them details of the job and asked if they could do it, choosing instead to just do it and message me a week later when they had finished. I, of course, had already given the job to someone else, assuming they weren't interested. Some of them simply sent me messages that had no structure and looked like they had been written by a teenager on a mobile phone. Obviously, I didn't hire any of these.

This is a professional environment. You wouldn't walk into a real job interview dressed like a slob, refusing to answer questions, and occasionally spitting on the floor, so why would you do this online? Yes, you will have to go through this interview process many times and it's easy to lose heart, just as it is easy to try and take the shortcut. However, you're only prolonging the torture. It doesn't take two minutes to structure a message properly, yet that professionalism and that attentiveness could be the difference between you getting the job or not.

While the work you do is of a high importance, it is not as important as the attitude you have and the way you talk to the client. You can be the best writer in the world, but if you are rude, late, hard to work with, and hard to understand, they're not going to hire you. I like to think of it like self-publishing a book. It is easy to focus on the writing only and to think that the quality of the writing and the story will sell the book for you. But if you don't have a good cover or an enticing synopsis, your book won't even be picked off the shelf. The quality of the writing is important, but without a professional package, it will be ignored.

Chapter 7 Summary

- Some sites are easier than others where the feedback system is concerned.
- Most bad feedback can be deleted, but it might cost you.
- Upwork has a fourteen-day wait period in which the client and freelancer can leave feedback without seeing his or her own.
- On Upwork, your "recommended" score is given more of a priority than your feedback, but both are just as important.

- Clients have been known to blackmail freelancers with feedback, another reason why understanding your client's personality is essential.
- Bad feedback can be the end of you, so be selective early on and do what it takes to get good feedback.

See Also

- *Applying for Jobs* **(Chapter 3.0)**
- *Excuses* **(page 102 – 5.6)**
- *Suspensions and Bans* **(page 150 – 9.1)**
- *Give Clients a Nudge* **(page 249 – 16.1)**

Chapter 8

CLIENTS: PERSPECTIVE AND ATTITUDE

There is a lot to get through when it comes to working with clients. We've already discussed the protocols of applying for your first jobs **(see Chapter 3.0: Applying for Jobs)** and working those jobs **(see Chapter 5.0: Your First Job)**, but in this chapter we'll look at the client/freelancer relationship in more detail.

8.1 — KEEPING IT NEUTRAL

Elsewhere in this book, I have discussed how important it is to be friendly with your clients, and even, on occasion, to treat them as if they were your friends. Obviously, you should never break from professionalism, and there are boundaries (they don't need to know about the man/woman you picked up on Friday night, how much you drank, or why you ended up tied to a lamppost in nothing but your birthday suit). Try to treat them like you would a high school teacher or headmaster, assuming you weren't a miscreant in your schooldays. Be open when it is called for, make a joke or two, but always show them respect and always make sure they know you are working hard.

How you treat them and how friendly you are to them depends on how they treat you, on how friendly they are to you, and on their personality. If they are strict, talking only of work and never deviating from that, then you should act the same. If they start to talk to you as if you were a friend, using a relaxed language, calling you "buddy" or "mate"—as is so often the case for British and Australian clients—and filling messages with emoticons, then you can be a little more open.

Even if a client is acting like your new best friend, always try to keep your beliefs out of it. We are all different, and while your beliefs might be accepted and appreciated in your town, they might not be treated with the same respect by a client halfway across the world. This goes for any sort of political or religious beliefs. These things are just best not discussed. Keep it neutral, keep it vague, because even though it sounds right and natural to you, it could easily piss the next person off, and this is not the sort of relationship you want with a client. These things affect the way clients perceive you, which in turns affects future work, feedback, and bonus payments. If I hire you to do some work for me and in the course of conversation I find out that you're a bigoted KKK member, I'm immediately going to have a negative opinion of you, even if you do a good job.

Even if you think the other person shares your beliefs, no matter how fucked up those beliefs are, keep them to yourself. You're not here to find like-minded people; you're here to work, get paid, and get good feedback. I consider myself a very liberal and tolerant person, and I would hope that the clients I talk with the most and the clients I enjoy working with share the same beliefs, but I would never express them. They don't need to know my stand on religion and politics; they don't even need to know what football team I support—although humiliation often keeps me from disclosing that piece of information anyway.

Your opinions should also be in line with the client. If they hate a text and it is your job to edit it, then you hate it as well. If they love a website or a book and they want you to emulate it, then don't point out its flaws and just do what they ask (although I do like to casually mention areas in which my writing is better, letting the client know

I can give them something much better). Many clients are in high positions and like to think they know what they're talking about. If you question their beliefs, any friendly rapport you have generated with them could be gone in an instant.

8.2 — CLIENT'S PERSPECTIVE

If not for my experience as a client, I wouldn't understand just why my own clients have valued my punctuality so much, because nine out of ten people I have hired, and nine out of ten people they have hired, have missed a deadline. The same goes for producing highly sellable and professional work, because so few freelancers do this. That has no bearing on how good they are as writers either, because the vast amount of freelancers I have hired who have produced poor work have struggled with basic grammar, spelling, and punctuation. I would paste an excerpt here to show you, but I deleted most of the work they gave me for fear that if I met an early demise, someone would find that content on my laptop and believe it to be mine. If there was ever a fate worse than death, that would be it. This is discussed at greater length, with a surviving excerpt from one of these freelancers, in a later chapter (see Chapter 11.0: Outsourcing).

This book is all about giving clients what they want, while also getting what you want from them. The main goal for many freelancers, though, is to get a long-term client, someone who will constantly supply you with jobs and will limit your need to search and apply for more. To help you understand just what these clients are looking for, I asked my own long-term clients what they look for in a freelancer.

8.3 — KHALED: ALL-ROUNDER

Over the years, I have grown quite close to one of my clients. He lives on the other side of the world in Kuwait and we couldn't be more different. He's a very religious man from a very religious part of the world. I respect all religions and consider myself very tolerant. However, I am the least religious person you could meet, having grown up in a household and an environment with no religion. We speak different languages, have different goals and interests, and live completely different lives, but I consider him to be a friend, and one I would happily share a drink with—if his religion permitted it, of course. This is what it means to have a long-term client; this is what you should aspire toward. Not only does he give me a lot of work, but he understands my work and my work ethic more than most. He knows that if he needs anything, I'm happy to help, even if it means the occasional unpaid synopsis for a book I wrote or an unpaid report on a film I wrote. Conversely, he is happy to help me when I need him, and when I asked him to write something for this book, to tell me what he looks for in a freelancer and to help others find clients like him, he didn't hesitate for a second.

His name is Khaled, and as well as being my favorite client and one of the few that I consider a friend, he is also prolific. He hires many designers, writers, developers, and more, and he understands the client side of things better than anyone. His English is very good, but I have edited the grammar while ensuring I didn't alter any of the meaning.

This is what he had to say:

> I have used freelancing platforms for a long time now, more than four years. I always preferred Elance (currently Upwork), because of the quality of the freelancers there, which is much better than sites like Freelancer, which I have occasionally used for design work. I think I'm probably addicted to freelancing sites as they make my work and my life much easier. It also introduces me to new people and hidden talents around the world, while helping my business to grow faster.
>
> From a personal angle, I love to tell stories, and freelancing sites help to make my dreams come true by helping me find people who can tell them properly and professionally, like PJ. He became a friend and understood my way of thinking and what I wanted to tell the world. English is my second language, but freelancing sites have helped me to finish comic books and novels in English.
>
> Once I have created a job, the first thing that catches my eye is the ambition of the freelancer and the interest he shows in the project. I look for someone who expresses a need to work on the

job, someone who shows me that he/she is willing to go very far to give me exactly what I want, and not someone who is in it just to fill in the lines and collect a paycheck. I want freelancers who really want the job and will give me their full attention and focus—and of course I check the quality of their work throughout each stage of the process.

Price is important as well, but it depends on the work. If the project is huge and needs a professional head, I choose quality above all else. If the job is simple, like a data search or a brochure design, I always focus on price. While many clients will avoid certain countries and nationalities, this is of no interest to me. I just want people who show a good work ethic.

Of course, everyone has both good and bad experiences. For example, I once hired a comic book artist from Colombia to work on a project that PJ actually helped to script. He was an amazing artist, one of the best in the world in my eyes. But sadly he lives in an area that is riddled with drug cartels and rife with violence and unrest, so he doesn't always have access to the Internet and can't always work as quickly as I would like. This means that one "quick" project actually took over eighteen months.*

This is my advice for professionals and business owners who want to hire freelancers:

1. Choose someone who displays a passion for the subject matter and a desire for the job, because this freelancer will give you the best results.
2. Always save the biggest payment for the end, after you check the work. Never pay more than 20 percent in the

---

*Khaled is a very smart man. I am personally dubious of all excuses that I hear and usually reject them outright (**see Section 5.6 on page 102** for my reasons why), but as far-fetched as this seems, I trust that it has some basis in truth. While Khaled is trustworthy, I know he wouldn't just accept a far-fetched excuse as the truth without any proof. Also, while these guys were very late with the work, he left them very good feedback. This is because he is genuinely a great guy, and if you please him, he'll reward you. Clients like this are very rare, and you will often get poor feedback if you are that late.

beginning; otherwise you will be begging the freelancer to finish the work.

3. Always check the history of the freelancer, and double check to make sure they really did the work, rather than only a small part of it.

4. Always be fair to people, and never lie to them or hide any information about your work. Hiding information in the beginning will always lead to bigger problems further down the line.

5. Keep the contact details of the best freelancers so you can always work with them when you need them. Try to create a circle of creative men and women who you can always turn to when in need.

6. Talk to the freelancer over the phone before you hire them to make sure they understand the job.

7. Be nice to the freelancer and the freelancer will be nice back to you. Once they like you, they will give you an even better result.**

8.4 — POLLY: WRITERS, DESIGNERS

Polly is a committed client, one who relies on freelancing platforms to get a number of jobs done. She runs many websites by herself, hiring writers to create the content, and she also works on behalf of

---

**I have already discussed the importance of dealing with individual clients differently, and this is a prime example. Khaled is from the Middle East, and as well as being very warm, God-fearing people, they are also very respectful in business. They will begin messages with "Good morning," "Good afternoon," etc., and they will always wish you well. This is considered polite, so you should return the favor. While I am not at all religious myself, I have made a mental note of Islamic holidays, during which I always wish Khaled well and am also understanding when he might be unreachable because of them. If the client was very cold and standoffish, I wouldn't do this; but Khaled is a warm and friendly person and that sort of personality will always appreciate greetings and well wishes.*

another company doing the same job. She has commissioned content in many categories over the years, and she has also used freelancers to help her with a speech for her brother's wedding, her daughter's application letter to a college, and a few personal projects as well. She understands what it is like to hire at all different levels and is familiar with the frustration that can be a result.

I spoke to Polly about her experience. The below was written by myself, based on the conversation that we had:

> Sites like Upwork seemed like an easy way out. They were perfect, an answer to all of my problems. I needed a lot of content, often by different writers, and there was also a growing need for designers, programmers, and other skills. When I first started though, it was less of a dream and more of a nightmare.
>
> The first freelancer I hired produced work to a very poor standard. I had assumed he would be good because he was charging a fairly big fee, but that was not the case. If he had been thirteen years old and I had been his English teacher, I would be keeping him behind after class so he could brush up on basic English. The next few freelancers all abused the deadlines, and while one of them did produce good work and did hit the first deadline, after that the excuses just rained in.
>
> I had all but given up when I found a capable freelancer. They just make life so much easier. I have worked with many talented writers and designers, and my favorite freelancers definitely fit this mold, but that's not the only reason I keep returning to them. It's the fact that I can trust them. If I have a tight deadline for something that needs to be done, I know these guys can do it for me. There is nothing worse in this industry than having such a deadline, finding a freelancer who says all the right things and makes all the right promises, and then doesn't show up when you need them.
>
> To be a good freelance writer, you don't necessarily have to be a great writer. You just need to meet deadlines, to do what clients ask of you, and to do it in a timely and professional manner. You certainly have to know how to write. If that wasn't the case, I would still be praising the very first freelancer I hired, a man who met the deadlines but couldn't write. But succeeding in this industry

is more about being professional, having the right business sense, making the right decisions, taking on the right jobs, and having the right attitude.

If you are a great writer and you keep missing deadlines and feeding me excuses, I will drop you in a heartbeat. If you are a terrible writer who meets deadlines I will equally lose interest in you. If you do exactly what is asked, if you are competent, and if you meet deadlines, then you will be hired and you will get good feedback.

I would have been delighted with an "average" writer who was very professional when I first started using these sites, but these days I expect my freelancers to be the best in all aspects. Still, that doesn't mean that average writers can't build up a very profitable career and eventually improve those writing skills and take that next step.

Chapter 8 Summary

- Clients are different and look for different things in a freelancer.
- Feedback isn't always the most important thing, but a good attitude can be.
- You don't have to be the best writer to make a good living, but your skills will need to improve if you want to take it up a level.
- All clients respect freelancers who are punctual, professional, and friendly.
- Clients value freelancers who show a passion for their project and a dedication to get it right. If you're not feeling it, fake it.
- Some clients may be easier to please than others, but they all deserve the same respect.

See Also

- *Applying for Jobs (**Chapter 3.0**)*
- *Understanding Clients (**page 57 – 3.5**)*
- *Negotiating (**page 81 – 4.3**)*

- *Your First Jobs (**Chapter 5.0**)*
- *Excuses (**page 102 – 5.6**)*
- *"Offline" Clients (**page 120 – 6.5**)*
- *Outsourcing (**Chapter 11.0**)*
- *A Client Didn't Leave Feedback (**page 208 – 13.8**)*

L6

Chapter 9

SUSPENSIONS, RULES, AND DISPUTES

This is a scary industry, because it's one where customer support is more or less nonexistent and one where the people at the top are completely indifferent to the people at the bottom. A freelance platform relies on big clients, and while they also need good freelancers, it's not their top priority. After all, if a client joins the site and spends $50,000 a year, someone will be ready to pick that up. It doesn't matter if they do a great job or an average job—as long as the money is exchanged, the platform will get their cut. There are always freelancers willing to take a share of that $50K, and when one goes, another five will take his place. Never expect to be valued more than a client on these sites, and never expect to be given fair treatment if you are wrongly banned or suspended. These platforms do appreciate their big earners. They are rare in this industry. But part-time freelancers and amateur workers are ten a penny.

Before you work your way to the status of respected freelancer, you need to stay in the shadows. Don't break any rules, don't give them an excuse to ban you, and don't give the client a reason to open a dispute. A lot of freelancers don't realize how persistently close they are to the edge until they're shoved off.

9.1 — SUSPENSIONS AND BANS

I have been suspended from a freelancing platform and I have also been threatened with a suspension from another, and on neither of those occasions did I do anything wrong. The former was oDesk, before it became Upwork. Back then it was a part-time site for me, playing second fiddle to Elance. I took a risk on a big contract with a guy who had no feedback but who was verified, but because that guy had joint nationality (British-Nigerian), there was an issue with his deposit. Add to the fact that I asked for a large upfront payment, which he paid, which raised so many red flags for oDesk that they tripped over themselves trying to screw me. They suspended him, suspended me, and then spent the next two weeks asking what my relationship with him was, while apologizing for the chaos they had caused.

The second time was on Freelancer. The client listed a job with a respectable hourly rate, but when he offered me the job, he insisted that I only work for $0.50 an hour. Obviously I canceled the job there and then, only for Freelancer to warn me that if I did that again (despite the circumstances), they would suspend me. This is one of the many reasons I avoid Freelancer. They basically told me that I should have agreed to the client's outrageous demands.

In researching this book, I encountered many other freelancers who have been rightly or wrongly suspended. Of course, many of them said the suspension was unjustified—though after a little digging, it seems that they did break the terms and conditions and knew full well they were doing so. However, there are those who get suspended and have no idea why, and this is an incredibly scary thing.

If this happens to you, don't get worked up. Keep your cool. I find that it's best to take a break—to give yourself time to assess the situation, read any emails they send, and check your account—before jumping into a reply. Your first reaction after getting such a shock is likely to swear at them, to call them a bunch of incompetent pricks, and to tell them to fuck off (or maybe that's just me). This might be acceptable with a utility company (If we don't tell them they are useless, then how will they know?), but it's not with a site you rely on to pay the bills when that site does not care whether you work there or not.

Once you have understood all of the angles, then respond professionally and politely. Be firm, by all means, but don't fly off the handle. They don't suspend you without reason, and while their reasons are often absolutely bat-shit insane (refer to previous), the tight controls they have on things like fraud, money laundering, and general bad service means that these things do happen. On many sites, not just freelancing platforms, I find that they will generally ignore you if you send them emails and use the standard contact forms. This is exactly what oDesk did to me for two weeks. However, once you air their dirty laundry for all to see, things change. As soon as I voiced my complaint on Twitter, exposing them using every relevant hashtag and making sure I "mentioned" them, they changed their tune. After two weeks of nothing but apologies and stalling, it took one Twitter message and three hours for my account to suddenly reappear. It doesn't matter if you don't have a lot of followers, or even if you don't have Twitter. Facebook will do.

You can't really avoid suspensions and bans. This is something that could happen to you at anytime and could be the result of a system cock-up or a misunderstanding. The vast majority of suspensions and bans occur because of a handful of reasons, some of which are more innocent than others.

Poor Feedback

I'm not sure whether it exists on Upwork, but on the Elance terms and conditions, there was a sentence that basically said they could ban you outright if they deemed you to be a discredit to the service. I looked into this and discovered that anyone with a string of bad feedback, disputes, and general poor job satisfaction fell foul of this code. If you are banned for this, there is no way to overturn it. These sites don't want freelancers who can't do a good job, because it gives the service a bad name. This makes sense, and while it seems a little harsh, you can't fault them for this. And don't think that just because your average rating is above four or five you won't be banned, because you don't know what clients are saying behind your back or who is complaining. Many of these sites have an option for the client to anonymously report your performance when finalizing a job.

Multiple Accounts

When I first signed up to a freelancing platform, I asked my partner to join as well. She is a fantastic designer, and while it's only a part-time hobby for her, I knew she could make some money on the side. I contacted the site in advance and asked them if it was okay. They basically told me that as long as those two accounts were not linked, as long as they were not exchanging work or feedback, it wouldn't be a problem. There are freelancers who look for an easy way out, creating multiple accounts to swap jobs and build feedback. This is very easy for the freelancing platform to spot though, and it will get you banned. You will also be flagged if your first jobs are all completed for $5 or so, and if all of them generate positive feedback. I spoke to many freelancers who seemed to have been banned for no reason, and I was genuinely baffled, only to discover they were all returning freelancers, with all of them having been banned in the past. If a free-lancing site has banned you in the past, it will ban you again as soon as it makes the connection.

Offline Work

Many freelancing sites do not care if a client abuses you, if they try to blackmail you, or even if they steal all of your work. They are facilitators, mediators—they want their cut and nothing else. However, if there is so much as a suggestion that you have taken a job off the platform and worked through PayPal or another means, they will ban both you and the client. I get a lot of requests like this, and you will too. Under no circumstances should you accept. It's not worth the hassle. Although reluctant to mention it initially, I discovered that many of the banned freelancers I spoke to had done this.

Dispute

If it comes early enough in your career and if it's big enough, it is possible that a single dispute will lead to a suspension. Unfortunately, there are writers out there who will sign up to a platform, post an impressive but fake portfolio, take an upfront payment for a job, and then disappear. The sites want to cut down on this, so if your first job—or even one of your first few jobs—ends in a dispute, it could be over much sooner than you'd like.

Profile

Two months into my time as a freelancer, the platform I was working on threatened me with a suspension if I didn't change my profile picture. They had actually restricted my access to the site because of this and they were ready to pull the trigger. At the time, my profile picture matched the fact that I used a pen name. It was me, but it was me obscuring my face. In no uncertain words, they told me that is was against the terms to use a picture that was "not of me" or was an "illustration or cartoon." It was none of those things, but arguing with these people will get you nowhere, so I changed it. Be sure to follow the guidelines in the profile section **(see Chapter 2.0: Setting Up Your Profile)** to avoid this, because they can be trigger happy at times.

Mistakes

All platforms make mistakes. My only major suspension was a direct result of stupidity on their behalf, and this was not an isolated incident. The only way to avoid this is to refuse to work for anyone without an extensive history, including those marked as "Payment Verified." Because apparently that means nothing.

If you are banned, then it's game over. If it was a wrongful exclusion, then you can fight your corner, preferably out in the open. Show your proof, and give your case as much PR as possible. If you made a mistake, or if your account wasn't very profitable to begin with, just forget about it and move on. There are many more freelancing platforms, many chances to rebuild. You should also look to get involved with other areas, such as self-publishing, blogging, and website flipping, all of which will be discussed in more detail a little later **(see Chapter 15.0: Websites and Blogging)**.

9.2 — DISPUTES

There is a dispute process on all freelancing platforms and they all work in pretty much the same way. A dispute can be filed by a free-lancer or a client, and it can be the result of nonpayment, poor work, or a number of other issues. I have only been involved in one of these, but I know many others who have been dragged into them. As a free-lancer, I would advise against initiating a dispute unless you have already been left feedback for that particular job (unlikely) or unless the client is refusing to pay you a very large amount. Otherwise, a dispute will only anger the client, and while it may get you the money in the end, it will also leave a big red mark on your profile.

Don't panic if a dispute is filed against you. On most sites they are commonplace and the platform will not make rash decisions. They will wait until they have heard both sides, they will take their time, and they will then decide the best course of action. If a client is saying something that is not true, then prove it—this is why it is important to keep all work and all correspondence **(see Section 12.2 on page 190)**. Always be professional, never lash out against the mediators, and never badmouth the client in front of them. There's a good chance that the client will not be able to refrain, so keep your cool, look like the bigger person, and you'll come across as the one who's right. In most dispute processes, the client will be able to see the messages you send to the mediators, so use this to your advantage. Say something, a passing comment, that you know will rile the client and cause them to act out. Once they do, you will gain the upper hand.

When this happened to me, the mediators already knew about the client. They knew he was prone to lies and abuse. And the reason they knew this is because I had already laid the foundations.

As soon as the client threatened me, I got in touch with the platform and showed them his threats, along with every other piece of twisted insanity he had sent me.

If you come across as a bitter, obscene child, they won't listen to you; if you act calm and professional, they will. You're not dealing with robots here; you're dealing with people who have seen their fair share of bitter, blackmailing, lying clients and badmouthed, petulant freelancers. Be neither and let your opponent dig their own grave.

On Upwork and Guru, you can expect fair and equal treatment. If the client is demanding a refund and it's not justified, don't feel you need to give it to them. If you're working on Freelancer, then things might be a little different. That site seems to be geared more toward the client, and I have had too many bad experiences to ever trust them to initiate a fair dispute.

Regardless of the site you use, experience rarely comes into it. They don't care if you have a flawless record and if the client is new to the site. They will treat every case equally, and while that can work against you as you progress, it will benefit you in the beginning.

> **Upwork Verification**
> Although it has not happened to me (yet), there are occasions in which Upwork will ask you to verify your account with photo ID, utility bills, and more. These include:
>
> - Suspicion of duplicate/linked accounts
> - Account suspension/limitations
> - High-risk/suspicious activity
> - Random checks (also known as "because they feel like it")

9.3 — "HIDDEN" RULES

I mentioned some of the lesser known rules above, including the fact that you can be banned just for having a poor work history. If this is going to be your career and your workplace, you need to understand the rules. The rules of a typical workplace come down to common sense. You know it's wrong to swear at your boss, to relieve yourself in his stationery drawer, and to hit on his secretary. But on freelance platforms, there are some strange rules that can easily pass you by. Here are the biggest ones on Upwork and Freelancer, many of which are universal. There are rules for both freelancers and clients, as many of you will need to outsource at one point or another (**see Chapter 11.0: Outsourcing**).

Upwork

- *Freelancer & Client*: One account per user. No sharing or duplicating.
- *Freelancer*: Do not lie on your profile (including falsely claiming you work or have worked for a company).
- *Freelancer*: Do not display contact information on profile (Skype ID, email, etc.).
- *Freelancer*: Spamming job applications—repeatedly applying for jobs that do not match your skills and copy and pasting irrelevant cover letters—may result in suspension.
- *Freelancer*: Do not copy from other users' profiles.
- *Freelancer*: Repeated refunds may result in suspension.
- *Freelancer*: Poor use of English (brought to Upwork's attention via the "invisible" client feedback section) may result in suspension.
- *Freelancer & Client*: Do not leave overly negative, defamatory, or libelous comments on job feedback (rarely enforced).
- *Client*: Do not post the same job multiple times (rarely enforced).
- *Client*: Jobs that discriminate or express preference based on sex, culture, or race are not allowed. "Native writers only" posts are okay.

Freelancer

- *Freelancer*: Do not sell or give away your profile to another user.
- *Freelancer*: Failure to verify account within three months of request, or nonresponse to such requests, will result in a ban.
- *Freelancer*: Their cut (10 percent) will be taken from your chosen payment method (usually a credit card) when the job begins, and

not from the final payment amount. If the client does not pay you upon completion, there is no guarantee that that money will be returned.

- *Freelancer*: Direct quote from the terms and conditions "We may close, suspend, or limit your access to your Account without reason."
- *Freelancer*: Do not post contact info (Skype ID, email, etc.) on message boards, in profile, or in job proposals.
- *Freelancer*: Canceling a job after a client accepts your proposal will result in a warning. Following another cancellation your account will be suspended.
- *Freelancer & Client*: A negative account balance for more than thirty-five days will result in suspension.

I was going to include Guru here, but one of the main benefits of this site is that it seems to be very difficult to get suspended or banned. They are far more relaxed than other freelancing platforms, and in all honesty, I prefer dealing with them. They have absolutely no issue with you posting email addresses or Skype IDs on your profile, they won't harass you about any profile images you use, and they won't suspend you at random. They also tend to be more responsive than others. I asked them a series of inane questions to verify this and received a response within two hours each time, regardless of the time of day I sent the message. It's just a shame that their platform isn't the best.

Chapter 9 Summary
- Don't lash out if you are suspended. Take some time to calm down and assess the situation.
- If you are caught breaking the rules, the game's up and you need to move on. If you did nothing wrong, calmly prove your innocence.
- Air your grievances on social media for the world to see.

- Stay calm and professional during a dispute. Win over the mediator, prove your innocence, and try to incite the client into exposing themselves.
- Pay attention to the rules that can get you banned.

See Also

- *Setting Up Your Profile* **(Chapter 2.0)**
- *Outsourcing* **(Chapter 11.0)**
- *Organization* **(page 190 – 12.2)**
- *I Have Been Suspended* **(page 207 – 13.6)**
- *Horror Stories* **(Chapter 14.0)**
- *Websites and Blogging* **(Chapter 15.0)**
- *Don't Put Too Many Eggs in One Basket* **(page 252 – 16.3)**

Part 3

PROBLEM SOLVING

"... motivation is a huge factor in whether you make any money or whether you spend your days eating ice cream, watching reruns of '90s sitcoms, and talking to your cats (I'm speaking from experience here)."

Chapter 10
ODD JOBS

I don't want to hold your hand through all of this process and I won't need to. Even if you've just started out, you will be able to rely on your writing ability, common sense, and knowledge of the Internet (if you made it far enough to sign up to these sites, then you have all you need) to work on many article writing, content writing, and even creative writing jobs. There are a few jobs that are a little more complicated though, jobs that might be second nature to experienced writers but will come as a complete surprise to novice writers and novice freelancers.

In this chapter we'll take a look at a few of these, explaining them in full and hopefully helping you to get the most out of them. Don't worry if you have never worked on jobs like this before, and don't let that stop you applying for them. I didn't have a clue when I started, and a few of these, including Guest Posts and Memoirs, are part of my regular schedule now. Even if you already know what these jobs are, don't dismiss this chapter, as there are things about them that all freelancers should (but may not) know.

10.1 — GUEST POSTS AND SEO
In the days of oDesk and Elance, you would encounter a small number of guest post jobs, maybe one out of every twenty. After the merge

into Upwork, these became much more common—most likely the result of a handful of clients creating countless jobs and spamming the search pages. If you have never been involved with building a website, and if you are new to online freelancing, then these jobs might be a little confusing.

Nearly a third of all jobs on freelancing platforms relate to SEO, or search engine optimization, which is the name given to the method of increasing the value of sites within the Google algorithm. Google attaches a value to all sites in its engine, and the greater that value, the higher a site will rank. The goal of SEO, and of the SEO writer, is to improve that ranking using a number of methods.

I don't consider myself to be an expert on SEO, but I have taken on many jobs where SEO was prioritized. In my case, I avoided all jobs that mentioned "meta tags" and "keyword density," because this requires a little bit of technical know-how. However, for jobs that simply focus on SEO, the only thing you need to do as a writer is include the keywords that the client gives you. Think of it as a high school writing experiment where you have to write a creative piece that includes a list of words.

One of the most important aspects of SEO is something known as a "backlink." If there is a link to your site on a site that Google already trusts and values highly, then by association Google will think more of your site. The goal of many webmasters is to get something known as a "guest post," whereby they produce an article for another site and within that article place a link to their own site. It's not as simple as "we give you a free article, you increase our SEO," because the value of a link like this can be worth considerably more

SEO in a Nutshell

- SEO aims to improve a website's position in a search engine.
- That position relates to one or more keywords.
- SEO includes image searches, blog searches, web searches, and more.
- SEO includes the use of keywords, tweaked layouts, meta tags, and backlinks.
- The best SEO marketers command thousands of dollars a day.
- Some methods are frowned upon, getting results but risking penalties.
- Black hat SEO refers to practices that are prohibited and not advised.
- White hat SEO refers to methods that are accepted by Google and recommended.

than an article. In fact, if you can get such a link on a site like Huff Post, or another high-value content site, you're looking at a value of hundreds, if not thousands, of dollars.

This is why you will see jobs that advertise the need for a "Huff Post Contributor" or a "High-Value Contributor." Many of these jobs, like so many other jobs on freelancing platforms, are a joke. You will genuinely see jobs like this that offer freelancers less than $50 to write an article and then get it posted on a high-value site. To do this, you need to be already writing for that site. If you're already writing for that site, you're earning much more than $50 for your articles.

The jobs that offer hundreds of dollars for single posts are a little more realistic, but contributors for sites like this can't simply write and publish guest posts at will, and when you consider that they will be risking their job—or at the very least their reputation—for what amounts to a fraction of their usual pay, they would be crazy to do it. In fact, very few people do, and that's why these jobs often amount to nothing.

The clients will keep trying, simply because they believe they can spend a few hundred and get something that is worth much more; they believe this because they see similar jobs posted by other clients. Look at it this way: The minimum fee for a campaign on BuzzFeed, which includes "sponsorship" articles that are similar to guest posts, is $100,000. I know this because I enquired. If you think you can get the same value for just a few hundred dollars, you're either very optimistic or very naive.

From a freelancer's perspective, these jobs are best ignored. You might think that the added incentive is worth the effort it takes to try and get an article published on a high-value site, but you'd be wrong. "Backlink" posts are always blatantly obvious, and the biggest sites turndown hundreds of these a week. This is because while it benefits the client and the freelancer, it does not benefit them.

There are smaller sites that can qualify as well, but only if the client specifies it. If they focus on the big-name sites only, and on

Google Change
In 2015, Google made their biggest algorithm change for many years. This change forced all websites to accommodate mobile users. If they did not, they were penalized with decreased rankings and PR. This had been in the pipeline for several years and was the result of statistics showing that more people access the Internet (and therefore use Google) via mobile devices than they do through desktop computers.

"high-value backlinks," then ignore them. If they open themselves up to a wide assortment of sites, and if you have access to such sites, then try your luck. Some writers have their own sites, some write for friends, and some are part of a bigger community. You can check the value of the site you write for with a "Page Rank Checker," which gives you a number from zero to ten after you input the site's URL.

Anything under four is useless. The bigger sites tend to be eight and above. If you write for a site above six, then clients will probably be interested in backlinks. If you write for a site between four and five, it's still worth a shot. Of course, the issue here is that clients looking for backlinks usually place no value on the actual article itself and therefore may only offer you a price based on the value of the backlink. That wouldn't be too bad, if you didn't have to write a 1,000-word article just to include that backlink.

Although rarer, there are also jobs that require you to write for a specific site, one which accepts guest posts and asks you to follow certain guidelines. These are completely different. The site is open to accepting submissions, but the article needs to be very good. I have taken on jobs like this for long-term clients, but only under certain circumstances. You should expect to earn more money for these jobs, and you will need to factor in rewrites and edits. If the payment and deadline does not allow for or cover that, you're better off ignoring them.

10.2 — SPINNING

There is an episode of the sitcom *Friends* (which my partner insists on watching day after day, even though it finished over a decade ago) where Joey discovers a thesaurus. Excited by the prospect of making his writing sound intelligent, he goes to town on a letter, using the thesaurus on every word. By the end none of it makes sense. This, to some extent, is "spinning," and the end product is often just as terrible. There are two forms of spinning, though, so this requires a little more explanation.

As with guest posts, "Article Spinning"—often written as just "Spinning"—relates to search engine optimization. Google values originality over anything else. Otherwise you could just steal a strong SEO article from another site to use on your own. So, when a webmaster wants to replicate an article to go on all of his or her sites (a person who makes their living creating and running websites will rarely have less than ten on the go), he or she needs to ensure that each variation is 100 percent unique.

You will find rewriting jobs that pay you to duplicate articles manually. I have taken on many of these myself, and while they are incredibly tedious (especially when you are tasked with writing the same article hundreds of times), it's easy money. These jobs are occasionally referred to as "Spinning," but most of the time this word is used to refer to a cheaper, quicker, and more automated process. And it requires a detestable type of program known as "Spinning Software."

This is not something I would ever endorse and it is something I have despised since I started, because the end result is always—without exception—absolutely terrible. You feed this software an article and it churns out a duplicate of that article that is 100 percent original. It sounds amazing, but as you may have guessed, we're not quite in the realms of science fiction here. The software uses

Price for Manual Rewriting
Rewriting doesn't necessarily take half the time, and in many cases it will take just as long as writing from scratch. But as there is no research or thinking time needed, these jobs move fairly quickly. Clients will expect you to reduce your rate by at least 50 percent for these jobs, so if you charge $0.07 per word to write from scratch, charge $0.035 to rewrite. "Automated spinning" jobs will never pay more than $0.01 per word, and you'll be lucky if you can find one paying $0.001. In many cases, freelancers earn less than $2 an hour for such jobs.

a simple algorithm whereby words and phrases are altered slightly, making them completely different to the original, while still getting the point of the original across. That's the theory anyway, because in practice these articles rarely make any sense. The job of the "spinner" is to go through these articles and ensure they do make sense.

The latter part of that job isn't always included though, and in many cases clients will require the freelancer to simply feed the articles into the software.

Clients find it much easier to create a job and offload their work to a freelancer willing to work for pennies than to just do it themselves. Also, if anything goes wrong and if the articles make no sense, they have someone to blame and can insist that the freelancer fixes the issue, even though it's not the freelancer's fault. They'd have to be utter contemptible bastards to act like that, but if they're willing to initiate a job that produces a diabolical end product, and one where the freelancer makes approximately fuck-all per hour, then it's clear we're not dealing with the Dalai Lama here.

In the cases where they do include the latter part of the job, asking freelancers to make the articles legible, they rarely get what they want. That's because those freelancers are working for pennies and have little grasp of the English language. They can't really expect anything else for the price they pay, yet these clients often do, which means these jobs result in a bad experience and bad feedback for all.

Whether you are willing to work for pennies or not, "automated spinning" jobs should be avoided. Not only will you get very little money for very tedious work, but you're also contributing to the millions of content sites out there that read like riddles written in pidgin English.

10.3 — NAMING JOBS

In the real world, if you want to find a name for your company or your product and you don't have a creative bone in your body, you go to a marketing team. In the world of online freelancing, for reasons that I only partially understand, you ask a writer. We're creative people and some of us have business and marketing sense, but the vast majority of us do not.

If you are a client and you need a good name for a product or company, post your job in the marketing section. Not only will you get the creativity you need, but you'll also get some marketing expertise, potentially from someone who understands your industry and your customers.

From the point of view of a freelancer, don't turn these jobs down, as they can make you a quick buck. Be very careful when undertaking them, though, because things can turn ugly fast. You're in a unique position, and one where your work is only good or bad based on the opinion of one person, who may be a complete and utter numbskull.

I worked on a few of these jobs early on. One of them was for a client who had me name his company. I thought it would be fun so I undercharged him and I gave him a few really good names. That's not just my opinion either, as I ran them by several others and they all agreed on one of them. However, when I gave that list to the client, he ignored them all, delayed payment and response, and then, eventually, created one of his own. When he told me the name he had chosen I couldn't believe it. It had nothing to do with anything. It was not smart, and it didn't correspond to his industry, his demographic, or his products. Everyone agreed with me, but the one man who didn't just so happened to be the one making the final decision.

Still, I ended up with good feedback because the client was thankful for the work I did—and there's the clincher. While quality is always better than quantity, that doesn't apply when the "quality" is subjective. I was disappointed that he didn't use a good name and that I didn't help, but I soon got over that. I realized that with these jobs, the goal of the freelancer is not to find the perfect name but to do enough for the client to think they have tried. After all, you could find the best name in the world, and the client could opt for a tired cliché instead.

You need to show the client that you have worked hard. You'll probably think of thirty names before you find a good one, and many freelancers will only give the client that good one. Bad idea. Instead, pick another ten or twenty from your "discarded" list, putting your best one at the top of a new list with the others underneath. Tell the client that you enjoyed the job so much that you decided to devote more time to it and to create more names for them. Don't gush, but let them know that you wish them well and that you were happy to do what it took to help them.

You might not find a name that they will like or use, but you'll get paid, you'll get good feedback, and you can move on. That's all that matters.

10.4 — MEMOIRS

Andy Warhol once said, "In the future, everyone will be world famous for fifteen minutes." Much to the anathema of many—no doubt including Warhol himself if he was alive to see it—that has come to fruition courtesy of reality TV and social media. We're seeing something similar in the publishing world. There is a whole subsection of society that wants nothing more than to be famous—people who think that the world would be interested in knowing what they do, think, and see every minute of every day. This perception leads them to commission freelancers like you and I to write their life stories.

I was once headhunted by a client on Elance who insisted that I write about his life for free, being so kind as to offer me 10 percent of the royalties if I wrote, published, and marketed the book for him. Before I realized he was insane and I ran a mile, I was forced to listen to his nonsensical attempts at proving he was worldly and well read. I have no idea why he was determined for me to believe this, but I found it amusing when he quoted "someone" as saying, "Everyone has a book in them," before adding that "that guy" was right and "[his] book will be a bestseller." What I didn't stick around to tell him was that the quote—attributed to everyone from Karl Kraus to Christopher Hitchens—was actually, "Everyone has a book inside them, but in most cases that's where it should remain." If this client hadn't stopped at the first sign of a comma, then he might have saved both my time and his.

Writing someone's memoir can be a rewarding experience, but it can also be an incredibly tedious and frustrating one. It's all about the luck of the draw, and there are far more bad clients in that draw than there are good ones. These days I turn down most of the invites I get for memoir writing jobs, but if you want to wade through the insane, the dull, and the time wasters, you might find something worthwhile, and, more important, you might find a client who is actually willing to pay you real money.

To make the process easier, it's best to avoid any personal memoirs where the job application looks like it was written by a child. If they can't appreciate or understand basic grammar, they will not appreciate good writing and will refuse to pay for it. These clients genuinely believe that writing is writing, and that as long as their dictations and their plot is the same, it doesn't matter who pens the final product.

You should also avoid anyone who stresses the need for someone local or someone who can travel. This is mainly because most of the time the client just wants an ego fix. They want someone who will listen to them as they recite their life story. And the vast majority will expect you to do this for free. You're not a shrink and you don't work for free. If they are not willing to pay for travel expenses and to cover your costs every time they talk your ear off, then they are not worth it.

Providing a client can write emails, use a telephone, dictate to an audio file, or simply send messages through a freelancing platform, then you don't need to be in direct contact with them to write their memoir. Of course, professional memoir writers will travel the world to sit with their clients, but those guys are getting in excess of $500,000 a book, and you'd be lucky to get 1 percent of that.

The best memoirs to write are ones where the client is not the subject (sons and daughters who want books about their parents to show the grandkids, widowers who want to preserve the memory of their loved ones, etc.) and business memoirs, where the subject is a rich entrepreneur who wants his ego stroked in written form. The former client will not want to devote much time to the project. He or she may have already attempted to write or research the memoir and will therefore have something for you to build upon. The latter will be too busy to get involved, will often direct you to information you can use, and will be willing to pay big for good writing.

If you do insist on getting involved with a personal memoir, then be sure to ask for an hourly contract, tell them in advance that you will charge them for any discussions and any research, and make sure you get everything signed and sealed before you let them talk shit to you for hours on end. There are clients out there who string dozens of writers along with no intention of paying them a penny, purely so they can talk about themselves for a few hours.

10.5 — EDITING PERSONAL WRITING

I avoid editing jobs where someone's novel or other personal project is involved, only undertaking them under specific circumstances and with specific clients.

This can go wrong in so many ways, but the basic issues stem from the fact that a lot of people believe they can write when few of them actually can. I have seen some appalling examples in my time and have been asked to edit them. This included one "novel" that was actually only twenty pages long. It consisted of a James Bond–obsessed middle-aged man's wet dream. Half of that "novel" was actually devoted to one fight scene, where the "writer" had clearly enjoyed himself and gotten carried away. A lot of people write for fun, and if that's how he gets his kicks, so be it. But he wanted me to give this novel a "quick clean" so he could, and I quote, "sell it to a publisher."

I had to be the one to crush his dreams, because he paid me to be honest. I was lucky with him, because he understood my honesty and saw his own flaws, but he was a rare case. There are many writers out there who don't understand their own ability. This applies to good writers who think they are worthless, but more so to bad writers who think they are the dog's bollocks. In fact, experience has taught me that the best writers think they are terrible, while the worst writers think they are amazing. If you're the one smashing their dreams with a paid edit, they're not going to be happy with you. They might argue with you, they will almost surely give you bad feedback, and they might refuse to pay you.

A "friend" of mine once told me that he had tried to find an editor for a quick polish of his book. He blew up on this editor because, in his words, they were trying to rip him off. Basically, the editor had told him that it was not the quick proofreading job the writer had promised; rather, the book was in such a poor state that he would need to charge more than what had been previously agreed upon. The writer was furious with this, so sure it was a scam and that his book needed a handful of corrections at the most. I asked for a copy of that book, and I am not exaggerating when I say that it was the worst thing I have ever read. The twenty-page Bond porn mentioned earlier looked like Tolstoy next to this.

This is the mentality you are dealing with on such edits. They often don't realize their true ability and instead think that you are trying to rip them off and/or you are just being a dick. I liken this mentality to the tone-deaf singers who head for the *X Factor* auditions every year, inciting calls of "How do they not know they're terrible?" from viewers nationwide. We're not talking about writers who lack a certain polish either. I have worked with many writers who have poor grammar and very messy writing but who also have moments of greatness and glimmers of genius that signify potential.

The same goes for many published authors looking back on their old work. It looks terrible, but the potential was there. With many writers, though, there is no potential, and while they think they are worthy of publication, they are a long way off.

You should always ask for a sample if someone asks you to edit their book. A simple paragraph will do. That should be enough to tell you if that client can string two words together. They could still be a poor writer, but dealing with someone who understands English and can string sentences together is completely different to dealing with someone who writes like their cat is napping on their keyboard. If you tell someone that their work needs a little polish, or "this and that" needs changing, they'll be okay with it. If you tell them they need to scrap everything and find a new career, they won't be.

There is another negative aspect to editing as well: deep down, most people are idiots. I would like to follow this up by saying that I don't really mean that—but I do. Editing jobs really bring this out in people, because as soon as someone thinks he knows more than the person working for him, he becomes obnoxious and even mean. Albeit laughably so. For this, I have an example that happened before I started on these online freelancing sites. It was an unpaid job for a friend of a friend. As it turned out, he held some unexplained bitterness toward me, even though I was taking time out of my day to help him with his shit.

It was a small edit, but in it I used a serial comma, also known as an Oxford comma. Many of you will know what this is, but the "client" did not. He pointed it out (again, I was doing this for free), drew my attention to it, and then berated me for not understanding how commas work. I mentioned the serial comma, and with the look he gave me, you'd think I'd just told him I was a Power Ranger. When I used the word "sic," which follows a misspelled quote to show that it was like that originally, he genuinely thought that I was saying the quote was "sick," like some 1990s stoner. And he also had an issue with the use of quotes and italics, all of which were used correctly.

In the end I told him to do it himself. That experience left me wondering if there was anything about the English language he *did* know, while he was presumably left thinking that either I knew even less or that I had invented my own language and had been trying to impose it on his novel.

I know of other editors who have encountered similar issues. Everyone is a grammar Nazi these days, including those who don't understand basic grammar. You'd think Google would solve these issues instantly, but I'm not sure these guys know how to use the Internet. It would certainly explain a lot.

Chapter 10 Summary

- A vast number of jobs on all freelancing platforms relate to SEO.
- Jobs asking for "High-Value Backlinks" only benefit the client and are rarely completed as needed.
- Unless you want to work for less than minimum wage and get abused by clients, avoid Article Spinning jobs.
- Avoid personal memoirs unless the client is paying you to travel and listen.
- Approach personal editing jobs very carefully, and always ask for a sample of the client's work first.

See Also

- *Searching for a Job* **(page 43 – 3.1)**
- *Sending Proposals and Communicating with Clients* **(page 135 – 7.6)**
- *Horror Stories* **(Chapter 14.0)**
- *Take Risks* **(page 256 – 16.5)**
- *Researching a Job* **(page 292 – 19.1)**

Chapter 11

OUTSOURCING

Outsourcing is crucial to your success as a freelance writer, but while it can make your life easier if done properly, it can also break you. I have already discussed how a lot of freelancers on sites like Upwork do not deliver on time and do not deliver quality work. When it comes to outsourcing, you're the client, so you will have to deal with these freelancers yourself.

The first step is to know when to outsource. There is only one instance in which I will outsource a project, and that is when the client knows about it. For one of my oldest and closest clients, I used to run a number of sporting blogs. I wrote content on everything from soccer to snooker. I know a lot about sport, but I can't cover every sport myself, and I know very little about baseball, golf, and MMA. To ensure the site had this content, and knowing I was in full control of the site and everything that was posted on it, I suggested that I find qualified writers to write articles about these other sports. I hired them for less than I was earning, I rewrote and edited everything they sent me, and I posted them. In essence, I was being paid to write and I was also being paid to edit. At the end of the day, the client was happy with all of it.

Now, if I had done this without informing him, I am sure he would not have been happy and he would have had every right. If a client pays you a lot of money to complete a particular project, they expect *you* to complete it. Simple as that. You are deceiving them if you do not, and by doing so you are running the risk of losing that client and getting bad feedback.

That's not to say that you should avoid it altogether. Personally, I have been so put off by the process of finding a competent freelancer within my price range (I have to offer less in order to make a profit, which means I am scraping the barrel) that I do not outsource for any other projects. If you can find a competent writer, though, and if you are confident of your ability to edit their work (never send it straight on), then there is no reason why you shouldn't work this angle.

Outsourcing can be a great way of rationing your time when you establish yourself. In the beginning, you will be working cheaply and there will be no chance of finding someone even cheaper than you to outsource to. When you establish yourself, when you get more contracts and for more money, then you can consider hiring someone who was in the same position as you were when you started. Their work will be just as good, but the fact that they have only just started and are offering a low price means you can hire them and still take a substantial cut.

Once you outsource the work, it is your prerogative to ensure it is up to scratch and is exactly what the client ordered. If the outsourcer does not deliver and still demands payment, do not then send that work onto the client and also demand payment. The client should not be held responsible for the failings of your outsourcer. Pay them and then do the work yourself, before writing that particular experience off as a loss.

Outsourcing Accounts

On Upwork you will be given a client account as soon as you sign up as a freelancer. If possible, always look to use a different account when working as a client. If you can't do this through Upwork, use one of the other platforms. Simply put, freelancers will expect leniency and may even cut corners if they know you also work as a freelancer. Some of them may look to hurt your status as a freelancer if you leave them bad feedback. They may even inform clients you were looking to outsource their work. There are many ways it can work against you, so keep these accounts separate.

Such instances are rare, and once you get into the rhythm of it, you will find that you have a number of outsourcers that you can go to on a regular basis. You know the standard of work they produce and you know how much they charge. When you get to this stage, the money is easy to come by.

If, for instance, you have a full schedule but have stumbled onto a job that offers a lot of money, then apply for it with your rate and give them a sample of your outsourcer's work. This way they know exactly what they will get. If they agree to hire you, it will be because you have great feedback and a solid profile. And because they are expecting exactly what you will give them, you shouldn't have an issue with feedback. At the end of the day, you will be earning a large cut for acting as a middleman and doing very little.

It should be noted that I have never done this myself. I have certainly been in situations where my schedule is full and I have been offered other jobs, but I have yet to find a freelancer I trust to deliver as well as cover a wide range of subjects. I'm also very critical of everyone else's work and this makes it difficult to pass anything on without spending a lot of time editing it.

11.1 — THE WORST WRITERS

I have not outsourced much, but I have hired writers for other projects. As I will discuss under a section on blogging and website creation **(see Chapter 15.0: Websites and Blogging)**, running a website is a very useful thing to do as a writer. I set a number of these up myself and wrote for all of them, only to get inundated with work and no longer have the time to keep them updated. Instead, I decided to pay writers to create the content for me. Cue weeks of the worst writing and the most unprofessional behavior I have seen in my life.

One man actually swore at me when he misunderstood something, and he still expected me to continue hiring him and paying him. I had been nothing but polite, but even when he realized the mistake was his own, there was no apology. He was actually shocked when I closed the job, and right after some more swearing and needlessly rude behavior, I left him bad feedback. I hired another client to give me some funny images of his own creation, only for him to Google "Comedy" and take the first image he found. When I asked him, he claimed it was his own image and when I confronted him with the truth, he ignored me and disappeared. Another woman sent me the most appalling writing I have ever seen, and I asked her to change it. Several hours later I returned to find she had sent me a string of messages needlessly attacking me. She had clearly been stewing, and in those moments of madness, when she was getting herself worked up—imagining what I must have been thinking and what I must have been saying behind her back—she retaliated in a fight against herself. Of course, I hadn't said or thought anything, but I did begin to think those things when I stumbled on her neurotic backlash.

I have worked with writers who insisted they were capable and that they were the best, only to receive work that I wouldn't expect from a child. If my ten-year-old niece produced anything so terrible, I would slap my brother.

I will admit that I do have high standards, but I wasn't looking for a great writer—someone who understood English would have been nice. It's not as if these were nonnative speakers either—they were from the United Kingdom, United States, and Australia. They were English, they just didn't understand their own mother tongue. As an example, look at the following excerpt, used to begin an article on binary options. This writer valued her services at $0.03 per word.

> A binary option trading is not small, radical investment channel. That is accessible just from a small number of online platforms. Numerous binary trading platforms for operatives have developed with identifying capabilities.

Not only is that exactly how I received it, but that's the edited version—that's what I was sent *after* I handed it back with a perplexed

"What the fuck?" I mean, what was she thinking? "I used big words and punctuation in there. That's what writing is, right?"

What's more, this was just the first paragraph. The rest of the article was much worse, but she had good feedback and she charged me $0.03 per word, which works out at around $30 an hour. Now, you take a look at that paragraph and tell me if that writer deserves $30 an hour.

If your answer is anything other than "Hell no," you are not only demented, but you are also the dream client of every half-arsed writer out there. Don't get me wrong. I am not one to pick faults with the work of others, and I definitely don't like to mock or to point out flaws. I get a lot of aspiring writers coming to me with their work, and I find it difficult to be honest because I don't want to hurt their feelings. However, this woman was charging me, and she was charging me an amount that I had actually worked for myself as a writer. I would have never produced anything so incomprehensible, and she shouldn't have done either.

Luckily, I learned how to avoid writers like this, how to find the best of the best, without paying over the odds for it.

11.2 — THE BEST WRITERS

I'm going to go against everything I have said in this book. I have extolled the virtue of never lowering your price and I have moaned about clients who pay peanuts and expect the best writers in the world. However, when you're standing on the other side of the fence, your goal is to spend as little as possible while also getting as much as possible. I wasn't making anything from those websites to begin with, and for quite a long time after that, so I couldn't afford to pay a lot to keep them going. I needed cheap writers. As an outsourcer, you will also need cheap writers, because you could be working with very fine margins.

Still, you should never sink to the levels of some clients. You should never expect good work for anything less than $0.01 per word; if you're paying that amount and it's not for a bulk job, you should understand that it's not going to be perfect. You can find very good writers for just $0.03 per word, but they need to be new to the platform and they need to be inexperienced. You won't get published authors for this price, but you will get writers with the talent to be published who lack the experience to realize or accomplish that.

Post a job on Upwork and state a random fixed-price budget. Never tell them exactly what your budget is or what you are looking to pay per word. If you offer a top-end budget of, say, $500, you would expect to receive varying offers from varying talents. In reality, almost miraculously, everyone who applies—from bestselling authors to those who can barely spell their own name—will quote a price of $500. If you create the same job for $50, you'll get many of the same freelancers applying. I actually ran a test to prove this, creating two similar jobs that required identical talents and identical time-frames. On one I set the budget as $300, and on another I set it as $50, asking that people ignore the budget on both jobs and set their own value. There were three different freelancers who quoted their "minimum" rate as $300 on the first and then $50 on the second. (This is a terrible thing to do as a freelancer, because clients know you are doing it and will lose respect for you because of it.)

Do not mention a price per word or per hour. The budget for the job is there as a placeholder only, and it should be above $300 to entice the right people. Don't worry if you can't afford to pay this amount, you won't need to.

Upwork will ask you how many freelancers you want to hire, and at this point you're looking for at least ten. You can also insert some custom questions into the proposal that all applicants will need to answer. I like to use these two:

What is your price per word? Bearing in mind that I have a tight budget.

Will you be willing to complete a sample article for a lower price?

You should get a flood of applicants. Your first step is to ignore all those who go way over budget. Next, pick out half a dozen that look promising. At this point, don't focus on their profile or their history; focus entirely on their cover letter and their cohesiveness, because many queries are a mess, and if they can't get that right, they won't be able to write a decent article.

Find a set price that you can easily afford to lose and ask them all to complete paid sample articles to be delivered in forty-eight hours. You should ensure these sample articles will be of use to you if they are good, so make sure they are on the topic you are trying to outsource. From these jobs, you will learn who is professional, who can meet deadlines, and who is a decent writer. Make sure you run all articles through Copyscape or another plagiarism checker, because at least 10 percent of freelancers you hire will give you plagiarized content.

Keep doing this until you find someone decent. Once you do, strike a deal with them. To begin with, keep them on a low price. I have worked with decent writers and have watched them mess up time and time again. Only when they are consistent should you look to give them more. Be upfront about this—let them know that if they do what you ask, the price will increase. How much you give them is up to you, but if you're earning $0.06 per word for the job and they are doing 100 percent of the work, you can pay them as much as $0.04 per word.

Of course, many times you will find writers who need a lot of polishing before they can be relied upon. Luckily, there is a way around this, and it will also give you a way to use that mass of badly written sample articles you will have undoubtedly accumulated.

11.3 — MIDDLE-GROUND WRITERS

I have always worked on fine margins. I only outsourced for one job and it was a bulk job, paying very little. I took 50 percent of the cash, but the writers were never good enough for me to simply pass their work straight on. Instead, I edited it. This was more than a simple polish—usually more like a rewrite—but it was very quick and easy for me, taking a third of the time it would to write the article from scratch.

You will encounter a lot of writers like this. The better they are, the less you need to rewrite. All articles can be fixed, unless they come from really bad writers, such as in the excerpt shown previously. In those cases, it's easier to write from scratch, so there is no use for them. This is a balancing act, and if you get it wrong, you could eliminate all of the benefits that outsourcing brings.

Let's imagine you find a job that pays you $0.05 per word for 10,000 words a month. You want to outsource this as you're busy elsewhere and can't focus all of your time on it. Of that $500, you will get around $450 once the site takes their cut. If you have done the legwork, as mentioned above, then you might have a writer on standby who will work for $0.04 per word, but then your profit is only $50 a month, and for the time it takes to delegate, it's not worth it. However, if you find a decent writer for around $0.02 per word (look at the Pricing Chart **[see Section 4.2 on page 78]** for a detailed analysis of price and ability) then you can simply edit their mistakes, polish their articles, and pocket $300 a month. Rather than earning $500 for writing 10,000 words, which many writers will do in around six hours, you're earning $300 for a simple edit, which may take you as little as two hours plus thirty minutes of delegation.

What's more, if you give them a big contract, paying them in bulk for a batch of articles that you drip-feed to your client, you should be able to get them down even more. After all, negotiation **(see Section 4.3 on page 81)** is as important from the client side as it is from the freelancer side.

Always try and give a little back though—always try and keep the cycle going. If you manage to find a great writer who agrees to work for very little and you find yourself taking a huge cut, then slip them some extra money. You're in this game to make money, but so are they, and they're taking your cast-offs, so they clearly need it more than you.

11.4 — EXPERIENCE

Even if you do not need to outsource a project or hire for your own project, this is still something that you need to experience. I learned more as a client than I did as a freelancer, because it was only when I tried to hire writers, artists, and coders myself that I realized just why everyone had valued me as a freelancer.

I work hard, don't get me wrong, and I think of myself as a good writer. However, I am confident that 95 percent of my success is not down to my ability as a writer, but rather to my commitment as a worker. I'm a slave to many of my clients. I respond to all questions, offers, and interviews within minutes. I work fifteen or more hours a day. I never miss deadlines. I am always friendly, polite, and professional. Basically, I follow all of the rules laid out in this book, very few of which actually have anything to do with my abilities as a writer.

I thought that was standard practice until I began to outsource, at which point I realized that what I had understood to be common sense was actually missing from most freelancers. This has to be seen to be believed. The ineptitude is astounding, and on many occasions it defies belief. Yet, this is your competition; this is what you're up against. These are the people who will be hired ahead of you when you receive those "I'm sorry it didn't work out" messages. These are the people who will fuck up, deliver shitty work, or even just disappear, leaving the client to either give up on the freelancing platform or to turn to a competent freelancer.

Professionalism is what makes you in this industry. On many occasions, I have delivered way short of my best work and have received nothing but praise for it. I always try, of course, but if you do the same thing for fifteen hours a day, eventually your mind switches off. By the thirteenth, fourteenth, or fifteenth hour, you will probably lose the fluidity that you had on the first, second, and third. Providing you never lose that professionalism and work ethic, though, none of this matters.

I'm not saying that I'm the best freelancer on the site. Far from it. I'm not egotistical and I don't claim to be the best at anything. However, I know I am a hard worker. I know I am always committed to reaching my end goal, and that alone has put me where I am.

From my experience, these sites are awash with useless freelancers. Your goal is to avoid becoming one of them. But first, take a look at what they do and how they operate. Create a few jobs, spend a little money—the experience alone will be worth it.

11.5 — WHERE TO OUTSOURCE

While Upwork is probably the best place to outsource, there are other platforms that can be useful if you can't quite find what you're looking for on Upwork. Freelancer, which I have written several negative things about, is okay if you are the client. And just because I hate the site doesn't mean you will.

The issue with Freelancer is that it is open for exploitation, and that puts freelancers in a very awkward position. "Contests" rely on complete and utter trust from complete and utter strangers, and while the system is willing to ignore clients who don't play by the rules **(see Section 1.1 on page 3)**, freelancers are always treading on thin ice.

Offline Outsourcing

If you have the connections, you can make a lot of money outsourcing work to freelancers you know in person. Established writers tend to know amateur/aspiring writers who look up to them and ask for advice. You might know a younger, unemployed family member or friend. If so, you will know exactly how reliable and talented they are. Because you're acting as the middleman and taking all of the stress and logistics out of the job, they might just agree to help you with a few projects. Everyone wins this way. You're giving a talented amateur some experience, some writing credits, and a little money on the side; and, following some light editing and some delegation, you're picking up a healthy profit.

Fiverr also has its uses. Again, these can be exploited, as there are good writers willing to sell their soul for $5; but if you invest your time in finding the right people, and you give them bonuses when they deserve it, there's no harm in it. Just search for "writing," "article," or "words," and you'll find gigs from writers who are willing to open their soul for the price of a cup of coffee. They usually have samples of their work, and you can often tell how good they are by simply reading their profile and gig description. The same goes for People-Per-Hour, but the issue with this site, Fiverr, and sites like them is that you have to do the work to find the freelancers. On freelancing platforms, you create the job and you wait for them to come to you, while on these sites it works the other way around. If you don't have a lot of free time, this is not a viable option. If you do have the time and you're prepared to use that in order to save a few bucks, then go for it.

As you begin to outsource more, you'll start believing you can make a career out of it. Think again. There are ways to do this, but the time it takes to find useful writers, to keep them in check, to put up with their missed deadlines, and to polish their shoddy work means that it's often easier just to work as an individual. You can read more about this in Chapter 16 **(see Section 16.2 on page 251)**.

Chapter 11 Summary

- Outsourcing can increase your profit without increasing your hours.
- Your reputation is in the hands of the person you hire.
- Always create "sample" jobs in order to whittle down the applicants.
- Remember to remain polite and professional at all times, even when the freelancer does not.
- If you can afford to pay more, do so.

See Also:
- *Freelancer (**page 3 – 1.1**)*
- *Pricing Chart (**page 78 – 4.2**)*
- *Negotiating (**page 81 – 4.3**)*
- *Websites and Blogging (**Chapter 15.0**)*
- *"Companies" Are Doomed to Fail (**page 251 – 16.2**)*

Chapter 12

PRODUCTIVITY AND ORGANIZATION

If you don't enjoy writing, you're not going to sustain yourself for long. All freelance writers begin with a passion for the craft, and after a couple of years, when clients, deadlines, and demands have worn them down, they despise the thing they used to adore. At that point, they have worked for long enough and established themselves well enough that they can work on autopilot and/or they can afford to take a break until they rediscover their passion. If you didn't have that to begin with, if writing is not something you enjoyed, you won't have the will to push through those difficult times.

Will Self, a freelancer himself, and a great author as well, said that freelancing is all about willpower. Just like any other career path, you need the strength of will to push through the stress and the tedium. This is definitely true, and willpower is not something I have ever had an issue with.

Patience is important. There will be times when you're waiting for the client to review your work or to pay you, times when doubt and paranoia take over. You have to be resilient and thick-skinned too. Also, just like anyone who works for themselves, motivation is a huge factor in whether you make any money or whether you spend your days eating ice cream, watching reruns of '90s sitcoms, and talking to your cats (I'm speaking from experience here).

I often get asked how I can find the motivation to work from home—how I can avoid the distractions of TV, computer games, and a fully stocked drinks cabinet. The truth is that I don't. I sit on my ass watching TV all day and write at the same time, but only because much of the work I do, and much of the work you will do as well, requires very little concentration and can be completed on autopilot.

In the beginning, however, especially for inexperienced writers, this is not advised, because even the most tedious of work needs your full attention.

12.1 — NO DISTRACTIONS

Find a room in your house where you can work free of distractions. All writers need an office, somewhere away from noise and distractions. It should be cozy and quiet, and there should be no TVs, game consoles, or any other major distraction.

My own office is away from the main room in the house and there is a lock on the door. The walls are decorated with my favorite art prints, there is a fully stocked bookshelf, and there are also enough intoxicating substances to kill a small herd of elephants. This is my haven. It is where I work on my novels, and it is where I spent my first year as a freelancer. But when the tedium set in and I realized I didn't need silence to write half of the stuff I was writing, I took my laptop downstairs and set up shop in front of the big-screen TV. Of course, my partner works for most of the day, so it's usually just me and the animals in the house. If there are others in your house throughout the day, you will need that solitude at all times.

As for motivation, this should not be an issue. If the work is there and your career and a large paycheck are on the line, you shouldn't have an issue doing it. If you do, you're in the wrong profession.

You can't slack as a freelancer, because every minute you spend pissing about on Facebook equates to a missed opportunity, to lost money, and to a pissed-off client.

If you're struggling to find the motivation, remind yourself what will happen if you miss that deadline, if you don't apply for more jobs, etc. It could be the difference between paying the rent and getting evicted, the difference between achieving your goals and spending the rest of your life in your parents' basement. We all have different levels of ambition and we all have different goals, but if you don't really want this, you're not going to find the determination you need to succeed at it.

Don't try and kid yourself with excuses either. No one cares. You are in this alone. The pressure, the stress, the deadlines, the disputes—all of it is down to you and you alone. Don't lie to yourself, don't feed yourself excuses—*I'm not feeling too well today, I missed my morning coffee, I hurt my finger*—just put your head down and get on with it.

One of the biggest concerns I hear is from people who have been out of employment for a while—people not used to the discipline of work. This is not an issue and it should certainly not be an excuse. I have worked all of two days in my life outside of being a writer, and both of those were when I was seventeen. From the age of eighteen to twenty-eight, I was an unemployed writer, one who wrote novels, short stories, and query letters for a "living." Yet I had no issue transitioning from that into a full-time writer working seven days a week and fifteen hours a day. In fact, I find that people in the same position as myself tend to handle freelancing better. They may not be used to the regime, but they understand what it is like to have nothing and to do nothing all day. They don't value free time as much as others; they are happy to work every minute they have. Those used to full-time employment and strict schedules tend to value their time off; they expect longer breaks; they set themselves strict working hours; and they usually take the weekend off.

Being a successful freelancer is a full-time job, and by that I don't mean a nine-to-five that comes with holidays and weekends off. You are literally expected to work from morning to night, from Monday to Sunday, and from January to December. If you half-ass it, if you try to cut corners, you'll still make money, but you won't get the sort of respect, jobs, or money that the very best freelancers get.

12.2 — ORGANIZATION

When you get into the swing of things, you have to stay organized. That's pretty hypocritical of me, as I am the least organized person you could meet. Still, that works for me, I'm happy with it, and I don't make any mistakes with it. You will find your own way of handling things, although to begin with, it's irrelevant. You will have one or two jobs at a time, and unless you have a terrible short-term memory, then you shouldn't have a problem.

I don't keep any sort of calendar. I don't write down what needs to be done. I don't keep track of deadlines, etc. Instead, I open all necessary documents relating to an active job, and I keep them minimized on my toolbar until that job is finished. This means that at any given time I have up to ten tabs open, including word-processing documents, spreadsheets, scripts, and web pages, and I cycle through these accordingly.

I have a relatively good memory, but that's not why I do it. I just can't be bothered to keep an appointment book. If you don't want to rely on your memory, then an appointment book is a good idea. Keep the book filled and keep it open on your desk. You can also use the note programs on your computer, or simply write down all your ongoing jobs and deadlines in a Word document. The freelancing platforms will keep track of this, but eventually you'll get to a stage where you're working jobs away from freelancing platforms, and where you're working for long-term clients and simply adding milestones to jobs that have already been completed. In this case, you can't rely on the freelancing platforms to keep track.

You should also keep a folder of all of the work you do. Simply create a folder marked "Freelancing Work" on you computer, and then create individual folders for each client, storing all the documents, images, and more that you complete for them. This is not only a good way to keep track of your work, but it will also come in handy if you ever need samples or if you ever want to look back on some old work to help you with some new work. You will also encounter clients who lose work. This doesn't usually happen with clients on freelancing platforms, because old files are easy to find, but I have had it a couple of times with "offline" clients **(see Section 6.5 on page 120)**, and it looks good if you can resend that work. In fact, if your client is of a certain mentality, then they will actually expect you to redo the work for free if they lose it and you haven't saved it.

You should also keep all messages that you exchange with the client. Many of your clients will be busy, dealing with dozens of other freelancers and employees. It is not unusual for them to receive work from you that was completed exactly as requested, only for them to inform you that you missed the brief. They might not still have the messages or emails, but if you do and you can prove that you did as they asked, then you can diffuse any dispute before it begins. This is far more common than it should be, and it has happened to me at least half a dozen times. On each occasion, the client eased off once I proved that the work was done exactly to spec.

A lot of freelancers miss the important details of jobs because they have several on the go and only remember the key points of each. You can use workstation programs and note-taking tools to keep track of this, but you can also just copy and paste all important points the client gives you directly onto the top of the document you're using to complete the work. This is what I do, and it hasn't failed me yet.

My methods are not ideal. They are cluttered and disorganized at best. If you prefer a little more order, you can download some programs to help. I have listed a few examples below, but there are many more available. I haven't used any of these myself so I can't recommend them directly, but I know of freelancers who rely on these programs and programs like them.

MindMeister

I hate mind maps. Let me get that out of the way. I don't know what it is, but when my brain sees ideas in perfect formation, it goes into revolt. For some reason, the creative process has always been easier for me when it is entirely mental and completely disordered. Some people swear by them, though, and they don't come much bigger than MindMeister. If you work on creative projects, you might actually be referred to this program by a client, as they will always expect you to "show" your creative thinking. Ninety-nine percent of clients out there assume that all writers and all creative types rely upon chalkboards, mind maps, and brainstorming sessions to figure out their ideas. If you tell them that you, like most writers, write and create on the fly, they'll assume you're up to something.

Evernote

This is a "workstation" that simplifies the note-taking process. It is ideal to keep running in the background and to jot down any research and ideas, or even just to keep track of clients' specifications.

Things

This app is available on all Apple devices and can sync across those devices. It is a time-management tool that keeps track of your to-do list and simplifies each item on that list. It is one of the better apps in this category, but it is also one of the most expensive. It is also exclusive to Apple at the time of writing.

Google Calendar

This is a free tool for Android devices and can help you in a similar way to Things, albeit without the extra functions. With apps like

CalenGoo (a paid app), you can also sync this program with other apps and devices.

Rescue Time

This is a useful app for all freelancers. It monitors where you spend your time online, letting you see just how much of that time you're wasting. This could be the kick up the arse you need to tell you to stop wasting time on social media and start spending more of it working and applying for jobs. There is always something you can do, because when you're not applying for jobs or updating your profile, there are other projects you can work on. There is never an excuse to procrastinate, and you might be shocked if you discover just how much time you waste.

Toggl

A popular time-management app, Toggl has its uses in online free-lancing, but only if you're pedantic about your time. It is a little more useful to contractors, consultants, and offline freelancers.

Remember the Milk

A simple but effective app that syncs with all of your devices and reminds you of important deadlines, dates, notes, and anything else you want to be reminded of.

Focus Booster

Designed for those who procrastinate, which is a big issue in this industry, Focus Booster looks promising. If you have a big issue with time wasting and organization, it might be worth checking out.

Focus at Will

This works in a similar way to Focus Booster and promises to boost your attention span. Quite a bold promise, but it does have positive reviews from freelancers.

12.3 — PLAN AHEAD, KEEP EARNING

I always like to plan ahead, writing articles that I know clients will request, albeit only when I also have an alternative use for them. In the early days, when you have established a few long-term contracts and completed a few sporadic contracts for clients you worked with briefly, you will find yourself working on a specific subject. This often has something to do with your interests and knowledge, but it also has a lot to do with luck and with what most clients need.

Let's assume that your first ever job is to write articles on gambling. This is a popular subject and there are many jobs like this on all free-lancing platforms. It doesn't matter if it's the first time you have ever written on that subject or not, because as soon as you do it and as soon as that client pays you and leaves you good feedback, you will become an expert in it. You can use a sample from that job, as well as your experience working on it, to win over future clients and to get future jobs on the same subject. After a time, they'll start coming to you.

When you have some free time, when you have sent as many applications as possible and are waiting for more jobs to come in, you should look to write more articles on this subject. The more you write on it, the easier it becomes and the quicker you will be able to do it in the future, effectively increasing your hourly rate. More important, there's a good chance that a long-term client will request another batch of articles and an equally good chance another client will come along and request them. At that point you can give them what you have, completing part, or even all, of the job right there and then. This means that all of those "wasted" hours you would have spent refreshing the Job Applications page in the hope someone would get back to you have now turned into fully paid hours.

I have done this many times before, and I have always ended up selling those articles—letting the client believe I wrote them specifically at their request. As a backup, I also created a sports site where such articles could go if I was unable to sell them to a client. This is actually another good way to make money when times are slow, and one which I'll discuss in a little more detail later on **(see Section 15.3 on page 244)**.

Give yourself time to get used to the freelancing platforms and to the needs of the market before you do this, because some subjects are just too niche. If it helps, throughout my time on these sites I have discovered that the main article topics (as well as rewriting and Spinning, discussed in **Section 10.2 on page 164**) tend to be based around gambling (slot machines, sport, casinos) and finance. Listicles, which is what sites like Buzzfeed are built upon, are also popular and often based around celebrities and life-hacks. There is also a constant demand for YA fiction and erotic fiction. You'll work out yourself what sells and what is popular, and if a long-term client doesn't specially request them and you don't want to publish them on your own site, you can sell them. A message along the lines of "I have just completed a batch of articles for my own site, all of which relate to [article theme]. I know you publish similar articles and was wondering if you would be interested" will suffice.

12.4 — TAKE A BREAK

In freelance writing, there is no such thing as writers' block, but at the same time, being a full-time freelancer will cause it. What I mean by this is that at no point should you find yourself struggling to write, simply because most of the work you will be doing will not be creative. You'll be writing articles to predefined guidelines, and most writers will be able to do this in their sleep. However, after a year or more of doing this, it'll suck the life out of you and you might struggle to write anything creative.

As I write this, I have been writing professionally for twelve years, and this is the longest I have gone without working on any short story or novel of my own. It's not in me anymore. It will come back, but only when I take a break from writing shit day after day. I fully intend to take a break when I finish this book, but it's easier said than done.

When you get to this stage in your career, you will have countless clients getting in touch with you. Long-term clients will expect work; new clients will hope to get you onboard for their projects. And every single one of these will assume that the work you do for them has your full attention; many of them will even assume you will be working on nothing else.

It is very hard to turn long-term clients down, but at the same time, if you want a life outside of freelancing and if you want your sanity intact, you need to. Don't just stop, though. If you find that things are getting a little too much, whether it is eating into your other work or even your sanity, then slow down. Stop applying for jobs, stop replying to invites. When long-term clients get in touch, agree to help them but tell them you can only spare a few hours.

It will take you a few weeks to wind down if you have been freelancing for a long time. And if you're anything like me and many of the people I have spoken to, once you're down to writing for just a few hours a day, you'll be content with how things are going and you won't need to reduce any further. If you make it to this stage and feel comfortable taking on more work again, then you can gradually build back up, which shouldn't be an issue if you have the experience.

If you have only been freelancing for a short time and already feel burned out, there's not much you can do. It will happen, but you have to suck it up and keep going. Taking a break so early on, and restricting the work you do for long-term clients who have only been working with you for a few weeks or months, is going to hurt you in the long run.

Chapter 12 Summary

- Find somewhere to write where you won't be distracted. In the early days, you will need peace and quiet.
- As time goes on, you might find that you can work on auto pilot, writing anywhere you want. You should still find solitude for those difficult and creative jobs, though.

- Don't focus on strict organization. Don't follow methods that others suggest. Find one that suits you, regardless of how chaotic it seems.
- In your downtime, when you can't do anything but wait and hope, try to guess what your biggest clients will need and write those articles in preparation. If you're going to write large quantities, make sure you have a website to publish them to if the client doesn't want them.
- Articles and content writing might be easier and it might pay better in the long run, but if you're a novelist on the side, be prepared for it to suck your creativity dry.
- If you work hard and for long hours, take a break after a few months to stop yourself from burning out.
- Don't take too many breaks early on. You need to be prepared to work indefinitely.

See Also
- *"Offline" Clients* **(page 120 – 6.5)**
- *Spinning* **(page 164 – 10.2)**
- *Websites from Scratch* **(page 244 – 15.3)**
- *Take Risks* **(page 256 – 16.5)**

Chapter 13

TROUBLESHOOTING (ISSUES THAT MIGHT ARISE)

A lot of things can happen over the course of a single job or a single day. You're always on the go, always facing new problems. As a free-lancer, you're on your own, and that can be a little daunting. Luckily, I have encountered many of these issues myself and have learned how to deal with them. In this section, I'll discuss some of the most common issues that might arise. Not all of these will apply to you straight away, but this is definitely a chapter that you will want to come back to time and time again.

13.1 — A CLIENT IS BLACKMAILING ME

I won't go into detail, but this has happened to me. Unfortunately, it happened when it was too late for me to do anything about it and I had to take a hit. However, in most cases you do have some recourse. Just bear in mind that whatever happens, you can't think that Upwork (or any other freelancing platform) will help you, because they will not. I was at the very top of the system, earning more than most and making a pretty penny for them, and I was still wronged in a very bad and one-sided way. The response I got was to basically say there was nothing I could do, while also admitting I was right.

The first thing to remember is that a client cannot leave feedback unless they have paid, and you can erase bad feedback by giving a 100 percent refund. This applies to Upwork, but there are similar solutions on other platforms, as discussed **(see Section 7.1 on page 125)** elsewhere in this book.

If a client is threatening to give you bad feedback and promising to give you good feedback only if you refund them, remember this is not possible. If you created work that was written from scratch and was not an edit or a rewrite, then you can claim ownership of it and refuse to give them control, threatening legal action if they do (how easy this is depends on your country of origin).

The best course of action, however, is to avoid it in the first place. Clients like this typically don't have a lot of good feedback, which is why you should only work with clients who have a proven track record and have given plenty of good feedback in the past. On Upwork, you should also look through their job history for the words "Job Canceled." If there are many instances of this, be very cautious. It means they gave the job to someone and, more than likely, that freelancer completed the job, but the job was canceled before any payment was made.

You can also get a good idea of what a client is like by talking to them. Send a few messages back and forth under the pretense of getting more information about the job. I do this all the time and usually I can spot the ones who will cause trouble. Are they demanding, strict, rude? Ignore them. Are they happy-go-lucky, polite, friendly? Sign up. Many clients will ask you to go on Skype or for a phone call. This is not a necessity and it can cause problems, but if you are unsure and the client suggests it, then go for it. A face-to-face conversation, so to speak, will give you a better idea of what they are like and whether they will rip you off or not.

If you do find yourself in this situation, there may be something you can do. The freelancing sites do not seem to care if you contact them directly, but I know that they care a lot more when you expose their inadequacies to others. So, take some screenshots, get some proof. Show everyone that you have been wronged in a horrible way, and then expose that via Facebook or Twitter. Not only will you expose the client, but you'll expose the site as well. This takes some doing, of course, so it's only worth it if you stand to lose a lot. If you don't, then as painful as it is to do, you might be better off letting the client win, after which you can fight to keep ownership of the work they are trying to steal.

13.2 — A CLIENT WANTS TO TALK ON SKYPE

In her broad Geordie accent, my mother always used to tell me, "Shy bairns get nowt," and if you were to believe many freelancers and clients, that also applies to the world of online freelancing. It seems that a Skype account is essential, as are Skype conversations prior to being awarded jobs. This is not true, though. Not at all.

When I first started out, I downloaded Skype and reluctantly talked with clients. I am one of those "shy bairns" my mother always talked about, but I'm also business minded and thought it was essential to get what I wanted. There was one client in particular who insisted upon it. This client came early in my career, so the price I offered him was small. He had an even smaller budget and I felt bad for him, so I cut it in half. In the end, it would have been better for me to flip burgers at McDonalds, but I persisted. He was a night owl, working on a hectic project that kept him up all night. It was hard *not* to feel bad for him.

Meeting Clients

Be very wary if a client asks you to meet in person, especially if they ask you to travel to see them. This is very rare, and while the image of the freelancer seems to be of someone who is regularly traveling—meeting and negotiating with clients across the country—that definitely does not apply to online freelancing. Unless they have a memoir to write, unless you can verify that they are who they say they are, and unless they are willing to pay for your travel in advance, stay where you are.

That stopped one morning when I woke to discover that he had phoned me half a dozen times and sent me a number of texts **(see Chapter 14.0: Horror Stories)**. I expected the worse, but what I got was something so tedious and pathetic that I felt like slapping him. He treated me like a friend, and one whose existence was based around helping him with his problems. He took my generic, friendly, and informal words of "whenever you need me, give me a shout" to heart. After that I deleted Skype, blocked his number, and told him I was busy whenever he emailed me. That might seem rude, but so is harassing a stranger in the dead of night. Fast forward a year and I have made more money than ever freelancing, and I have never used Skype. I don't give clients my phone number either. (I didn't give it to this particular client either. He took it from an invoice submitted automatically by the freelancing portal.)

Unless they are paying you, you should not give them your time. Messages are okay, because you can get to them when you're ready and they are fairly quick to deal with, but a full-time, or even a part-time, freelancer cannot afford a conversation with a client who will waste their time talking about nothing—especially as this rarely leads to the client giving that freelancer a job.

Still not convinced? Before the Attack of the Persistent Insomniac, I worked with an aspiring author who I conferenced with on Skype. The project was tiny and related to a website, but as soon as I was on Skype, he asked me questions about getting an agent and a publisher, and then he rounded off the conversation by asking if I would listen to him recite his short story and critique it for him there and then. I was too polite and too British to tell him where to get off, so I turned off my laptop and blamed connectivity issues.

The long and short of it is, if you use Skype, then people will use you. Your job as a freelancer is to find jobs, discuss them briefly through a handful of messages that can be sent at your convenience, complete the job, and then get paid. Add in endless conversations from insecure clients and you're limiting your income.

13.3 — I HAVE MISSED A DEADLINE

Deadlines are incredibly important, and you should do what you can to ensure you stick to them. But mistakes happen. In my time as a freelancer, I missed one big deadline and that was more down to stupidity than anything else. I had finished the work early and put it to one side to send. The client expected it to be a long job and I didn't want him knowing I completed it as quickly as I did. I then got caught up in something else and forgot. I didn't remember I hadn't sent it until the client asked for it after the deadline.

In this situation the job was a quick one and the client was a good man. I apologized deeply, told him the truth, and told him that he didn't have to pay me the full amount. In the end, the gesture was enough. He paid me the full amount, left good feedback, and continued to hire me.

You need to show that you care in these situations. The absolute worst thing you can do is let the deadline pass and then not say anything until the client complains. I have had many freelancers do this to me as a client and it is very frustrating. What's more, they all knew the deadline was there, they all knew they were missing it, and they made no attempt to message me or to deliver the work. This told me all I needed to know about their professionalism, and I never hired any of them again.

Always let the client know as soon as you can that you will miss a deadline. Never leave it to the deadline day or after. This way they can make arrangements. They can fix any issues that might arise, and they won't be so frustrated with you as a result. When you do let them know you are going to miss a deadline, be honest. Your dog/grandmother doesn't have to have died for it to be a valid excuse. I've already discussed the importance of simple excuses, because you won't be believed otherwise **(see Section 5.6 on page 102)**. Also, make sure you offer a small refund, along with an apology. If money is tight, then promise to make it up to them, and when you deliver the work, deliver more than the job stated. If they are paying you for 500 words but you know more would be better, give them 1,000 words. If they asked for twenty articles, give them twenty-one or twenty-two.

The best way to avoid this happening is to make sure you always give yourself a big deadline. If I know I can complete a job in twenty-four hours, I will ask for three days. This is a respectable deadline to ask for, and when I deliver early they will be delighted. If I have any unforeseen delays, I'm also covered. If a job will take you a week, ask for two. The vast majority of clients have no idea how long it takes you to complete a particular job. I had one client who was amazed when it took me thirty minutes to write a 500-word article, because he genuinely thought it would take me at least six hours. I have no idea why, but while everyone isn't this extreme, they do have a hard time understanding just how quickly many writers can work.

When you give the client a deadline, always finish with ". . . if this is okay. If not, I'm sure I can move things around and get it to you earlier." Nine times out of ten, they will agree to the deadline, and the one time they don't, they'll never cut it short by more than 50 percent.

There is also a "trick" you can use to buy yourself some more time, as discussed a little later **(see Section 5.6 on page 102)**.

13.4 — A CLIENT PROMISED A BIG JOB AND ONLY GAVE ME A SMALL ONE

This will happen, and it's not something you should worry about. Many jobs will begin small, with the client promising something bigger. You might write one article on the promise that more will be delivered. You might edit/write one book on the promise that the client has more books for you to work on. Many times, though, you won't hear from the client again.

There are a couple of reasons behind this. The main one is that clients understand freelancers want long-term jobs; they understand the need for big jobs, big money, and long-term security, so they play on that. There are also cases where the client simply changes their mind. We've all had moments when we've let an idea take us over, moments when we've gotten very excited about something and have put our hearts and souls into it, only to lose interest days later. Clients are the same, and when this happens, that extra work they promised just isn't needed.

Many times, they simply realize that you're out of budget. I had one client who paid me good money and got great work in return. However, he then realized he could get a nonnative speaker to do it for ten times less. His eyes flashed with dollars signs, and despite being excited about my work, he hired another writer. Unfortunately for him, he was only a content editor working for a bigger company, and when his bosses saw the reduced quality of work, he lost his job. I know this because those same bosses apologized to me and begged me to work on the project again, a job that began with me rewriting all of the articles that had been written by the previous writer.

There are also clients who just take their time to deliver on those promises. My very first job was a sample piece, a comedy script with the promise of more. I did it, he loved it, but I never heard from him again. I let it get to me and wondered if he really did like it and if it really was good. I ended up forgetting about that job, only to hear from the client eighteen months later, by which time he had turned that first script into a video and was ready to go with the other scripts.

Don't let it get to you. Don't stress yourself, worrying that they didn't like your work. If that was the case, it would show in the feedback or the recommended score. Clients are not parents—they are not going to praise poor work, slap it on the fridge, and then blow smoke up your ass. They will tell you it's terrible and demand better. If this didn't happen, then it doesn't matter if the big job didn't come—circumstances change. Sometimes they change in your favor; but if they don't, there are many more jobs and many more clients out there.

13.5 — THE CLIENT HAS ASKED FOR MORE WORK AND ISN'T OFFERING TO PAY ME

One client asked me to write an article about horror novelists. I did what he asked, but when I finished, he said the subject had changed. The subject it had changed to was completely different, relating to sporting superstars, and it meant I needed to start again. This client was not the easiest to work with and he offered no payments for these changes. In this situation, the best thing is to just rewrite the article, take your money and your good feedback, and then never work with the client again.

If you discuss the job in advance, going through all of the minor details, you will limit the chances of this happening. When I have a job figured out, I like to send a message to the client with my plans, detailing my understanding of what they want me to do and including a small sample of it. It is also a good idea to split the job into milestones so you get paid as you complete smaller parts. This means that if you are paid to write a batch of two hundred articles, you can request 10 percent of the payment for every twenty articles you deliver. It also means that problems will be picked up early on, so you won't write all two hundred articles and then have the client demand you change them all before they release the money.

If the job you have done is small and the client has yet to pay, you would be better off just canceling it. They can't leave you feedback and you don't want to work with time wasters like that. Just be sure to remain polite when you tell them your reasons for leaving. If you have put some time and effort into the job and would like the money, you should probably just do what they ask and be polite about it. I have seen many client/freelancer relationships turn sour, ending in terrible feedback, disputes, and even suspensions because a client made such a request and the freelancer retaliated. Obviously, the client is in the wrong, but they rarely see it that way and no amount of arguing will change it.

13.6 — I HAVE BEEN SUSPENDED

These things happen, and the freelancer isn't always at fault. This happened to me, back in the days when Upwork was oDesk and Elance still existed as a separate entity. I had used them both, although I had used Elance much more than oDesk. In fact, this was when I decided that I would spend more time on oDesk and make it into a big account that would resemble my Elance account. I mentioned this experience earlier **(see Section 1.3 on page 10)** and won't bore you with it again, but needless to say that this was the job that told me to stick with Elance and to all but give up on oDesk.

When clients have no feedback on Upwork, the only way to check they are "legit" is if they are "payment verified," which is when Upwork basically validates their credit card, doing the hard work and giving you the thumbs up. In the case of this client, they *had* verified him.

There is very little you can do when something like this happens, and it's a constant worry knowing that it could happen at anytime and for no reason. Luckily, now that oDesk and Elance are no longer separate, there has been an improvement. I never had an issue with Elance customer service, and since they moved to Upwork, it seems that quality of service has moved as well. This is a big company, and while mistakes do happen, they are not vindictive and they are not there to screw you over.

If you are in the right, your account will be reinstated once you prove it. Do not lose your head and do not worry (easier said than done, I know). Just bide your time and keep pushing them for a resolution.

If you have been using multiple accounts, you have had too many disputes, or you have had too much bad feedback, you might not have a leg to stand on. In the first instance, you are breaking the terms and conditions, and in the second and third instances, they may just decide that you are not a credit to the service. They do this, and they do it more than you might think. They want a professional environment after all, and one where clients get good work. This is another reason why it is important to get good feedback and to ensure your clients are always happy with your work.

Don't think that this is reserved for Upwork either. This can happen on any freelancing website. Pay close attention to the chapters on dealing with clients and courting good feedback and you should be okay.

13.7 — I AM NOT BEING PAID BY THE SITE

If you have just joined the site, then it might take some time before the payments go through. All of the online freelancing platforms work a little differently, though, so it depends on which one you use. As an example, when Elance and oDesk existed, their payment systems couldn't have been more different. With Elance, you could make a withdrawal one day and the money would be in your account the next. With oDesk, it took a week from a client paying you to that money even showing in your oDesk account, and then another week to go from your oDesk account to your bank account. Unfortunately, Upwork adopted oDesk's system and not Elance's.

Freelancer are slowest in this regard. They have a rule in place whereby all first withdrawals are delayed for fifteen days. Because of this, if you use Freelancer, it's best to withdraw early on with whatever money you earn. That way, when you complete the big jobs, you can get the money more or less straight away.

If you have waited and waited and the money is still not in your account, then get in touch with the site. If you are using one of the sites mentioned in this book, you should have no issues. These sites process millions of dollars a day, and they use the latest banking software for the safest transactions. They are not immune to small mistakes, but customer service should be able to help you with those mistakes.

13.8 — A CLIENT DIDN'T LEAVE FEEDBACK

There can be a number of causes for this. The main one is that the client is busy and simply overlooked it. This happened a lot with one of my biggest and best clients, and I had no issue with it. In those cases, when you trust the client, you know they were very happy with your work and you have since created another job, then simply ask them if they wouldn't mind leaving feedback. Remind them that it helps you, but do not suggest that they give you five stars; that's just rude. Of course, if you have a suspicion they will give you less, then don't say anything, a job with no feedback is no detriment to your profile, but a job with low feedback is.

If the client was a one-off client who you didn't speak with much, then I would also ignore it. For all you know, the reason they didn't leave feedback is because they were not entirely happy, and they didn't think you deserved five stars and didn't want to leave less. On some sites, it is not possible to close a job without leaving feedback, and on sites like Upwork you can only see that feedback when you leave feedback, or after a fourteen-day period. This makes things a little tricky at times, but it's always best to leave them good feedback and hope they do the same. Be the bigger man, because the feedback you leave will show next to theirs, and even if they give you bad feedback, at least future clients will know you are not bitter.

13.9 — I AM NOT BEING PAID BY THE CLIENT

There will be times when the client delays payment. In their eyes, it's nothing, but for you, it could mean the difference between paying the rent or moving back in with your parents.

You will generally find that most clients pay quickly, but this doesn't apply to all of them. However, the worst thing you can do is pester them. I know of one freelancer who actually pestered the clients in advance, telling them that she would need to be paid within twenty-four hours of completion and would send reminders every twelve hours if not. You can't make such demands; the client needs time to review the work and cannot be expected to rush around to cater for you. Most clients refused to give this particular freelancer work, and of the ones that did, many gave her bad feedback.

When you complete the work, send it across and ask the client to contact you if there are any problems. Do not mention money. If they have not responded after a couple of days, even to tell you a date and time they will review it, then send them a polite reminder. Again, don't mention money. A message like the following will suffice:

Hey [Client]

It has been a few days since I heard from you, so I just wanted to check in to make sure everything was okay with the work. If you have had a chance to read it that is.

If you need anything, or want to discuss anything, let me know.

Regards,

[Your Name]

I know of some freelancers who will add, "If you want any changes, I'll be happy to make them," but this is a mistake. If the client expresses dissatisfaction at the work, fair enough, but making such a comment at this point will make them more inclined to spot issues with your work. As you should be making these changes for free, this is time that you cannot afford to waste.

If the client still does not respond, give it a few more days and then send another message. By now, though, you should have heard something from them, telling you a date and a time you'll have probably been paid. In all of my time as a freelancer, I have only had two clients with whom this happened indefinitely. One of them owed me just $20 and was banned from the site before he could pay me (probably for the best, as it seems he turned into a rogue, despite being respected for several years). The other owed me $100 and disappeared. I also had one client who owed me considerably more and did not pay for weeks. It was the first time I had worked for them and they had little feedback at the time. I was worried, but they were a big company and the intent was always there, even if the haste was not.

You should never be quick to jump into a dispute, and you should never jump into a dispute if you can't take the bad feedback.

Ask yourself how desperate you are for the money. Is it a big enough payday to offset one-star feedback? Because if you dispute the job and force them to hurry up and pay, they will leave you bad feedback. If it is not worth it, then bide your time. There's nothing else you can do.

Some freelancing platforms have upfront payments, where the client is forced to put the money in escrow; but not all of them do, and it is not good practice to ask clients to do this in advance. You need to come across as someone whose mind is on pleasing the client, doing the work first, and getting the money second.

13.10 — THE CLIENT WON'T CLEARLY ANSWER MY QUESTIONS/I DON'T UNDERSTAND THE JOB

Such instances are rare, but they are uncomfortable when they occur. You need to know the specifics of a job before you begin, and with some clients, you will prefer to know these specifics in as few emails as possible. (It's easy to tell if they are the sort of client who prefers short, sharp conversation and will get frustrated by too many questions.) If you are asking questions, are still not getting the replies that you want, and are still not sure about the scope of the job, then this is what I would do:

Clarify Before Accepting Job

- **Deadline:** If the client is not clear, ask. If the ball is in your court, set a deadline and confirm that this is acceptable.
- **Milestones:** Clarify each individual deadline deliverable.
- **Payment:** When will you be paid? For big projects, request milestone payments.
- **Style:** Don't begin in full until a writing style is agreed upon.
- **Formatting/Design:** Are they expecting you to format the project? Some clients expect writers to do everything.
- **Rights:** If you're unpublished, they'll want to take credit. If you're published, they might want to use your name. Clarify this in advance, and don't sign your name away to a freelance project unless you have control over the end product.

Ask for a sample of what the client wants. Do this as early as possible. Ask them if they have a similar job completed by a previous freelancer, if they have similar content, or if they have content from a rival site or publisher. Make sure you tell them that this is just to give you a "feel" of what you need to do, because some clients will think you want to steal that content or even put it through spinning software **(see Section 10.2 on page 164)**.

Tell the client that you think it would be best for both parties if you completed a small sample first. This, you can tell them, is so you can be sure you're both on the same page. No job needs to be created, no money needs to be released. You're not promising the world and are only doing something that will take twenty minutes or less.

Complete the job as you understood it, with whatever information you can glean from the job post, the client's messages, and any other information they gave you. If they love the work, then you've hit lucky. Take the job, repeat what you did, and get paid. It might sound strange to finish a job when you're still not entirely sure of what you have to do, but in my years as a freelancer this has happened to me a few times. There are so many different jobs, so many niche jobs and strange reasons for commissioning them, that these things are more common than you would imagine.

If you completely missed the point with your sample, you'll find that the client will point out the reasons you have missed it and will most likely give you an idea of what a correct sample would be. If, looking at that, you are still none the wiser, then apologize and go on your merry way. You need to wing it a lot of times in this game, but you can only push it so far.

13.11 — THE CLIENT IS ACCUSING ME OF PLAGIARISM

The client will have a reason for saying this, and that's what you need to confront. This has happened to me once. I wrote a lot of content for one particular client and he picked out two words. To this day I still don't know why he insinuated what he did, but English was his second language and it seemed that he didn't think the tense was incorrect. As a result of what he assumed was a sudden change in tense (there was no such thing), he asked me, in an accusing manner, if I had plagiarized the work. He was perhaps assuming that because a change in tense was so out of place, it must have been copied and pasted from elsewhere.

The client had been nice until that point and was probably having a bad day. I told him that I would never plagiarize any work (I never questioned his understanding of English, as that would have made things worse), and I showed him a screen-grab of Copyscape, which told him the work was 100 percent original. I then finished that particular job and refused to work for him again. He had been relying on my work until that point, and I had been questioning whether it was a worthwhile job, considering the money offered. It was all I needed to tip me over the edge, and after getting good feedback, he proceeded to beg me to return.

Copyscape can be your best friend. It's the only thing you have to give you concrete proof that your work is original. Of course, if you are plagiarizing work, they will use Copyscape against you, and you probably deserve that. I have dealt with freelancers who have plagiarized work. I even had one guy who copy and pasted from Wikipedia, leaving the hyperlinks in place. What's more, he had the nerve to deny it when I picked up on it.

You should never plagiarize work, and you should be ready to defend yourself if someone wrongly accuses you of it. Of course, there is another side to this coin. Many articles require quotes, and if you use a lot of quotes, then because they have been published elsewhere, your article will show as being plagiarized to a certain extent. In these situations, I like to notify the client in advance and tell them that as there will be quotes, it may show up as being plagiarized to a degree. At the same time, you should inform them that it doesn't have to be like this and that you can simply remove the quotes. Let them choose, and save yourself the trouble. I know of many freelancers who have submitted work with quotations in them, only to be blamed for plagiarism and shown the proof via Copyscape.

13.12 — THE CLIENT MADE A MAJOR MISTAKE ON THEIR PROJECT

This will happen, and you should point it out, but only before the job begins. At that point in time, you may be paid extra to fix it. They may even close the job down to amend the errors and focus their time elsewhere. Either way, you won't be wasting time or money. However, if the job has already begun, it could be tricky. I once worked on a children's book about a number of characters, all from different countries, all with a visual representation of what they looked like. Imagine my surprise when I encountered a young boy from New Delhi, India, who was dressed up like a Native American, sometimes referred to as "American Indians." Obviously, the person writing the description and the bio was not the person designing the images. Wires had been crossed and the result was amusing but also very ignorant and incredibly offensive. No one wants to tell the world that they don't know the difference between Indians from India and Native Americans, and when I informed the client, they immediately told me that they had to pause the job to focus on "something else." Basically, they hadn't spotted the error (and presumably didn't know the difference either) and needed to stop production on that book immediately.

I lost a job, and I lost money, because a milestone was halfway to completion when that happened. It was their error and they wouldn't have spotted it without me, and while it's the right thing to do, the only person who was suffering by doing the right thing was me. Also, when you tell clients they have made major mistakes, you're telling them they have wasted time and money, and they will need to spend more time and money fixing it. Whether you did the right thing or not, whether it was your fault or not, they're going to hate you. So, in this case, keep it to yourself.

13.13 — I HAVE TO WRITE CONTENT WITH WHICH I AM NOT COMFORTABLE

I have had at least three clients who have asked me to write mature content and have warned me beforehand, making sure I was okay with it. Most of the time, this sort of thing will be specified in advance. With one of them, the mature content was mixed in with other content and was therefore not specified on the job proposal. Still, they knew that some writers would have an issue with it so they checked to make sure I didn't.

I never had such an issue, but there are a number of things I would have an issue with. If the content was in any way inflammatory, be it racist, sexist, xenophobic, or anything of that nature, I would refuse the job. Many writers in my position would, and 99 percent of the time, the client will warn you about this content in advance. For the other 1 percent of the time, it will be so obvious they'll feel they won't need to.

There are less than obvious things. Personally, I am against hunting and any sites that promote it. However, few clients feel the need to warn me about certain things in advance. One client gave me a list of hundreds of sites to write about, warning me about a handful of "mature" sites, but not about the hunting sites. This is where you need to make a decision as a writer and a professional. I didn't find those sites until I was well into the project, and I knew that by not completing them, my option was to deliver a project that was only partially finished. Yet I would still be requesting full payment and that would make life difficult for my client. In such cases, it's best to bite the bullet and to realize that, while not pleasant, it's the best solution all round.

Of course, if the content had been deeply disturbing, things may have been different, and the client would have no doubt understood if I skipped it. As I said above, highly controversial content is often pointed out by the client. If you are offended by things that might not be obvious to the client, and if you are working on a job that will involve writing on many topics at once, you should inform them of your issues. If you do not and you get content you're not comfortable with, you'll be sacrificing your relationship with the client by omitting it.

If your beliefs are controversial, and you have issues discussing or promoting homosexuality, equality, or anything of the sort, then keep your hatred to yourself. You're not going to endear yourself to a client if they discover you have such beliefs (and rightly so). It is also very important to keep things neutral, as discussed previously **(see Section 8.1 on page 139)**.

13.14 — A CLIENT WHO LEFT BAD FEEDBACK WANTS TO START ANOTHER JOB

This has never happened to me personally, but I have come close and I know of a few instances in which clients have done this. The simple fact is that while most clients and freelancers know that anything less than five stars means they are unhappy with the work, this knowledge doesn't extend to everyone.

You could work with someone who seems happy with the job, pays you, and then asks if you want to start another job with them, only to discover that they have left you three- or four-star feedback. If you follow the instructions listed earlier in this book **(see Chapter 7.0: Feedback)**, you can avoid these situations by only working with clients who understand the feedback system and the necessity of five-star feedback. However, even then you might still encounter such clients.

The best thing to do is to be honest with them, but only if they want you to start a new job. Tell them that you try your best to get five-star feedback because Upwork/Guru/Freelancer/etc. tends to look down on freelancers with anything less. You can also let them know that if work that was completed on time, to standard, and to specification was still not able to achieve this, then you don't feel it is within your power to satisfy the client 100 percent. You're not doing this out of spite for the bad feedback they left you; you're doing it to avoid getting more bad feedback, because by opening a new job, you will be giving them the chance to give you more feedback. If you work to the best of your abilities for a client, pleasing them 100 percent, and yet they still don't leave you five-star feedback, imagine what they will leave you if you miss a deadline or make a mistake. It's not worth the risk.

The best thing to do with such clients is to recommend that you simply add a milestone onto the previous job. This is not possible on all sites, but it is on some. This basically means that they will be unable to leave you any more feedback, and it also means that if you mess up in the future, it won't result in terrible feedback.

13.15 — I CAN'T GET A RESPONSE FROM THE FREELANCING SITE

This happens with all sites. In the days when Elance and oDesk were separate entities and had yet to form Upwork, you could not get any sort of immediate response out of oDesk. They had a phone number on their website and they directed all members to this, yet for about two years that phone number did not work. If you rang it, you would discover it was disconnected. Add to this a Live Chat facility that was supposed to be available at certain times but never was, and you had the recipe for a lot of frustration.

Elance were good at responding, but when they merged with oDesk, before the formation of Upwork, they slowed down. Freelancer tend to be a little quicker, but trying to get sense out of them and their practices is a surefire way to send you insane. I have not had issues with Guru.

If you have a problem, try to fix it yourself. If it is a problem that cannot be fixed yourself, go to Twitter. These platforms operate on small margins and therefore don't want to pay staff to answer calls and deal with problems all day. However, if those problems are aired in the open and run the risk of damaging their reputation, they will fix them immediately.

I have already mentioned some of the issues I had on the old oDesk site, when I was incorrectly suspended and received nothing but empty apologizes—that is, until I complained on Twitter, at which point I was reinstated. The same happened to a close friend of mine who had issues with a withdrawal. For two weeks nothing happened, but after a complaint on Twitter, she got a response within minutes.

It doesn't matter how many followers you have either. I have told this story to a few freelancers in the past and their response is usually, "But you have tens of thousands of followers." At this point I direct them to my friend's Twitter account, where they can see that she has just a dozen followers.

Find the Twitter account of the platform you are having issues with and send them a mention. Be sure to target your followers, as opposed to sending a message directly to the freelancing platform. Word it like an angry rant. You want to come across as someone who is telling the world how bad [freelance platform] is, and someone who is ready to open up a debate on the subject, as opposed to someone who is directly messaging the freelancing platform and looking for some easy compensation or pity points.

Chapter 13 Summary

- Blackmail is common and there is little you can do to stop it except trying to avoid these clients in the first place.
- Skype requests will waste your time and they are not necessary. Make your decision regarding Skype and stick with it.
- Always anticipate a missed deadline and message the client beforehand. Apologize, reason, make a deal, and make sure they forgive you.
- Clients will lie about big jobs and future jobs to get you to work on small projects.

- Clients will ask for more work without payment. You should give them edits for free and never demand extra payment, but if they keep asking, think about closing the job.
- If wrongly suspended, voice your concerns on social media. If you broke the rules, there is nothing you can do.
- Platforms may delay payments, but they will always pay in the end. Contact them, be polite, and be patient.
- If a client didn't leave feedback, it might be because they couldn't say anything nice. Don't push them unless you're sure it was an oversight.
- Don't push the client for payment, but send occasional and polite reminders if it drags on.
- If you don't understand the job, offer to compete a small sample. If you fail to hit the mark and still don't get it, just cancel/refuse.
- Use Copyscape to prove you did not plagiarize anything. Explain that quotes will show as being plagiarized.
- If a client makes a mistake on their project, then don't rush to point it out. It could hurt you more than them.
- You shouldn't be forced to write anything you're not comfortable with, but weigh up your options before you refuse. If it's minor and it will hurt you, the job, or the client if you refuse, just do it.
- Don't start more jobs with clients who have left bad feedback. Let them know your reasons why.
- Freelancing platforms are not the best at responding to emails or calls. Social media is usually the best way to get in touch.

See Also

- *Keeping It Neutral **(page 139 – 8.1)***
- *Spinning **(page 164 – 10.2)***
- *Horror Stories **(Chapter 14.0)***
- *Missing Deadline Day **(page 258 – 16.6)***

Chapter 14

HORROR STORIES

You won't make it a year in this game without running into a bad client or five. I wouldn't wish these clients on anyone. They will make you question why you do what you do, they might make you want to quit, and they will waste your time. On some occasions they may even threaten to end your career. Unfortunately, there are a lot of selfish people out there—a lot of people who will not think twice about lying in order to destroy you, simply because you refused to give them free work or because you refused to pander to their bullshit. A lot of this book is dedicated to avoiding clients like that, but you will still run into them from time to time.

To give you a better idea of what to expect, take a look at some of the worst experiences that long-time freelancers have had. I have already related my bad experiences throughout this book, and many of those will be clarified here. There are also stories from other freelancers, all of whom have several years of experience. The details of these reports have been changed, because even dickheads deserve some dignity (and I don't want to get sued).

14.1 — STALKER
Job: Articles
Freelancer: Myself
Client: Ernie

In my very first year as a freelancer I worked for a friendly—albeit naive—man named Ernie. He ran an e-commerce website, selling electronics, video game consoles, etc., and he was looking for some irreverent viral articles that would boost his site numbers. It fit in perfectly with a recent contract I had done, so I was able to attract his attention in a proposal and then win the job. He didn't have a big budget and I took pity on him, so I didn't mind when he insisted on spending an hour chatting on Skype before paying me half of what I had been charging other clients.

I enjoyed the work and he let me do as I pleased in regards to the content. The piece I produced was very good, in my opinion, and he also loved it. Before he released payment, though, he wanted to chat some more. We discussed everything about his site and what he wanted to do. I had absolutely no experience with e-commerce, but I have a business mind and I didn't object to throwing some ideas his way. I began to lose my patience in the end, knowing I was wasting a lot of time, but I knew he was stressed and potentially depressed, so I gave him more of my time than I should have.

The next day he asked me to go back on Skype so he could tell me he wanted a different article. There was no mention of more money and even though he could have told me that in one message, he preferred to drag it out over an hour-long Skype session. Although annoyed, I hid my frustration, finished another article, and then sent it, finally receiving payment.

Before he left me alone, he began to talk about his site, how he wanted to run unnecessary and absurd promotions instead of focusing on what he should have been focusing on. Here was a site that was getting no visitors and had no sales, but rather than fixing a flawed layout, security errors, poor product descriptions, and broken links, his priority was to set up a chat site, a newsletter, and a competition. I entertained him, agreeing to his craziness in an effort to get away without swearing at him, and eventually I shut down Skype vowing to never return. At this point, I had worked two hours on a job that should have taken thirty minutes—and for a price that matches what I now charge just for ten minutes of work—and I had spent a further six hours listening to his bullshit.

The next morning I woke to half a dozen missed calls, text messages, instant messages, and emails. All from Ernie. He was in a panic, and thinking I had made a big mistake, I contacted him. I never gave him my number and never implied it was okay for him to contact me via this method. He took my number from an Elance invoice.

As it turned out, he needed to fix an HTML issue with the site, and because I had expressed a (clearly fake) interest and had wished him well, he actually thought I cared about his business—not only enough to work for him, but enough to be dragged out of bed on a Saturday morning in order to fix an HTML issue for free. I am as technically minded as a hedgehog and had never expressed anything to the contrary, so there was nothing I could have done. I told him to contract a coder, spent half an hour telling him that I was not qualified and couldn't help (despite his pleas), and finally lost my patience and left.

Make of this story what you will, but it was clear to me that Ernie didn't have the best grasp on social etiquette. As I dug a little deeper into his profile history, I discovered that while he had left and received five-star feedback, I wasn't the only freelancer he had hired to complete a job and then assumed they were his best friend and would be prepared to work around the clock free of charge.

After Ernie, whose site sunk without a single sale, I refused to use Skype ever again.

Moral of the Story: I'm not going to tell you to keep clients on a long leash. You need to be friendly, polite, and helpful, and unfortunately some of them will take that the wrong way. What you can do, however, is avoid Skype. You will miss out on a few jobs by doing so, but it won't matter in the long run. This was the only time I really used it, and while I did miss out on jobs by refusing to use it, I still did okay for myself. You should also look a little deeper into a client's history, paying attention to comments and job cancelations, as well as feedback scores.

14.2 — DEVIL
Job: Bulk Articles
Freelancer: Myself
Client: Satan

As was the case with Ernie, I began working for a guy I felt sorry for. He had a lot of issues, and because of that I was happy to give him my time and a big discount, even though the work was tedious and his messages were abrupt. In the beginning, he claimed he had a debilitating physical condition that my own mother had been diagnosed with, and as I had seen the impact it'd had on my mother, and the impact it had on me as a result, I was happy to forgive the obvious insanity he displayed. As it turned out, he didn't have this condition at all. He did have something wrong with him, but he had attached the name of this particular condition seemingly because he thought it was a "fashionable" illness.

The warning signs were there, but I ignored them. The first of these came when he "shortlisted" people for the job and included me on that list. In order to prove my worth to him, he tasked me with visiting the British Museum and doing some research for him, all of which he expected me to do for free. This is messed up on two levels. The first is that he had already planned to hire someone else for the job (he hired her, she realized he was insane and quit, and he then returned to offer me the job), and the second is that I live a good seven-hour drive from the British Museum. I'm not sure whether he thought Britain was one of these islands that can be walked in under an hour or whether he actually expected me to make an fourteen-hour round trip just to please him, but either way this was a warning sign that I ignored when he returned to offer me the job (which, thankfully, had nothing to do with the British Museum).

This client was every bad experience rolled into one. He hired me to write a bulk batch of articles. He would accept them, and then, two weeks later, he would decide that they needed changing and that I should do it for free. When I made those changes, he would okay them, and then, another two weeks down the line, say that more changes were needed. He paid for them initially, which was a relief, but the work was never-ending and I was never paid for any changes. It was long, slow, and tedious. I needed a lot of info from him, and while he was forthcoming with it, he provided me with way more than I needed. In the beginning I received more than 150 emails in three days, many of which had links to websites, attachments of his ramblings, and other useless information that he expected me to read. I copied them to a single document in the beginning, but after I hit 700,000 words and they continued to arrive, I gave up.

After a year passed, I had written the ten articles he had paid for, but the silly little changes were still coming. Only one article, written in the first two weeks, had been fully accepted, with no "I think we should do *this* instead" coming for more than eight months. However, I then received an email that casually mentioned that he thought the first article needed to go down a different route after all, and that after I finished rewriting the other nine, I should get to work on it. Not only that, but during his "editing phases," he would refuse to use track changes (which show any changes made to a Word doc) and would instead highlight words or phases he wanted me to change, without telling me anything about why he wanted them changed or what he wanted them changed to. My work was often flawless when I sent it to him, purely because he was abusive and very mean, and not the sort of person you want noticing mistakes. On one occasion, he returned a 10,000-word document with a single highlighted word. That word was "purse" in reference to the contents of a woman's handbag, and to this day I have no idea why he didn't just change it himself, or even what he wanted me to change it to.

Believe it or not, he wasn't joking. There is a good chance he had some screws loose, but by this time so did I. Prior to this, I had actually given him a bigger refund as he had been going through some financial hardship and I felt bad, but when this happened I decided enough was enough. I quit the job, I apologized, and I even refunded over $1,000 as a goodwill gesture. In the end, I had done well over three hundred hours of work and had been paid for a little under twenty. Enough was enough.

This was not the end for him though. I had actually been the twelfth freelancer he had hired to do this job, and while the others had quit sooner, with many of them refusing to put up with him (he was very abusive toward the end), my persistence and politeness had worked against me. He snapped, sending me an email that threatened to end me and then trying to do just that. I kept my cool. I never lashed out and told him what I thought of him, but despite this, he never stopped being abusive.

It was my own stupid fault for not following the rules I set for myself, and for giving too much time and compassion to someone who was not fit for the human race. The fact that many freelancers had quit on him and many friends had turned against him was not a reason to feel sorry for him—it was a warning to stay the hell away from him.

Moral of the Story: If you have a bad feeling about a client, if they are short with you, if they treat you like shit, then run. It doesn't matter if you feel bad for them. Sometimes it's their own fault their lives suck.

14.3 — SLAVE DRIVER
Job: Bulk Articles
Freelancer: Myself
Client: Hotel Site

This was another job taken on during my first year, and another I had doubts about from the outset. I had no other jobs to do, and while it was paying next to nothing it seemed like it would be easy (but as I have mentioned many times already, clients who pay little expect a lot). The job offered about $2 per description, and as most of that info could be rewritten and reworded from other sites, I figured I could do an average of one every five minutes, earning $40 an hour. Not a huge amount considering where other future jobs could lead me, but it was acceptable at the time.

As soon as the job began, the client threw a book of guidelines at me and the job immediately took a different turn. These guidelines were very strict, ridiculously so, but I didn't want to give up and pushed on with the job. Ten hours later, I had gotten through just twenty-five descriptions, earning $50 for my efforts. I was tired, ready to call it a night, but the client was not. He nitpicked, forcing me to make the tiniest and stupidest changes. Like the evil client mentioned earlier, he also refused to make the smallest changes himself. On one occasion he noticed a typo, and instead of correcting it, he pointed it out in a message to me, wrote an entire paragraph on why this was a mistake (because apparently I genuinely thought that "ther" was a word and needed telling otherwise), and then insisted that I correct this typo and return the document to him.

I spent an hour fixing these descriptions, even though I was dead on my feet. But before I could send them, he sent me a message to basically say, "You know what, I changed my mind. I think you should rewrite them." As you can imagine, having worked for less than $5 an hour all day, I wasn't in the best of moods and I certainly didn't want to decrease my total earnings to just $2 an hour. I canceled the job and refused payment. His final words to me were to insist that he wasn't "that sort of person," and that I deserved to be paid for my time. Before I could even begin to entertain this idea, he tried to pay me $15. He definitely wasn't "that kind of person," if "that kind of person" was an honest, respectable human being.

Of course, I could have taken the $15. Money is money. But doing so would have allowed him to leave me feedback. I had been nothing but polite and professional (even in the face of absurdity), but because I hadn't responded to his whips and shouts, I doubted that he would leave me positive feedback. Breaking out of those chains, finally getting some sleep, and writing that day off as a lost cause was the best course of action.

Moral of the Story: Do not drastically reduce your fee, and remember that low-paying clients are often much more demanding. After all, anyone who thinks it is acceptable to pay someone less than $2 an hour is a slave driver, and those guys don't deliver the best employee satisfaction.

14.4 — FORGETFUL

Job: Academic Contract
Freelancer: D
Experience: 5+ years on and off freelancing platforms

In early 2010, D worked on a project for a husband and wife team. The husband gave D all of the information she needed. He was polite, upfront, and seemed very professional. The agreement was established away from a freelancing platform, but the client worked for a prestigious college, so D trusted him to come through as an okay client.

She worked hard on the job and finalized it several months later, only to hear nothing from the client. She emailed him again after another week, asking what he thought of the work, and he replied to say that it was perfect and that payment would be sent soon. Within fourteen days the client paid, but as D waited for the money to clear, the payment was retracted. After more correspondence, the client told D that his credit cards had been stolen and that he had been advised to cancel all payments. He promised her he would sort out these issues and pay within the week.

Another week passed and then several more followed, with nothing coming from the client. When D finally heard from him, he apologized deeply and offered to pay more money to make up for the inconvenience. Several more months of excuses followed before the money was finally transferred into D's account, only for it to be retracted again before she could withdraw it. In the next year D persisted and contacted the client many times, before eventually giving up.

In 2013, nearly three years after completing the job and never seeing a penny, D decided to investigate. She tracked down the client's wife, who had since parted ways with her former husband. She informed D that he worked at a new college and she gave D his address.

D emailed the client to tell him how cheated she felt and how, if he didn't pay, she would tell his new boss. In the end, the client paid up in full, giving her the extra money he had promised her initially and proving that persistence does pay.

Moral of the Story: Persistence certainly worked in this case, and the thing to remember here is that while the freelancer always has something to lose, the client rarely does. The freelancer needs payment, but the client has the work and can simply disappear without paying, facing no consequences. So, always try to find something that holds that client to a payment—whether it's escrow, an extensive work history (that they are unlikely to risk losing), or, in this case, a connection with their new job and new life. You don't have to limit your correspondence to the freelancing platform, and if you can find them outside of this, you might make them anxious and put pressure on them to pay you. As mentioned previously, this is also why it pays to break a job into small milestones and to take it slowly, waiting for them to pay before you move onto the next milestone.

14.5 — FREEBIE HUNTER

Job: Spy Fiction
Freelancer: M
Experience: 6+ years on and off freelancing platforms

M had a passion for writing and jumped at the opportunity to join Elance when she first heard of the site. In her first few months, she wrote bulk articles on obscure topics, jobs that many writers have to do and ones that pay the bills, but ones that also become tedious very quickly. When she was given an opportunity to write fiction novels, penning a number of books in a cozy mystery series, she was delighted.

The client, Louise, sent her information about the story, which she was to review prior to a Skype chat. While the story was a little unorthodox, she was happy to study it and to accept the Skype interview. As soon as the interview began, the red flags were raised. M had questions about the story, but these were avoided, and there were some strange and strict rules placed on what could be written and what could not. The client was happy with descriptive sex and intense violence, but not with any sort of bad language. She wanted a love story and she wanted the protagonist to be likable, yet she wanted that same protagonist to kill men, women, and children who had done nothing wrong, purely because he was paid to do so.

Louise also insisted that M write a sample there and then as they were talking. She agreed on the basis that she could research a few things and then return to live chat to write, which the client was okay with. M began to write until the client said she had to go offline, asking M to wait and not to write anything until she came back. By the time she returned, M had been working, talking, and waiting for many hours and she hadn't been paid, nor had she officially been given the job.

She continued to write and the client continued to waste her time, explaining at length things that she didn't need to hear, and asking for her opinion on everything in the story. Although frustrated and worried already, M became even more concerned when she enquired about payment and the client told her she didn't want to go through Elance and, even if she did, she didn't want to pay for a sample.

Eventually, after losing many hours, she cut her losses, severed ties with the client, and never spoke to her again.

Moral of the Story: You should be very wary when clients ask for a Skype discussion, because all of them will waste your time in one way or another, and many of them, Louise and Ernie included, will treat you like a free consultant who is there to guide them through life.

M acknowledges that she made a mistake, that she should have paid attention to the client's work history and listened to her instinct—the little voice that was telling her to flee when the client started to waste her time. This was a vital lesson learned for M, but it is one that you can easily avoid yourself.

14.6 — DELUSIONAL
Job: Edit
Freelancer: Y
Client: Michael

I worked closely with Michael at the time. I felt bad for the guy and allowed those feelings to get the better of me, as they so often do. He contacted me early on in my career and asked for help. He was in a similar position as I was and had come from a similar place, but he was having a very difficult time. He couldn't get jobs, and the ones he did get ended badly. He had self-published a short biography, but as well as struggling for sales, he had gotten a lot of bad reviews.

I never read this story, but judging by his messages to me, the synopsis on his book page and every other piece of writing I had seen him complete, I had a good idea about the quality of his book. He was terrible, and that's putting it lightly. I could never understand why he wanted to be a writer when it looked like he had never read a book in his life. This was a man who struggled to write two words without making a mistake, a man whose writing skills were akin to a small child's. His heart was in the right place, though, and I didn't have it in me to tell him the truth.

One day he contacted me to tell me that he had hired an editor—whom we shall name Y—to fix his book. Apparently, he had listened to the bad reviews and decided to do something about it. He told this editor that a simple proofread was needed, and he was adamant that was the case. However, as soon as the editor saw the book, she told him that it was much more than a simple proof, that the entire book would need to be rewritten and that she could not do that for the price he had quoted.

Michael, who was as clueless to his lack of ability as a tone-deaf singer auditioning for the *X Factor,* launched into a verbal assault. I won't repeat what he told her, because half of it was obscene and you probably wouldn't be able to make much sense of the rest. He then, indignantly, told me what had happened, suffixed with a general air of "How dare she do that?" and "What is wrong with this industry if freelancers are out to rip you off like that?"

Before I offered my opinion, I asked to read the book in question, after which I confirmed that everything Y had said was, in fact, true. At this point I was honest, telling him what I should have told him previously. That was only because I understood what the freelancer must have been feeling. She had been attacked when she had been right all along, which has also happened to me. It wasn't fair to let it slide. As it turned out, Y was a saint for agreeing to edit that book, even with more money. As far as I was concerned, the only way to fix it would be to delete it and then write another story.

Michael ended up accepting Y's offer based on my advice. Y took the job, did what was promised, and then, in an event that should have surprised no one, Michael was not happy with it. Y had cleaned it up and turned a messy nightmare into a legible story. But when your client believes that a messily written shit-fest of a story is actually near perfect, then it's clear they have no idea what perfect is. Michael genuinely thought he was a great writer, and because the only way to fix his work was basically to rewrite it and delete everything he thought amounted to perfection, it was obvious he wasn't going to appreciate the end product.

Despite Y doing a good job, despite Michael being a freelancer as well and understanding just how hard the industry is, he left Y terrible feedback and also filed a dispute, claiming she had destroyed his work. There are two sides to every story. I understand that (even if one of those sides is typically a lie or a delusion), but believe me when I say that this was entirely one-sided, and that Michael played the role of contemptible bastard to perfection.

After that, I decided that enough was enough, and I pretty much severed ties with Michael. I didn't like the way he treated the freelancer, and he was clearly deluded and beyond help. As it turned out, his freelancing career never got off the ground, because here was a writer who should be paying clients to accept his work, yet he thought he was worth the same price that best-selling authors were charging. On the rare occasions he was given jobs, the clients were so appalled by the end product that they filed disputes.

Because of my experiences with Michael, Ernie, and "Satan," I no longer let my feelings of pity get in the way of my work, and I also tend to refuse to help people who get in touch out of the blue (except for very rare occasions). Experience has told me that even when you try to help people, when you try to be honest, kind, and compassionate, it usually blows up in your face. Just ask Y.

Moral of the Story: If a client exposes himself or herself as an utter fool, if they attack you and offend you, then regardless of their reasoning or their excuses, do not return to them and agree to work for them. It is also wise to remember that this industry is full to the brim of people who think they can make it as professional writers yet can't put two coherent words together. On many occasions these will be the people you are outsourcing to, the people you are working alongside, and you people you are working for.

14.7 — MISSION IMPOSSIBLE
Job: Biographies
Freelancer: Q
Client: Magda

This story begins with a job that I was actually close to applying for, but one that I turned down. Later, by some twist of fate, I would actually correspond with Q, the person who took the job, and she would relate to me the insanity that followed.

The job was for sporting biographies, small one-hundred-word pieces about famous sporting heroes. I am a big sports fan myself and have taken on many jobs relating to all kinds of sports in the past. At the time I was searching for work and this job stood out. When I discovered what they were offering to pay, and when I read the guidelines, I immediately moved on. Q, however, did not do the math.

The client was polite enough, and even though she was new, Q was confident that good work would generate good feedback. She did a rough calculation and determined that she could complete the job in a week, which seemed to impress the client. The job itself was for $500, and as she had just started, Q figured this would be a decent sum for a week's work.

When she began, she realized that something was amiss. The job was not to write just any one hundred words, but to complete a checklist that meant she had to find the full name, date of birth, martial status, awards, and more about the sports star in question. And she had to do over 10,000 of these, working from a list of sports stars dating back hundreds of years and covering many different sports and disciplines and many different countries.

Somehow she had calculated that she would need to write 100,000 words, when in fact she needed one million. What's more, she had been given an upfront payment, which meant she was determined to finish. After more calculations, she realized that even if she didn't sleep or eat, she would still struggle to finish in a week. So, she determined that she could do 100,000 words, and that she could outsource the rest.

She found writers willing to work very cheaply and she assigned them batches. She had fifteen of them working for her in total, all agreeing to be paid on completion. However, as I explained in the Outsourcing chapter (see Chapter 11.0: Outsourcing) and as Q quickly discovered, these writers were not at all reliable. After six days she had just a dozen descriptions, totaling over 1,000 words. Half of the writers had quit, and others were not responding (one would reply three months later to apologize for nondelivery and then ask if she had any more work).

With the stress of dealing with these freelancers, which can be a full-time job in itself, Q had only completed 20,000 words. At the end of the week, she had barely slept, she was stressed, and she was desperate. She asked for an extension of two weeks, and it was given, but she went straight back to relying on cheap writers, and they continued to let her down.

After three weeks, she had worked with over twenty freelancers, all of whom had failed to deliver what they promised. Some of these filed disputes, demanding that she pay them for the work they had done, which meant that Q was even more out of pocket when the client also filed a dispute. She was ordered to pay back the upfront payment, though the client did leave her a small amount to cover the work she had done. As a result of this payment, the client was also allowed to leave feedback, and this destructive rating stopped Q from ever working on that site again.

Moral of the Story: Q did so much wrong here. She admitted that herself but said that the stress made her desperate. I have been in a similar situation myself, calculating wrongly because I was thinking on the fly and having to work twenty hours a day for a week just to deliver on time. I managed to pull it off, but only because my miscalculation wasn't as bad as Q's. She could have given the upfront payment back and canceled the job, but she had struggled to find work and didn't want to let a job slip through her fingertips.

She should never have relied on others to finish her deadline. I know from experience that most freelancers will fail to deliver. To rely on more than a dozen freelancers coming through was never going to happen. She could have also cut her losses at the end of the first week, but she refused to give in.

Finally, she should have refused payment in the end. She was forced to give the upfront payment back, and the money paid to her as "compensation" was meagre, not even covering what she paid the freelancers. She didn't want to leave the job empty-handed after everything she had been through, and that decision essentially meant that she forfeited her account for less than $50.

Summary

- Clients can be dickheads.

See Also

- *When to Run (page 67 – 3.8)*
- *Things to Looks Out for (page 88 – 4.5)*
- *Client's Perspective (page 141 – 8.2)*
- *"Hidden" Rules (page 155 – 9.3)*
- *Outsourcing (Chapter 11.0)*
- *Take a Break (page 195 – 12.4)*
- *I Have Been Suspended (page 207 – 13.6)*
- *I Am Not Being Paid by the Client (page 209 – 13.9)*

Part 4

OPTIONS

*"Everything comes to an end, but success
breeds success."*

Chapter 15

WEBSITES AND BLOGGING

Blogging is something that all freelance writers should consider. Before you begin your career, a blog can provide some experience. It is something that demands regular attention and constant writing, which in turn can help you integrate into the life of a freelancer. It can also bolster your CV and showcase your writing skills. Once you're working full time, a blog can fill in the gaps when you're struggling to find jobs. It can keep you going in those downtimes, and it can also provide an extra boost to your income.

Of course, this is 2016. Blogging has had its day and you'll probably be looking at these pages with bemusement. However, when I say "blogging," I'm referring to a wider scope of websites, not just personal blogs.

One of my favorite clients owns a number of websites. I have actually referred to him a number of times in this book, as both a client who encouraged negotiation, and one who was always ready to listen to any ideas I had or any deals I could offer. This client initially hired me to work on a single site. When I did what he asked and he was satisfied with the work, that one site grew to half a dozen.

In the end, I was writing for twelve different sites. As well as deciding on the article titles and writing the articles, I would also post them through WordPress. After doing this for some time, I worked with a close friend of his, and one who also became a great client. That's when I began to understand a little more of what they were doing. They were basically creating sites that used WordPress as a platform. They would set some very basic SEO in place, give me a few simple guidelines to follow, and then pay me to write the articles. They also paid for design work and for coding, but they didn't do any promotion and relied on the content. My content.

It occurred to me that if they could do it using my content, then I should be able to replicate it. They paid me a lot of money, so I assumed they were making a decent return on these sites, and as I would be writing the content, I knew I wouldn't have that expenditure. My partner is also an incredibly gifted designer, so the only thing I would need to pay for was occasional coding work, which I could outsource.

And so my part-time career as a webmaster began. I get a little help from these two clients, mainly from the second one I mentioned, who helps me with SEO, keywords etc., but much of it is down to the content. This is all centered on affiliates, because if you find the right one, you can make a lot of money. Once you start earning, you can sell the site on and start another.

It does require a lot of work and it's not as easy as it sounds, but it's a very viable option for talented writers who have little to no technical ability. I personally don't make a lot from these sites and have yet to score any sort of worthwhile profit, but only because I devote very little time to it. If I ever have a lot of free time, I know I can fall back on these sites, devoting more time to them and getting more money out of them. What's more, although it may take a year or two at the slow rate I am going, I could still sell these sites for a tidy profit further down the line.

15.1 — FLIPPING WEBSITES

On sites like Flippa, you can buy everything from start-up websites to fully established ones. If you focus on the ones that cost between $100 and $1,000, you can use common sense and basic writing skills to get a big return on your investment. The issue with these sites is that they are usually based on a standard template, one that wasn't very good to begin with. They are usually written in English, despite being created by webmasters in India, China, and other non-English-speaking countries. They are also created quickly, focusing on SEO. Therefore, while they have the traffic and are earning a little money (usually through AdWords), they are typically very ugly and have very poor content. There are also sites that plagiarize content from elsewhere. These are just as bad and can be treated just the same.

You should spend some time on Flippa first, getting to know the true value of these sites. Be sure to research the page rank of a site, and find out where it is in the Google searches, how many visitors it is getting, and how many of them are "organic"—which means they are coming through search engines and not through social media. This is very important; it is easy to slip Facebook $200 and watch as they send thousands of hits to your website, but this counts for nothing in the long run and merely inflates the statistics when you come to buy.

Once you are sure that you're getting a good deal on a site, buy it. You then need to go through the site and clean up the content. Swap bad English for good; add a few keyword-rich articles here and there. Fix the layout if needed, or find a cheap designer who can do it for you. Once you have finished, you should have a good-looking, well-presented website with informative and well-written content. From here you can either continue to build on it, using AdWords and other advertising to generate an income, or you can put it back on the market and try to sell it, knowing that the improvements will add significant value.

You're like a skilled builder buying and flipping a dilapidated house. You need to put your time and effort into fixing it and making some changes here and there. You may also need to subcontract some specialists in areas you know little about. In the end, however, you have something that is worth considerably more than it was when you bought it, something that can be sold on for a profit.

You will get a bigger profit if you sell away from Flippa, as it keeps a record of sites that have been listed before and previous buyers will be able to see how much you bought it for. It doesn't matter how much better it looks now; if someone knows you paid much less for it a short while ago, they'll be wary about paying more. Luckily, there are a number of sites like Flippa out there.

15.2 — BLOGGING

Traditionally, blogging has been a great way for a skilled writer to earn a bit of cash. It's far from easy, but typically the rules of SEO don't apply as much. With blogging, you're not trying to score success through search engines, but rather you're hoping for a viral hit— something that will be shared on social media, something that will essentially spread itself. And in this case, Facebook should definitely not be dismissed.

Your first step in this process is to buy your domain name and your web-hosting package. Do not purchase a shared hosting plan. This will put you on the same server as thousands of other websites, which means during peak times, your website will crawl at a snail's pace and may even timeout. Don't go over the top either, just because you anticipate 50,000 hits a day in the future doesn't mean you need to cater for that early on.

VPS hosting plans are good and relatively cheap. They will allow you to host as many sites as you want, and you can grow at will, paying a little extra to cover any floods of extra visitors that you might get. If you're not technically minded, get a "supported" VPS plan, as opposed to a "self-hosting" plan. Don't assume problems won't arise, don't gamble on a cheaper "self-hosting" plan and think you'll be okay. At the very least, you'll need to keep a coder on hand to fix problems, and in the long run that will cost you a lot more.

Once you have set that up, you need to download WordPress. You can find some simple instructions for downloading and installing WordPress on the actual WordPress site. Trust me, if I can do it, then you'll be fine. If you do have any issues, an experienced coder should be charging you no more than $40 to install it for you, as it will take them a maximum of twenty minutes.

This might seem like a lot of hassle when you can just get a WordPress account and go through there, but you have little to no control of your website if you do that. You will be indexed by Google immediately, and you will have access to the WP community, but if you want to truly profit from your site, with banners, ads, and even an eventual sale, then you need to go through the process explained here. There are other content providers as well, of course, but for ease of use and variety of templates, you can't beat WordPress.

Speaking of templates, that's your next step. But before you do anything, you need to discourage Google from indexing your site. I learned this the hard way and was schooled by a good friend and great client, who told me that if the site is indexed early on, before the content is there and before the template is set, Google will judge it poorly from that point on. So, under "Settings," you will find a section that says "Reading." From there, go to "Search Engine Visibility" and click the option that says "Discourage Search Engines from Indexing This Site." Once the site is ready to go, you can un-click this, but only do so when you're good and ready.

Once the website is up and running, the only thing you can do is keep writing. When it comes to writing for search engines, the rules are fairly straightforward. You find out what people are searching for on Google Keyword Planner, and you cover those topics in your article titles. The same rules work for a blog, but it is much easier if you stick to controversial topics, unique topics, and anything that will make people want to click when they see it on Facebook or Twitter. Always use between one and three words for your article URL. WordPress will automatically copy the title of your article into this space, so be sure to narrow it down. Also, all article titles should be less than seventy characters, because Google will ignore anything over this.

The process for getting your posts to display on other people's timeline is very simple and surprisingly cheap. Simply set up a Facebook page for your site and fill the page with links to the articles you have written so far. For this, you should give your articles at least one image each, something to entice the reader and something to show on the post. Once the site is ready, run a Facebook ad campaign to get more likes. This will expose your page and its content to targeted Facebook users, based on a set of criteria that you choose.

Depending on how "clickable" your page is, you can get anywhere from 100 to 1,000 likes for just $100. These are genuine people, and for everyone that likes your page, hundreds of their friends will be exposed to it. Once that's done, you need to choose a couple of your stand-out posts and run campaigns for them. Be sure to pay for "impressions," as opposed to "activity." That way, if your posts go viral, the campaign won't be cut short.

With a very attractive picture of a gorgeous Austrian town and a simple travel article, I once paid just $20 for an article that received 150 likes and more than twenty shares. I also got a few hundred visitors to the article itself, and because of those visitors and the fact that a few of them clicked links and one of them bought something from one of those links, I received a return of $50. This is not a great deal of cash, and as I write I have yet to break into a profit from doing this, but it no longer has my full time and attention. I have still made enough money to cover every penny spent, though, and I also have some assets to sell.

15.3 — WEBSITES FROM SCRATCH

If you want to create a content-based website from scratch, with the intention to flip it as mentioned above, then the process is similar to creating a blog. However, once you have uploaded your WordPress site and discouraged Google from indexing it, you should try and get a few basic pages on the site, aiming for at least 800 words each. It isn't always easy to get this many words, but that's where your skills as a writer come into play. These sections include a Homepage, which is the first thing visitors will see, as well as a Privacy Policy, Terms and Conditions, About Us, and Directory. These should all be linked in the footer or header, and for the Directory, be sure to link to pages that are relevant to your site and ones that have a high Page Rank and/or a .gov domain extension.

Steps for Website Creation

1. Purchase domain and hosting plan.
2. Install WordPress.
3. Discourage Google from indexing site.
4. Find a template that works.
5. Create some simple articles for Homepage, About, Directory, Terms and Conditions, and Privacy Policy.
6. Add a bulk batch of keyword articles with 800 words minimum. Aim for at least twenty.
7. Index site.
8. Keep adding articles. Aim for one a day until you hit 100.
9. Reduce to one every other day until you hit 200.
10. Keep adding at any rate you choose. Reduce to as few as one per week if you want.

You should also aim for at least twenty articles on launch. These should cover the basics of your chosen subject, and they should mention your affiliate. So, for a site about gambling that is affiliated with 32 Red, I would write content such as "Online Casinos with Free Bets" and "Online Sports Books and Casinos" and be sure to mention 32 Red in all. This can be a bit tiresome after a while. It is very repetitive. But I find that this sort of writing can be done when you're half asleep, when everything else has been finished and you're not in the right mind-set to write for clients. Once you have the twenty articles, post them to the site and let Google index you. Don't post any affiliate links yet, though; you should wait until you are ranking on the first page of Google for a number of chosen keywords ("32 Red

Reviews" would be a good keyword in this instance) and are ranking in the number one position of one of them. This sounds difficult, but for sites with no outbound advertising links, it's not that hard.

You need to keep posting articles until you achieve this. Aim for one article per day, at least 800 words each. Once you hit 100 articles, your ranking should have drastically improved. From there you can post at a rate of one every other day. You may also be ready to start posting affiliate links and to take the site to the next level. The key here is not to bother with AdWords. Your traffic will be small, maybe no more than 100 hits a day, but it will all be targeted toward your exact theme. If that theme is 32 Red Reviews and 32 Red Free Bets, that means everyone searching for your site and clicking onto it will be ready to sign up to 32 Red. They are perfectly primed to click on your affiliate links and complete that sign-up process, and once they do, you will cash in. Affiliates like this work on leads and tend to pay a lot. As an example, I work with some Forex and Binary Options platforms, who pay me at least $300 for every sign-up my site generates.

Obviously, this is not a faultless process. It takes time and effort, and it doesn't always work. But providing that you don't make any major mistakes, then you will always have something of value by the end of it. The worst thing you can do is get desperate and impatient. Because as soon as you start paying for backlink services from people who promise 10,000 or more backlinks for $5, then you're screwed. By all means, pay for a few high-quality guest posts, anything to get your link on high-value sites (although not essential, this will greatly boost your site's rankings and hits), but avoid anything that promises the earth for a few dollars, because it'll lose you more than it gets you.

15.4 — FREELANCER WEBSITES

One of the most basic ways of offering your services as a freelancer is through a simple website. These days it is easy to create a simple website that is able to accept payments. You don't have the security of a freelancing platform, of escrow payments and mediation, but that's the risk you take. Luckily, there are ways around some of the issues (such as asking for half of the payment upfront and retaining ownership until they pay in full).

When it comes to advertising your website and your services, we can go back to Facebook. At the time of writing there is a trend for "designers" to advertise their services on Facebook. They create simple websites, with little more than a price list, a portfolio, and an e-commerce setup, often courtesy of PayPal. With a well-placed book cover and a "one-time" offer, they can generate a $20 ad on Facebook that will give them over $200 in business.

Of course, I say "designers," but these guys have less artistic talent than I do. They don't make the covers; they go straight to Upwork, where a number of long-term freelancers (whose work they stole for their portfolio) awaits them. Those freelancers do the work for them, after which the clients pass it on and pocket the cash.

This works for book-cover designers in particular, because it is very easy to use Facebook ads to target self-published authors, people who generally need well-designed book covers. The process should also work for other designers, though, and even for writers. The trick is to offer a complete service on your website. Make sure that everything a prospective client needs to see is there, that they won't have any questions when they have finished browsing, and that they will be happy to complete a purchase. Once you have that, you just need to target the right people through Facebook ads. For editors, target the same people that book-cover designers target; for copywriters, target anyone in marketing and any start-up companies; for article writers, target website owners and bloggers.

This is a good way of running a small business on the side, and as well as showcasing your skills as a freelancer, the website can also display your credentials as an author, your bio, your contact details, and your social media links. If you are also an author and you have fans stumbling onto that site, they might just become your biggest customers. After all, how many people out there have an idea for a book or a film script that they just can't seem to write themselves, and how many of them would jump at the chance of having one of their favorite authors write it for them?

Chapter 15 Summary

- Writers should look to plug the gaps of their schedule with websites and blogs.
- Flipping a site is a great way to earn a little cash and experience, but do your research in advance and begin small.
- Everyone has a blog these days, but that doesn't mean you can't profit from yours.
- Always get a domain and a self-hosted site, as opposed to simply signing up for WordPress or another content provider.
- For blogs: use Facebook ads, find a picture that attracts the eye, and build your article (preferably something that will generate a discussion) around it.
- For websites: focus on affiliates and keywords. It's boring and tedious and it takes a long time, but the rewards can be huge.

See Also:

- *W-8BEN (page 40 – 2.5)*
- *NDAs and Other Agreements (page 111 – 5.10)*
- *Where to Outsource (page 184 – 11.5)*
- *No Distractions (page 188 –12.1)*
- *Offline Freelancing (page 272 – 17.2)*
- *Expenses (page 303 – 20.1)*

Chapter 16

TIPS FOR LONG TERM

There are a few important things that need to be said, and a few things I have mentioned in brief that need to be addressed in full. I could have worked these in elsewhere, but the point of this book was to create something that you could refer to time and time again; to create chapters you can read and find useful as you begin your career; and to provide chapters you can skim through, make a mental note of, and return to when your career is a little more developed and they are a little more useful. These "tips" are for when you're in full swing and will probably be at their most useful when you've been freelancing for a year or more.

16.1 — GIVE CLIENTS A NUDGE

I feel a little strange writing this segment when I know that I will be sending this book to some of my long-term clients, but I'm sure they will understand and forgive me.

When you establish a relationship with a client and that client turns from someone who provides you with the odd job into someone who provides you regular (and even constant) work, there will come a time when you don't hear from them. The majority of long-term clients are webmasters who have a job and a life away from those websites. This means that holidays, weddings, and even boredom can get in the way, and they'll just stop asking for content from you.

They might return in the future, but they are just as likely to give up, to find someone else, or even to do it themselves. The trick is to remind them you exist, to make them hire you again, without being too pushy.

As soon as a long-term client goes silent on me, I wait a week or so and then look for an excuse to message them. Usually, I will have established a rapport with them and can therefore find a personal link. This means I can message them with a "heads-up"—something I discovered that I think they would find useful. For a webmaster who owns a string of WordPress sites, I might discover an article about a sudden spate of WordPress hacks; for a webmaster who runs affiliate sites, I might bump into an affiliate that offers a better deal than the ones they have. Whatever the reason, and however tenuous the connection, the point is to make contact, to send them a message that they will appreciate, but one that is more or less meaningless.

Some of them will reply to tell you that they are thinking of doing an "XYZ" project and were actually thinking about getting in touch and asking if you wanted to work on it. Some of them will reply to thank you and then finish by telling you about an upcoming project that they will probably hire you for. Others will hire you there and then. It's amazing how many times this works.

If you can't find anything to say to a long-term client, a message like this will usually suffice:

Hi [Client Name],

I don't mean to sound presumptuous or anything, but I just wanted to drop you a line to ask if you had anything you needed doing. I have some free time coming up for the first time in a while, and I'm just making sure that my preferred clients don't need me to do anything before I start applying for jobs elsewhere. I wouldn't want to fill my schedule with new clients and then find out you needed something.

All the best,
[Your Name]

The first time I sent a message like this was to a client mentioned in this book, one of my closest clients, and it was actually true. I did have free time and because his schedule was as erratic as mine, I wanted to know if he had any projects so that I wouldn't let him down in the future. When it worked (and worked very well), I began to use it again and again. It has yet to fail me.

All clients are different, and all will respond differently, which is why you need to tweak this. Never send either of these messages to a client you are not friendly with, always add an offer of cheaper work to a client who puts a good deal ahead of anything else, and simply ignore clients who prefer minimal contact and get annoyed by too many messages.

You should send these messages to clients you're close with, even if you know they won't give you any work. It pays to keep the communication—and even the friendship—going. I do this with a couple of my clients and actually recently sent a message to someone I have become close with, someone who shares similar interests. As it happens, the work had dried up for a couple of weeks and he did respond with more work for me, but that was a pleasant bonus, as I genuinely wanted to tell him something and to play catch-up. Because, although this book (and everyone who knows me, for that matter) would attest differently, I'm not a completely antisocial pariah.

16.2 — "COMPANIES" ARE DOOMED TO FAIL

On many freelancing websites you can set yourself up as an "individual" or as a "company." It doesn't matter how long you have been freelancing, at some point you will find yourself toying with the idea of setting up a company, hiring other freelancers to do the work for you, and then simply spending your time delegating. There are many successful companies out there, but this is a minefield. After all, if it was that easy, everyone would do it, but there is a reason why individuals like myself tend to do so much better than the majority of these companies, even though we're working alone.

The successful companies hire people that they work with in the real world, people they know they can trust. If I were to get together with a few writers I knew, trusted, and understood just as well as I knew, trusted, and understood myself, I'm sure I could make something of it. But the majority of "companies" hire within the platforms.

Most of the "cheaper" freelancers you hire will mess up in one way or another. Finding a decent writer among them is a difficult task. Finding one who doesn't miss deadlines and is always professional and reliable is nearly impossible. And you can't increase the payment, simply because the clients won't be increasing yours. If a client is paying you $0.05 per word, which is considered to be a good amount, then you need to be paying around $0.03 per word to make it worthwhile, and you'll struggle to find what you need at that price. You could charge more, but clients are not stupid. They know that many companies outsource, so they usually don't pay more than $0.05 per word and typically pay a lot less. You'll struggle to make that in the beginning, because even if you have the credentials, you're not the one who will be doing the work, so those credentials mean nothing.

You could be dishonest, you could overcharge, and you could get incredibly lucky when it comes to finding capable writers; but even then, after all the stress of dealing with many demanding clients and many (often incompetent) freelancers, and after receiving a lot of bad feedback and going through many disputes (after all, few clients will be happy to pay top dollar for low-quality work), is it really worth it?

16.3 — DON'T PUT TOO MANY EGGS IN ONE BASKET

This has definitely been mentioned several times throughout this book, but I can't stress it enough. As soon as you start making money, as soon as you get a freelancing career off the ground, you need to devote some of your free time to other outlets. If you rely 100 percent on the money you make through online freelancing, you might get through, but there will be some very anxious and stressful times ahead.

The trick is to use your success in one field to exploit another, regardless of how big or small that success is. You should also focus on the outlets that require a lot of work now but very little work later on. That way, if you fall ill, if you lose patience with your work, or if you simply want to take a holiday, then you'll still get paid. As I write this, I am actually a snotty, throaty, feverish mess and have been for a week. In that time, I have written a handful of paragraphs on this book, done between one and two hours work elsewhere, and generally lost a lot of money. Thanks to my investments (both time and money) and despite this illness, I'm not completely screwed and I'll still make enough to cover the rent, bills, and all my frivolous spending.

I won't go into detail with these investments. Not because they are illegal—far from it. I just don't want to bore you with my own endeavors. That's what my partner is for. However, it is worth briefly recapping my own experience to give you an idea of just what I am talking about.

In 2012 I had nothing. I had been trying to make it as a novelist for close to ten years, had failed miserably, and was relying on the support of an amazing woman to keep me from being homeless.

My Own Success

2003 to 2012: Full-time, unpaid author/writer.

October 2012: Self-published a "tester" novel. Getting an idea of the market.

December 2012: Published first novel proper. Ten thousand copies downloaded in first month.

February 2013: Published two further novels to equal acclaim.

April 2013: Rewrote two old novels and published under a new pen name, which sold better than the others.

August 2013: Began on Elance.

January 2014: Freelancing for ten or more hours a day.

August 2014: Began heavily investing my expendable income.

November 2014: Made it to the top of Elance.

January 2015: Branched out into website creation. Took advice from clients and outsourced work.

March 2015: Sold all self-published books. Contracted to write this book.

January 2016: All books began to be republished. Took a break from freelancing.

In 2013, I self-published some of those novels and I made a success of myself. Toward the end of that year I began to use freelance platforms, and within a year I was making more money freelancing than I was through my books. In 2014 I branched out even further. I began commissioning other writers to write books that I would then publish; I joined more freelancing sites; I began working for companies away from freelancing sites; I created some websites and set up some partnerships with webmasters and businessmen; I even helped other authors with their books in exchange for a payment and for a cut of their profits. I also invested a lot of the money I made, keeping very little spare cash and instead making sure that it was invested in as many different enterprises as possible. This meant that by 2015, when I began writing this book, I wasn't worried that the work would dry up, and I could take some time off. It also meant that I could take some time to get an agent and a publisher and to sell all the books I had previously self-published, opening the doors to a career that had always been the end goal. I haven't been hugely successful and those investments have not made me a fortune, but I am happy with everything I have done. I am happy with the way things are right now and the way things are going. I have a great agent, some great contracts and contacts, and as much work as I am willing to complete. And all of this came just two years after I had nothing.

If not for my self-published success, I wouldn't have begun freelancing (the paranoia of relying on my books as my income stream sent me into this career); and if not for my freelancing success, then this book, and all my other books, would have never been published by a trade publisher.

This job can turn sour very quickly. You don't want to look back on a time when things were going well and wish you had used that to your advantage. Everything comes to an end, but success breeds success.

16.4 — NEGOTIATIONS: BE A BASTARD . . . BUT A NICE ONE

I have already mentioned how it is important to be strict when negotiating but to never piss the client off as you do so. Having experienced things from both perspectives, I have never encountered a freelancer, other than myself, who does things the "right way." I have had freelancers who replied to offers with "My time is far too valuable for me to work for such a low rate. I can't work for anything less than XYZ," and a freelancer who even finished with "If that's not good enough then I suggest you find someone else and stop wasting my time."

What happens when the client hires you? Do you think they are going to forget that you were an utter, contemptible prick during the negotiations? Not likely. They will have a seriously lowered opinion of you, and not only will they make your life difficult because of this, but they'll also expect more (they think they're paying more than you're worth, after all). They will likely leave you poor feedback as well.

Apologize that you are not able to work for the amount they are offering, remind them that you have never worked for less than what you stated as your lowest, and tell them you are only prepared to work for that because you think the job is interesting. You can even tell them that you're not a businessman/businesswoman and are just a writer, so you're sorry that your negotiation skills are not up to scratch. That's nonsense, of course, but that's what you want them to believe.

You shouldn't be too strict in the beginning, but as you advance, as work is easier to come by, then you can be. You can afford to walk away, but because good and trustworthy freelancers are so hard to find, they cannot. If they do, don't go running back to then. Give it time. Let them try and hire someone cheap, wait for that someone to screw up, and then watch as the client comes back to you, agreeing to pay you what you want.

If you have received a personalized invite (an invite to a job created solely for you [see Section 3.7 on page 65]) and you really want to be a bastard, then simply decline the job and leave them a message to thank them, to apologize, and to say that you are very busy and can't work for anything even close to their budget. It doesn't matter how big that budget is, although in the cases where they have quoted one and it's pathetic, it's best just to decline and block them from sending you any more invites.

They will likely create another job and invite you again, trying their best to open a dialogue. It takes time for them to do this and it shows desperation, so when they do, you can guarantee they will be ready to pay top whack for your services. You still need to be apologetic, but in this case, set your minimum rate high and never agree to budge unless they think you're doing it as a big favor. For instance, if they accept your demands of $1,100, bring it down to $1,000, remind them that it was difficult for you to do that, and let them know you did it because you felt bad about being so tough on them. Reiterate you're a writer, not a businessman/businesswoman, and/or you understand what it is like to work within a budget. They will have a high opinion of you before the job starts, which will make things much easier. In many cases, the client will think you have done them a favor and will be more inclined to leave good feedback and not to hassle you for changes.

16.5 — TAKE RISKS

There are a lot of paranoid freelancers out there, people who seem to think that all clients, regardless of their work history, are out to rip them off. One freelancer reacted in that way to me, telling me even before the job had started that as soon as she finished she would send me a payment reminder every twelve hours until I paid. It didn't matter that I needed time to review. It didn't matter that she delivered the work late and I didn't say anything. She still followed through with this bizarre procedure. When I quizzed her on it, she admitted that she was paranoid about clients stealing her work and not paying, even though the freelance platform would back her up, even though my client account has spent thousands of dollars and this job was for less than $50, and even though it had never actually happened to her before.

If you can't trust your clients and that lack of trust shows, then you're not going to succeed over the long term. By all means play it safe to begin with. You should never harass a client for payment, but you can break a job up into milestones, request a payment upfront, and follow the rules of playing it safe (**see Chapter 5.0: Your First Jobs**). Once you start working with long-term clients, though, they will take liberties and you need to let them.

You will get clients, both online and offline, who expect you to do thousands of dollars of work before they pay you a penny, and you will get clients who ask if you can complete the work several weeks before they pay you. This makes their lives easier, which in turns means they'll be more likely to give you a larger contract and repeat work. Show the slightest sign of distrust, however, and they'll walk.

You need to make sure they are trustworthy first, but even then, I find that it's usually worth taking the risk. I have taken many such risks with long-term clients and I have always been paid in the end. If I had turned down all of those jobs, I'd be $20,000 or more out of pocket, not to mention the future jobs that came as a result of accepting them. None of them screwed me over. Not a single one. In my years as a freelancer, I have had two clients who disappeared before payment, one for $20 and one for $100. Both had extensive profit histories, both were "payment verified," both were on big platforms, and I was working for both of them for the first time.

Everything considered, while it would have been nice to be paid for those jobs, I don't mind taking such a small hit. Remember that this is a business. Unexpected losses and nonpayments are common, but that shouldn't stop you from taking risks and putting your trust in preferred clients.

Of course, if someone gets in touch out of the blue, has no work history, and expects you to complete a large project before they release a penny, you can avoid them. Just don't treat long-term clients the same way.

16.6 — MISSING DEADLINE DAY

There are a few things you can do when you miss a deadline. Crying is one option. Working your ass off to finish in time and then apologizing like your life depends on it is another. Don't miss the deadline and then apologize, and don't miss the deadline and wait for the client to shout at you. Always tell them in advance and offer a bargaining chip.

There is also a way you can get yourself an extra night or day without the client getting angry at you. I didn't mention this in a previous chapter on deadlines **(see Section 6.4 on page 118)** simply because it's kind of cheeky, and I'm hoping that you won't have to resort to it. I would also like to reassure all of my clients that I have never done this myself. Honestly. I have thought about it a few times, but I have never really needed to follow through with it.

Simply send them a message on the freelancing site, or in an email, telling them the work is done and attached, as you normally would, and then add a few comments to back this up. Discuss the work, tell them what you did, confirm you wrote what they asked you to write, etc. And then simply don't attach anything.

It's best to do this on an evening. That way you can spend the night and the next morning finishing the work, and when the client messages you to say they can't see the attachment, you can apologize and attach it "again." It's best to let them know that you had been working all day and were tired by that point, a valid excuse for forgetting to attach a document. Let's be honest, we've all done this before, and the client has probably done it themselves a few times. While I have never used this method myself I have genuinely forgotten attachments many times. I can't count the amount of times I have done it to editors, publishers, and friends, and I'm sure I've done it to my agent and publicist on a few occasions. I have been less forgetful with clients, as freelance platforms are more accommodating than emails, but I can still think of at least four occasions in which this happened and on none of those did the client have an issue. Their reactions, and the fact that this is a genuine mistake we all make, tells me that you won't have an issue using this as an excuse should you need to.

If you really want to be cheeky, you can send them a file in a format you know they can't open. I work on a Mac and I use Pages. In the process, not only have I discovered that very few people use this software, but I also learned that clients are picky. Most people are. They have one software suite that they use and they like to stick with it. They don't want to download something else, and they don't want to do any conversions. They're paying you, after all. So, if you're sure a client works in one format, then use something completely different, mark the title of the document "[Name of Job] Final," and then send it along. By the time they see your message, download the document, and discover they can't open it, you've bought yourself at least twenty-four hours. Some clients will take days to review the work, giving you up to a week before they try to open it and realize they can't.

I should provide a few warnings with this: *Never* do it when a client needs that work immediately for a valid reason. Otherwise you're just screwing things up for them and becoming part of the problem. *Never* do this regularly, even with different clients. They might not find out, but it's still disrespectful and it's a really bad habit. And *only* do this when it is an absolute last resort and when you know the client is not the sort of person who will respond well to an extension request.

16.7 — BUILDING FEEDBACK

As with the last "tip," this is not something I have mentioned yet, as it's not something I recommend 100 percent or something I have done myself. However, if you're struggling to build feedback, or if you're just really worried about getting bad feedback early on, then it can help.

Look for small jobs. There are many of these around, and because experienced freelancers tend to ignore them (the logistics of applying and interviewing are not worth the effort for half an hour's work), they are available for inexperienced freelancers. You should still research the client's history a little, ignoring those who tend to leave bad feedback and overly harsh comments, but by all means take a chance with new clients if they seem trustworthy enough.

It's good to be pedantic about your average feedback score, to do your best to keep it at 5.0, but this won't last forever. The good thing is that most clients won't care as long as your average is still acceptable. Anything above 4.0 is fine, and anything above 4.5 is unlikely to turn any clients away. A score of 3.99 or less will raise red flags, and if you have 2.0 or less, you'll struggle to find a job that pays a respectable amount and most clients won't even read your proposal.

Don't spend too long in the interview process. If the client is not ready to go straight away, then move on. Finding a similar job won't be difficult. If the client is ready to go, then jump straight in. Do the work, complete it, and finalize everything. If the client asks for small edits, stick at it and give them a little more of your time. If they ask for anything bigger, or they keep sending the document back, just cancel the job and move on.

Once the job is finished and you have been paid, wait for them to leave feedback. On Upwork, you will have to leave feedback for them first and then wait a couple of hours for it to show. If the feedback is five stars, excellent. Job done. You can now move on and repeat the process. If it is less than four stars, give the client a refund, erase that feedback, and then try again. I have mentioned elsewhere that it's never a good idea to push for payment and to keep asking for feedback, but you're taking chances here and you need that feedback, so feel free to ask for it.

You're not doing this for the money; you're doing it for the feedback. The money is just a nice bonus. You should still never take jobs less than your usual rate, simply because clients who pay very little tend to be more demanding and harder to please. At the end of ten hours' work, you might find that you have been paid for five hours, have received a lot of good feedback, and can now start your career proper. You might only have a couple of good feedback comments, along with a few canceled jobs against your name. Either way, this can be done in less than a day and it should get the ball rolling for you.

You don't need this "quick fix." I didn't do it and many other successful freelancers didn't do it either. This is because there are risks involved. It won't look good on your profile if you have canceled so many jobs and given so many refunds early on, and some freelancers will also use this as an excuse to be sloppy, which in turn will lead to a higher ratio of failed jobs. If you can give those clients the same dedication you would give others, if you pay attention to their profile histories, to their personalities, and to the work, there is no harm in it. The only difference between this and freelancing as normal is the focus on incredibly short, low-paying jobs and the fact that you're taking bigger risks with new clients.

16.8 — ENJOY YOUR MONEY, PREPARE FOR TAXES

While it is important to invest and to put away for a rainy day, it is just as important to enjoy your money. You're in a unique position, working in a full-time job that you can take with you anywhere you go. I am guilty of not really enjoying my money, and I have spent the last eighteen months locked away, working. But during my first year was a different story. I saw Paris, Berlin, Nicosia, Athens, and several smaller towns and resorts with my partner, working on car journeys to the airport, communicating with clients at the airport, taking notes on the plane, and working from the hotel room when I arrived. That might sound like a sure-fire way to ruin a good holiday, but there was still plenty of time for me to enjoy myself.

It's very easy for me to work in crowded rooms, in airports, on planes, and on trains. This is probably the same reason why I have no issue working in my front room with the television blaring, and while it might not sound like something you're capable of emulating now, it won't take long for that to change. Of course, you need to make sure that your hotel has Wi-Fi, and if you're the one who does all of the driving, you'll have to limit the amount of work you do. But even if you can do an hour or two in the morning before you explore your destination and the same in the evening, you can earn enough to pay for the holiday and keep your clients happy.

This requires some strict self-discipline. If you're prone to dropping everything in favor of a night on the tiles, telling yourself you can enjoy your holiday and deal with the mess when you get home, you should probably give it a miss. That attitude can destroy you, and rightly so.

While it is important to spend some of the money you make and give yourself a reward for all that hard work, you also need to put aside a large chunk of it to cover your taxes. If you haven't worked for yourself before, this can seem alien. Many freelancers often forget to do it, only to wind up with an unexpected bill at the end of the year. The issue with taxes is that they take a while to kick in—it might take you eighteen months before you need to pay tax on the money you make today. There is also no concrete way of knowing just how much you should be putting aside or how much you will owe.

To make this process easier, I opened a saving's account that is attached to my online banking account. I can move money to and from it with a few clicks, and I tend to transfer a set amount each month. At least that's the theory. In practice I have used this account as an actual saving's account, dipping into it when times have been hard, when I have had to cut back on the freelancing to focus on other projects. When that happens, though, I simply deposit a higher percentage of my earnings into that account over the following months.

You will have a good idea of how much you need to pay based on the information found on tax calculators **(see Chapter 20.0: Taxes)** or on your previous tax year. It's just a case of trying to accumulate that money in your saving's account throughout the year. While this may seem like a pain compared to what those in standard employment need to do, it's actually much better this way. Instead of losing money on every paycheck, that money is yours to do with as you see fit until the tax year ends. Think of it as a payday loan, something that you can spend freely and enjoy for now, but something that will get you into a heap of shit if it's not back where it should be by the due date.

16.9 — FINISH BEFORE YOU START

Clients tend to have a lot of projects to cycle through, especially those who contract your services for one or more companies. These clients tend to be the most demanding, because they don't want flaws in your work to reflect on them. They tend to work on tight budgets and will be stricter with negotiations than others; but it's worth getting on their good side, because they will give you a lot of work if you're prepared to take it.

I have worked with many clients like this, and most of them will offer me something new as soon as I finalize a previous job. Sometimes they will give me another project while the former one is still ongoing. This can cause problems down the line, so be very wary of accepting them. These clients are often vague with what they want simply because content editing/gathering is usually only a small part of their job and not something they want to devote much time to. Therefore, requests for changes are very common.

The last thing you want after starting a new project with them is to have to edit or rewrite the old one, because now you have two jobs to work through and you probably still haven't been paid for the first one. As soon as they make such an offer, tell them explicitly that you'd prefer to finalize the first job, to put a big red tick next to it, before beginning anything else. As with everything, you don't need to be a dick about it. Just let them know that because of your tight and erratic schedule, it's hard to know when you will be free, and if you take on any more projects, then you will struggle to find the time needed for rewrites and edits.

Not only does this mean that you won't find yourself working on a job you thought was over several weeks ago (which happens), but it will also give them a kick up the ass. They like to keep the content coming, so when faced with a comment like that from a writer they trust and have come to rely on, more often than not they will draw a line under the first job there and then. They will release payment and promise not to come back and ask for edits or rewrites.

Not only do you get an extra job out of it, but you get paid quicker and you save yourself any hassle in the future. It's a win-win. For you anyway.

Chapter 16 Summary

- Give long-term clients a "nudge" to get more work from them.
- Individuals fare better than companies on freelance platforms, and they also get a higher rate. Unless you know and trust the people you're going to work with, don't start a company.
- Invest your time and money in other projects when and where possible.
- Be tough with negotiations, but don't be horrible.
- If a long-term client needs work and can't pay until you complete a lot, or until a certain date, trust them and take a chance.
- You can "forget" to add an attachment to an email in order to buy yourself a deadline extension.
- Take on quick, small jobs to build feedback quickly, refunding and canceling those that don't work out.
- Take holidays, travel the world, but take your work with you and always prepare for your taxes.
- Always finish one project with a client before you accept another.

See Also

- *Invites (page 65 – 3.7)*
- *Negotiating Bulk Jobs (page 83 – 4.4)*
- *Your First Jobs (Chapter 5.0)*
- *Deadlines (page 118 – 6.4)*
- *Outsourcing (Chapter 11.0)*
- *Taxes (Chapter 20.0)*

Chapter 17

BRANCHING OUT AND OTHER OPTIONS

Freelancing can open many doors for you, and if you want to make it as a writer, you should look to use success in one area to succeed in another. I did this myself when my books were successful.

I asked my own agent about this, a man who has helped me greatly, who made this book possible, and who has an abundance of experience in this industry. He confirmed that if you have some success as a freelancer, something to back up your credentials as a writer, then any submissions, even for a fictional novel, will attract more interest from an agent and from a publisher. I also know from experience that self-publishing success will also get you a lot more attention across the board.

Basically, everything leads to something else in this industry, and as a writer beginning your career, the best thing you can do is to open as many doors as possible and to keep them open for as long as possible. Sales can be cut short in an instance, and sometimes work dries up. Nothing that you will ever do as a writer is secure, but as well as doing your best to keep those plates spinning, you need to add more and more. Now, before I run out of trite analogies, let's look at some of the other things you can do as you try to make it as a freelancer or after you have achieved some degree of success.

17.1 — SELF-PUBLISHING

This job is not as easy as you probably think it is. My family and friends think I have it easy, that I am my own boss, that I can dictate my own hours, and that my clients are fair with me. Their attitudes change when I tell them stories, of course. The truth is that this is a job like any other—in some instances it is better, in some it is worse. You are not your own boss. Your clients are your bosses and you have dozens of them. These can be just as demanding and just as irrational as any other boss you have had in your life.

Freelance writing involves a huge amount of stress and frustration. I have been fortunate to experience both the life of an author and the life of a freelancer, and if you asked me to choose just one of those, I would run away from freelance writing faster than you could say, "Holy crap, what was that blur?"

I was able to make a lot of money as a full-time author. I was working a lot for it, and to keep the flow going, I once wrote two novels and a few dozen short stories in just a couple of months.

I began as an author and then worked my way into freelancing, but it's much easier to do things the other way around.

As a freelancer you will encounter publishing companies, aspiring novelists, marketing experts—a host of people that can help you and people you can learn from. You will likely be offered the chance to write books for small-time publishers, companies who use the KDP program much like I did; only instead of writing books themselves, they get others to write them and then simply collect on the royalties. By all means, accept these opportunities, but try to glean as much information, tips, and advice from these clients as you can (approach such questions carefully and politely).

Let freelancing build up your bank balance and your knowledge. I self-published with no budget at all, simply because I didn't have any money to spend. But I was very lucky. In reality you need a big budget to beat the thousands of other writers who are trying to do the same thing as you.

There are a few tips and tricks to Amazon publishing that you will pick up along the way, so do what I did: don't invest too much in your first project and simply use it to feel your way around. The trick is to continue freelancing at the same time as self-publishing. It will be stressful and you'll lose a lot of sleep. In the early days, I slept for an average of four hours a night and spent the rest of the time working. However, if this is what you have always dreamed of doing, it will be worth it. Of course, if you have another part-time or full-time job to do, this is not possible.

The things I learned from self-publishing, the tips I picked up along the way, would fill another book and can't be discussed in full here. However, there are some things that are crucial to your success as a self-published author, things that you should prioritize over anything else.

Polish Your Book

There are a lot of poorly written books self-published on Amazon. Some of these sell well, but the vast majority flop. Your first step as a self-published writer is to go over your book a number of times to make sure it is of a publishable standard. Writers tend to have a skewed view of their own writing abilities, especially early on in their careers. So, give your book to someone else, someone who will be honest with you. Once you have ironed out major issues and are confident that your book is good, then give it to an editor to eliminate the mistakes. You'd be amazed at how many readers will give a book a bad review because it has a few small typos, and these reviews can destroy you.

Reviews

In the beginning it was very hard for me to get any reviews, which is why my tester book didn't do very well. It became easier later on, as I had developed a following of people who would buy and read my books as soon as they were released and then leave reviews. Those first couple of books were hard, but this is where the tester project comes into play. Pass it around on Twitter and Facebook. Talk with avid readers in the same genre, with competing writers, with friends, family, and anyone else who will listen. If they read, enjoy, and review the tester project, they will be more inclined to do the same to other books you release.

Cover

You need a great cover and cannot compromise on this at all. If you have a small budget, then all of it needs to go into making a good cover. My tester project had one that I cobbled together myself. It was poor, but I was convinced the writing would do the talking. I was wrong. I asked my partner (a professional designer with an amazing eye) to design the cover for the next book, and I am under no illusions that this design was behind much of the success of that book and all others that followed. Never think your writing will do the talking, because if the cover is poor, prospective buyers won't even click onto your book page. You need a cover that looks professional, because you don't want to look like a self-published writer. The industry has a bad rep, thanks to poor-quality books, so you need to distance yourself from this.

Give Away Your Book

You cannot underestimate the effectiveness of a good giveaway. The people who tell you that you can't make money giving something away don't know how Amazon works. To make it onto the "Also Bought" and "Recommended" lists, which is how you sell a lot of copies, you need to sell copies. It is a catch-22. However, if you run a free book promotion on Amazon, for just a day or two, thousands will (potentially) download it and you'll be on these lists when the promo ends. You will need to be exclusive to Amazon to be able to launch these free promotions, but I have never seen a reason not to be. Nine out of every ten ebooks sold are on Amazon, and to get the attention of that remaining one buyer, you would need to get the attention of half a dozen other sites. Stick with Amazon, because the alternative is simply not worth your time and exclusivity has perks that no other site has.

Low Quality, High Supply

Self-publishing is easy, and literally anyone can do it. This means that everything from high school poetry to fan fiction has found its way alongside traditionally published titles, and while a few self-publishers insist on rigorous editing and proofreading, the majority do not. Add to that the slew of terrible self-designed covers, layouts, and blurbs, and all of the "indie publishers" who outsource cheap writers to write low-quality books that they hope to then publish and profit from, and you have an industry that is rife with low-quality titles, and one that is only going to get worse. In 2014, it was estimated that more than a third of all ebooks sold were self-published, and that figure seems to have climbed since.

When I first joined the freelancing websites, I used my success on Amazon to help others achieve similar results. I have worked with several other authors who have had less than half a dozen sales over the course of a few months. They had poor covers, and many of them had poor books. I often discovered that none of them had used the free promotions that they were entitled to. After a quick edit of their book page, a change of cover, and a free promotion (this needs to be promoted two weeks prior to the start of the promotion, which you can do using free ebook blogs and services), they saw their sales increase to at least half a dozen a day. This is not enough to live off, but it is a lot more than they were getting and if they had followed this advice from the very beginning, things might have been better.

Don't get your hopes up though. This is not some magic trick that will work for everyone. Amazon has changed a lot since I made my money there, and after signing the rights to my books over to a publisher, I have no longer been interested in studying the Amazon algorithms, nor have I paid attention to the new promotion methods. Still, if this is what you have always dreamed of, or even if you're just looking for another way to earn some money using your writing skills, then by all means go for it. You have got nothing to lose, and as a writer, one of the best feelings you can get is to know that there are thousands of people out there reading and enjoying your books.

Freelancing is to write in the shadows; being an author is to stand in the spotlight.

17.2 — OFFLINE FREELANCING

There are dozens of books out there that can help you with becoming an offline freelance writer. That was never the goal with this book, simply because I firmly believe there is more money to be made online. Online freelancing is also significantly easier, but it is not without its flaws, which can put some prospective freelancers off. The main flaw is that as an online freelancer, you are relying on one or more websites. Not only do you need these to remain online and to stay true to their terms, but you are also counting on them not to suspend you for no reason, which is a very legitimate worry in this industry **(see Chapter 9.0: Suspensions, Rules, and Disputes)**.

As an offline freelancer, there are no such risks. You are still relying on companies and websites, but these are your individual clients, as opposed to your entire platform. You also run many of the same risks involved with online freelancing, in that there is no security with this job and illness will essentially break you.

If you have read this book and don't think that online freelancing is for you, or you simply want to have more irons in the fire—which is always recommended—you should look to branch out. There are a lot of similarities between online and offline freelancing. You have to create a CV/profile to sell yourself and a portfolio to catch the eye; you need experience and references; and you need to find an ideal price point. Much of what I have discussed regarding online freelancing applies to the offline world as well, and this is different to "offline" clients, which we looked at in chapter nine.

Benefits of Online Freelancing over Offline Freelancing

- **Time & Simplicity:** Clients and jobs can be found quicker and with considerable ease.
- **Variety:** The greater volume of work allows for greater variety.
- **Escrow:** Escrow payment systems supply a certain degree of financial security.
- **Acclaim:** Building a reputation that leads to big jobs and money is easier.
- **Exposure:** Work well, and your name will automatically get the exposure it needs.
- **Quick Interviews:** It is rare for a client to insist on a time-wasting face-to-face interview.
- **Equipment:** There is no need for fax machines, printers, scanners, stamps, envelopes, or anything of the sort.

The hardest part about freelancing offline is that you can't rely on a platform to offer you jobs, to showcase your skills, and to handle your payments. You need to do all of this yourself. It gets easier as you go, but in the beginning there is a lot of hard work. The main things you will need to address are discussed below.

Basics

Before you begin, you need to create a CV. It doesn't have to be a standard CV, and it would actually benefit you more if it was a little unorthodox and included writing samples, awards, experience—anything you think would be relevant. You should also set up a PayPal account (make sure it is verified), a Skrill account, and an escrow account. If possible, create a separate bank account as well. A lot of clients will want to pay you via bank transfers. You will need to join social networks (particularly LinkedIn) freelancing communities, message boards, and anything else that is relevant. You should also create a website that showcases all of your talents and experience.

Networking

The next step is to find work. This is not easy and it will require a lot of research. It doesn't have to be done offline, of course. I'm using the term "offline freelancing" to denote freelancing that is done away from freelancing portals. Much of the work you do will still rely on the Internet. In the beginning things will move slowly, but it will get easier. Look on classified ads, Craigslist, freelancing portals, message boards, and social networks. Email content sites, e-commerce sites, and anyone else that needs content, and enquire if they are hiring freelancers. Google "write for us" and search the results for paying opportunities. You should also be willing to drop in to local newspapers and magazine offices, to send letters, to make phone calls, and to check the wanted ads.

Relationships

Developing a relationship with a long-term client is as essential offline as it is online. There is no feedback system, but you need these clients to act as references, you need them to keep hiring you, and you need them to put in a good word for you. One well connected client can give you work for life, but only if they enjoy working with you and only if they appreciate the work that you do.

Payments

You should be invoicing your clients. You cannot expect them to remember when they need to pay you and how much they need to pay you. Send them an invoice when the work has been finalized and be strict about it (you can find invoice templates on most word-processing software). By all means deliver edits and any other fixes that they need. Definitely do not pester them, but let them know that you are relying on that money to pay the bills.

Workshop

When it comes to offline freelancing, it is vital that you join the community. Get involved with workshops, and join message boards, clubs, unions, and organizations. Not only can they provide guidance and assistance where needed, but they can also help you network and grow your client base.

Communicate

My life as a freelancer is a lonely one. Prior to writing this book, I hadn't spoken with many freelancers, and because I work primarily on freelancing platforms, I can get away with this. However, as an offline freelancer, you need to have a network of freelancers around you. This will give you better access to bigger clients, and it will help you to keep an ear close to the ground, warning you of any trends and changes to keep an eye out for, and of any clients and jobs you should avoid.

Opportunities

This applies to online freelancing as well, but it is more relevant here. You will be working for clients who have a range of skills and experience, and you will be given the chance to take advantage of these. If a client is relying on your skills as a writer to get a project off the ground or to keep one alive, don't be afraid to ask them about a collaboration. This is not something you should do straight away, and it is something that you will need to feel out yourself as it is only advised with clients who are relaxed, friendly, and open. For instance, if they are creating a succession of affiliate websites, asking you to write the content as they do the promotion, then ask them if they would be interested in creating a website with you. Begin small and build from there, because if you go too big too early, you might find yourself working full time on a project that doesn't generate any immediate income.

Professionalism

An important aspect of all freelancing, this can be the difference between full-time employment and no employment. Always maintain the utmost professionalism. Double check to ensure you have the client's name correct and structure all emails properly, using this name and signing off with your own. Proofread your correspondence as if you were being paid to edit it, because clients will not hire freelancers who can't write an email without making several mistakes.

Records

You can afford to be lazy on freelancing platforms because they do most of the record keeping for you. Away from those platforms, though, you need to do this yourself. Keep track of every single job, every single client, and every single payment. You should know who paid you, how much they paid you, and when they paid you. It is also important to understand all of the clients you work for. Do quick background checks on them, make sure that they are how they say they are, and keep a record of that information and their contact details. If you're worried about a client's honesty, be sure to let them know (without being obvious) that you know where they work and that you can report any of their bullshit in a heartbeat if they turn nasty. In offline freelancing it is much more common to work on jobs where the client disappears without paying.

Submissions

To avoid spamming anyone with repeat applications, you should keep track of all applications you submit, whether it is through a message board, through a website, or via email. A client may ignore you now only to return to your message at a later date when they are in urgent need of work. However, they are unlikely to do that if, after you sent that message, you sent a further dozen messages applying for the same role.

Advertise

Advertising is all about selling a product, and as a freelancer that's exactly what you are looking to do. Many freelancers won't even consider doing this, but this is often how the best freelancers get started. Create a professional, well-written ad—including a picture or two—and then post that ad wherever you think it is relevant. This can be on writing forums or even in bookshop windows. One of the better ways to get attention is to advertise on a website or message board for self-published authors, as they are always on the lookout for editors, proofreaders, consultants, designers, and even writers who can enhance their books, collaborate, or write forewords.

Benefits of Offline Freelancing over Online Freelancing

- **Money:** The base rate for offline freelancers is higher than their online counterparts.
- **Networking:** Finding clients who are willing to recommend you is more common.
- **Reliance:** You are not relying on one website or one payment method.
- **Payment:** No one is waiting to take their cut of your earnings.
- **Deadlines:** Everything moves at a slower pace, giving you more time to work and submit.
- **Understanding:** Clients tend to be more understanding with regards to breaks, holidays, and delays.

Facebook

Facebook is a great advertising tool. Just set up a Facebook page, make sure your details are there for all to see and that the page points to a site or price list, and then use Facebook ads to promote it. If you target English-speaking entrepreneurs, small-business owners, and webmasters, you will generate a lot of interest from people who have decent budgets and a need for a good writer. If you target self-published authors, you will get a lot of interest from writers looking for editors and proofreaders—although in this case they rarely have big budgets, and many of them will waste your time with ridiculous offers and collaborations that only benefit them.

17.3 — TRADE PUBLISHING

This book came at a very strange time for me. It was proposed by myself and my agent just after I sold the rights to all of my self-published titles. As I write this, I am many months away from the first of those books being published, yet I know that this book will actually be published sometime after that date. This is very much a limbo period for me, and one that is dominated by freelancing.

Writing this book was very tricky for many reasons, not least of which was the fact that I didn't want to come across as high and mighty. I didn't want it to sound like I was bragging or that I was claiming to be the best freelancer on these platforms. None of those things are true, and I'm not that sort of person. Still, despite that, I do think it's relevant to return to my own experience again when discussing trade publishing. After all, I was in the same position as many of you probably are right now. I became a full-time novelist at a very young age, yet beyond a few short stories, I didn't publish anything. If I hadn't had been supported by my family (as is the case with all families, some were a little less supportive than others) and by my partner, I would have been on the streets. It was a reckless decision to make, and a selfish one, but writing was the only thing I ever wanted to do, and I couldn't see myself doing anything else. This "all or nothing" attitude worked out in the end, and this is why when aspiring writers ask me how they can repeat this success, I tell them the same thing that everyone else tells them: "Never give up."

If you write a book and it is rejected, then don't go back and edit that book only to send it out again. I know aspiring writers who have been working on the same book for ten years. Trust me, if no one wanted it back then, no one will want it now. Worst of all, you're not going to improve as a writer. My early attempts at writing were poor, and while I didn't realize it at the time, getting upset when the rejections poured in, I understand it perfectly now.

In the years that followed those early books, I wrote more and more. I discovered that I was actually better in a different genre and with a different style, adapted through years of starting a book, finishing it, and then repeating the process.

Freelancing, in one way or another, gave me my publishing contracts. It happened directly with this book and—although it was the self-publishing success that attracted my agent and publisher—it also helped indirectly. I have also grown as a writer because of my time as a freelancer. I used to write 1,000 words a day on my novels and be content with that. These days nothing short of 5,000 words will do. I have learned to meet deadlines, to write in many different styles and languages (British English, US English, and Australian English), and to improve my structure. It has killed a bit of my creativity—endless working will do that to you—but that will return when I take a break.

One of the best things you can do for your career as an author is freelance. Because even with moderate success, you still have something to put on your CV and attract attention from agents and publishers. You will still have made contacts that may be linked to publishing, PR, or marketing, all of which can help you get published and help you sell your books when you are.

What a Strong CV Needs

- **Contact Info:** Employers need to be able to get in touch with you should they want to.
- **History:** Showcase your employment history in detail.
- **Qualifications:** Include every certificate and degree you have.
- **Skills:** What makes you stand out; why should they hire you?
- **Layout:** A clean and simple design is best. Order your segments in terms of priority.
- **Ambition:** Let them know you're willing to work hard and that you want to succeed in life.
- **Clean Perfection:** There should be no typos, no grammatical errors, and definitely no doodles, outlandish designs, or garish colors.

I can tell you all of the things that other authors will tell you. I can say that you should never give up, that you should spend time researching the right agent and writing the perfect cover letter, but I firmly believe that the best thing you can do is freelance. Of course, you can self-publish as well, just as I did, but you could be the best writer in the world and still fail as a self-published author. No one will be impressed by that. However, if you have the skills as a freelancer and you read everything in this book, you won't fail.

Chapter 17 Summary

- Most writers aspire to be authors, and Amazon can help with that. Make your book as commercial as possible, make it free, and make a success of yourself.
- While it's not going to guarantee success, freelancing can help with a self-publishing career.
- If you do succeed, remember that self-publishing is as unstable (if not more so) than freelancing. Don't drop one just because the other is doing well.
- Online freelancing is not secure or guaranteed, so use your skills elsewhere.
- Offline freelancing, while not as relevant, is a great addition to online freelancing.
- If you have a back catalog of work, think about self-publishing. If not, write something in your downtime. This is the end goal of many writers, so you might as well start now.
- As well as being a very profitable career, freelancing can also lead to success elsewhere.

See Also

- *My Journey and Yours (page viii – 0.1)*
- *Tips for Other Freelancers (page 107 – 5.8)*
- *"Offline" Clients (page 120 – 6.5)*
- *Suspensions, Rules, and Disputes (Chapter 9.0)*
- *Websites from Scratch (page 244 – 15.3)*
- *Expenses (page 303 – 20.1)*

Chapter 18

INVESTING

The best way to give yourself some security as a freelancer is to simply invest. Once you have paid your bills and left enough cash to enjoy a reasonably easy life, then consider investing your expendable income. This will ensure that during any downtimes, and during any spells of illness, bereavement, or struggles to find work, you won't need to stress so much about your finances.

When I first decided to invest, I had no idea how to go about it. Beyond a savings account, I had no idea about the best way for someone like me to secure their money. I am young (or so I tell myself), but I have no interest in long-term investments and am generally looking to put some money aside every month. I also prefer investments that can be accessed when I need them (because you never know when work will dry up) and investments that have the potential for huge growth, without needing to wait for retirement. I had to learn all of this myself, but I was lucky enough to be given writing jobs on investments, precious metals, and some other opportunities. This basically meant that I was paid to research information I was desperate to learn, and everything I learned through that research, and through my own personal research, has been discussed in this chapter.

18.1 — PREMIUM BONDS (UK)

This is a personal preference, and one that might be slightly contentious within the UK. There may also be something similar in other countries. Basically, a premium bond is a government-run program that lets you invest your money in something that doesn't pay out interest but will let you take part in a monthly prize draw instead. This might sound a little strange, but premium bonds have been around for a long time and are generally considered to be a safe way to invest your money. Experts will tell you that based on an average premium bond return, there is less value here than in a saving's account. However, it is the prospect of getting so much more than average that entices people to invest. Personally, my return from premium bonds has been three to four times as much as I would have gotten from the best savings account. I should also add that as a big gambler, it is perhaps only natural for me to be drawn to premium bonds and the big prizes they offer. At the very least, even in the unlikely event that you don't win anything over the course of a few years, your initial investment will still be there in full.

You should not base your decision on my advice. Rather, you should see them as a way to store your money that is both safe and accessible, as well as one that could gift you a monumental return. There is currently a maximum investment of £40,000 on premium bonds, and you will need to wait a month before you can enter your first prize draw.

18.2 — PRECIOUS METALS

It is difficult to recommend precious metals as an investment, simply because I have no idea how strong the markets are as you read this. As I write, it is a great time to invest, but whether that remains as you read is for you to decide. Gold, silver, platinum, and even palladium are valuable metals that humans have attached a significant value to for thousands of years. They are used in industry and they are hoarded by investors. They tend to be a great way to guard against inflation, and they are also hoarded by people who are worried about an economic collapse. This is because when everything else fails, when the markets crash and currency becomes useless, there is a strong belief that these metals will still be given a significant value. This is not a radical belief, either, as this has happened many times throughout history, resulting in a tendency for countries to stockpile gold when things are looking bleak.

Reasons to Invest in Precious Metals

- **Inflation:** Gold in particular has always been seen as a great way to hedge against inflation.
- **Deflation:** When the world's economies suffer, gold and other metals tend to excel.
- **Demand:** Demand is increasing, but supply is limited.
- **Diversity:** Precious metals are a great addition to any portfolio as they tend to perform well when other investments struggle.
- **Variety:** There are many ways to invest, from bullion and numismatics, to ETFs, mining stocks, and bullion storage.

You can purchase physical bars or coins, and if you are investing solely for the precious metal content, then try and get as close to spot price as possible ("spot price" is the value of the markets at that time). It's not advisable to keep large amounts of precious metals at home, so the best way is to invest in a bullion storage company. They will hold the metal for you, giving you a certificate as proof and allowing you to sell whenever you want.

Some countries need to pay VAT on silver purchases, including here in the United Kindom. This additional 20 percent essentially renders it a worthless investment. If you order from abroad, you may also be stung by customs, who can stop the package and demand you pay the VAT before they give it to you. This happened to me when ordering from Australia. The package arrived when I was on holiday and all I received was a note, demanding I go to the post office, pay the 20 percent VAT, along with a surcharge, and pick up the item. However, if VAT has been paid in another country, then you're okay. This is why many UK silver investors choose to import silver from Germany, where VAT is applicable but is so small that you barely notice.

18.3 — INDIVIDUAL RETIREMENT ACCOUNTS (US)

These retirement plans are a great way for self-employed people to save for the long-term in the United States. This is as long term as it gets, though, with the money withdrawn upon retirement. There are several types of IRAs available, with slight differences for each, but traditional IRAs will suit most investors. To be eligible for these, you need to be under the age of seventy-five, and you need to be contributing a maximum of $5,500 per annum. Like ISAs in the United Kingdom, IRAs are tax deductible initially, but any profits received from them will be treated as ordinary income and therefore subject to income tax. This doesn't apply to all IRAs, though, as the Roth IRA offers tax-free payouts. As soon as the investor reaches the age of seventy the investment will be released to them.

You accountant can tell you more about IRAs and point you in the right direction based on your income and status. The Investopedia website is also worth a visit if you want to learn more about this particular investment opportunity and others like it.

18.4 — SHARES

As with precious metals, there is a good time and a bad time to invest in the stock market. It's not as restrictive as precious metals, because you're investing in individual companies and there is no shortage of these to choose from. However, if the stock market crashes, all of them will suffer. Such occurrences are very rare, though, and even when they do happen, it's not as bleak as you would think. If you had held shares in a number of companies prior to the global financial crises in 2008, you would have seen a huge dip during that year, but if you had held onto them, in 2015 there is a good chance they would have been worth more than when you bought them. Simply put, big crashes are rare, and when they do happen, they usually fight their way back.

Understanding a Crash
While stock market crashes do have underlying economic causes, the primary cause is panic among investors. As soon as they begin fearing for their investments and panic selling, those investments rapidly devalue, which triggers more panic selling and eventually leads to catastrophe for global markets. Such incidents can be caused by everything from uncertainty in major financial markets (such as the United States and China) to stock market "bubbles" (where stocks are driven above their true valuation, before the bubble bursts and they drop). They tend to occur after a prolonged period of rising stock prices and general market optimism, which means that when things are looking good and the markets seem invincible, that's when you should worry the most.

You need to do your research before you invest, and you shouldn't invest more than you can afford to lose. If you want small investments that can payoff big and over the short-term, then look for penny stocks, mining stocks, and energy stocks. If you're looking for something that will provide a little more stability, without any major rises or falls and with a regular dividend, then get your money in blue chip stocks. These are the biggest companies in the country, the Apples (AAPL) and Googles (GOOG) of the United States, the Diageos (DGE) and Glaxosmithklines (GSK) of the United Kingdom. The beauty of such investments is that while they're unlikely to make you rich, with their value typically sticking for many years, the fact that they pay a return of around 4 to 5 percent every year means that after ten years you will have made half your initial investment back without selling any shares.

These days investing in shares is easy. You don't need to meet with a broker in person or over the phone, and you don't need to pay high commissions. Get yourself an online share dealing account and you can start investing in global stock markets almost immediately.

18.5 — SAVINGS ACCOUNT

A separate bank account or savings account is very useful to a freelancer. It gives you a place to store some of that expendable income as you build toward your future or prepare for a rainy day. It can also serve as an account to hold your tax money. You can use two different accounts for this, a short term and a long term, or you can use one account to cover both needs.

Short Term

Simply put, as a freelancer you are self-employed. This means that no one is taking the required tax from your earnings every month. Instead, you have to tell the government what you owe them, and at the end of the year you have to pay them. Nobody wants to be surprised with a hefty lump sum, so you need to make sure you're prepared for this. Personally, I have a savings account that I can access at the same time I access my bank account. Every time I withdraw a large sum of money into my bank account, I take a percentage of that and put it into my savings. You don't need to calculate the exact amount, because with expenses and everything else (**see Chapter 20.0: Taxes**), you can't really know how much you owe until you're ready to pay it. Just put aside a reasonable amount every now and then.

You want an account that can be accessed quickly and easily, an account that will allow you to withdraw and deposit at will and will place no restrictions on you. These sort of accounts typically don't pay a lot of interest, but that shouldn't be your main concern.

Long Term

If you can find one account that suits the needs discussed above and also offers a big interest rate, then you don't need a separate account. However, to get a decent interest rate, you often need to place restrictions on your savings. This can mean not touching it for a few years. There are many savings accounts out there, so be sure to shop around. The worst thing you can do is go straight to the bank that provides you with a credit card or current account and rely on whatever savings account they offer. Use a comparison site, do your research, and find out if ISAs or standard accounts work best for you. Nothing is secure in this job, and you can't rely on any long-term earnings, so a savings account like this will provide some much needed stability when things get a little shaky.

18.6 — COLLECTIBLES

Freelance writing involves a lot of researching, as well as detailed writing across a wide range of subjects. This is one of the many upsides of the job, particularly if you love to learn new and random facts.

For one job, I researched first-edition books and other collectibles. It opened my eyes to an investment opportunity that at the very least allows you to beat inflation, and at the most generates a sizable profit. There is a wealth of goods out there that can be bought today and sold on for an almost guaranteed profit in a few years. You will have to do your research on particular products, with some requiring more research than others, but there is a wealth of things you can invest your money in.

Silver and Gold Coins

As well as the precious metal content of the item, which itself can increase and decrease, premium coins can generate huge profits over time. Coins that typically increase in value over time include the Lunar Series by the Perth Mint, as well as premium coin series by the New Zealand Mint and the Singapore Mint. Again, research is required here, but for an investor, precious metals is a great industry to get involved with.

Rare Single Malt Whiskies

You will need to find bottles from beloved distilleries that have been produced in limited runs. A good way to stay up to date with such offers is to sign up to newsletters from the biggest distilleries. Rare bottles from rare distilleries can be worth a small fortune, and nothing makes a distillery rarer than it closing down. Once you have your investment, try not to drink it.

First-Edition Books

First editions and signed editions are worth a lot of money. If you buy the book for a base price (the same price everyone else is selling it for), within months of its release, you should be guaranteed a profit in a few years. If you buy a first-edition book yourself (preordering is usually a good way to guarantee this), and then take the book to a book signing to get it signed, you will be increasing the value instantly. It all depends on the author and the rarity of the signature (which itself depends on how often the author does book signings), but typically you can buy a new first-edition book for $15, get it signed, and then sell it for $100. If you hold on to it for a little longer though, that price should increase.

Collectible Books

These books are not easy to find. As with the whiskies, the best way to learn about them is to sign up to author's newsletters and social media sites. These books carry a huge price tag, but they have low print runs and their value increases every time they are sold. As an example, during his last few book releases Stephen King (or his publisher) commissioned a collectible edition for about $100. These books were signed and included original artwork, slipcovers, and other original additions. There were usually less than five hundred printed, and when they were all sold, they instantly went onto eBay and Abebooks and were sold on for $200 a piece. A couple of years later, you could find them selling for as much as $300. Give it a decade or so, and who knows what they could be worth. The rarer the book, the smaller the print run, and the higher the demand, the bigger your profit margins can be. There is a reason that sellers on Abebooks and eBay make a living from buying these books as soon as they become available and then selling them on.

Original Art

This is perhaps the most profitable, but also the one that is the most difficult to acquire. If you can get original art from an up-and-coming artist, or from an artist who has already achieved a degree of popularity, then you are assured a big profit in the future. The best way to go about this is to follow the artist on social media and on their websites. There are popular artists who will release runs of limited edition prints, sketches, and more, making them available to the first one hundred people or so who pay the money and respond to the post. As an example, I follow an artist who offered for sale a small print for just $50. There were one hundred of these and they were gone within minutes of being offered. As soon as they were all sold, they were being resold for upward of $500. What's more, investors were paying that inflated price, knowing that in five years or ten years, those prints would be worth even more. If you have an eye for good art, this can be a great way to use money gained from freelancing to invest in your future. However, with a little bit of research, anyone can get involved.

These are by no means the only collectibles that can make you money, so if none of them are to taste, don't give up. The more irons you have in the fire, and the more money you have tucked away, the better. I know of writers and other self-employed people who do very well investing in comic books, action figures, video games (classics and special editions), and even playing cards. There is no end to the potential in these markets, and providing you have the capital and are willing to wait a few years, this is a great way to guarantee a return.

Chapter 18 Summary

- Freelancing is not as secure as other full-time jobs, so look to invest your money.
- Save money for a rainy day, because a storm is never too far away.
- Limit your high-risk investments.
- Spread your money around and ensure the majority of it is accessible. There will be times when you don't make a lot of money, so you might need to tap your savings and investments to pay your rent/bills.
- You don't need to be a financial mogul to invest in shares or precious metals, but while most of your knowledge will be picked up as you go, you should seek to learn a little before you invest.
- When it comes to buying for the future, go with what you know and what you like.

See Also:

- *The Right Price* (**Chapter 4.0**)
- *Plan Ahead, Keep Earning* (**page 194 – 12.3**)
- *Websites and Blogging* (**Chapter 15.0**)
- *Enjoy Your Money, Prepare for Taxes* (**page 261 – 16.8**)
- *Self-Publishing* (**page 268 – 17.1**)
- *Taxes* (**Chapter – 20.0**)

Chapter 19
RESOURCES AND REFERENCES

To paraphrase American author and humorist John Hodgman, a man who freelanced himself, "Several magazines wanted me to be an expert in every subject, whether food or wine or history or the life span of veterinarians. I was completely unschooled in all of these things." There are several reasons why freelancers struggle to make it in this industry, why they complain that it's just not for them, or that there are not enough jobs or enough good clients. Many of them don't have the patience or the willpower needed, but there are also those who focus on a single subject, purely because they know the most about that subject. You have a computer, you have the Internet, and you have a brain, so you have everything you need to become an expert in everything the client wants you to write about. No one is going to ask you to get a PhD in a subject that you've been tasked with writing about. You won't need to pass a test or consult with academics. Use Wikipedia, a bit of general knowledge, and a lot of common sense, and most of the time your research will take a matter of minutes.

At any given time, your desktop will be filled with dozens of web-pages, documents, spreadsheets, and more. The last time I rebooted my laptop and all of those went away, I panicked and thought there was something wrong. Without all of those minimized pages and documents, my toolbar looked alien. This is my way of organizing things—the way I know what I have to do and when I have to do it. I wouldn't recommend it as it's a little chaotic. You will find your own way, though, a way to accommodate the many websites, programs, and documents you will need for single jobs, while keeping these separate from other jobs.

In this chapter, we'll look at some of the sites you can use to help you to write, research, and complete jobs, as well as some resources to help with your career on the whole.

19.1 — RESEARCHING A JOB

My partner calls me a walking, talking encyclopedia of bullshit. At least, she would, but she doesn't want to hurt my feelings. When I was a penniless, clueless, aspiring author, I spent my days researching random information and facts and reading up on everything that interested me. I am also a big fan of random information and the shows, websites, and radio programs that divulge it.

This makes me a bore at parties. It means I am the guy people go to when they want an answer to an obscure question, and it means I would be everyone's "Phone a Friend"—if I actually had any friends. It's pointless, basically. Or at least it was until I began freelancing. This is where being a know-it-all comes into its own, because you will be given articles on endless subjects. If you can write those articles without researching, you can effectively cut a job in half and double your hourly rate (unless of course you're on the clock, in which case you should still research).

If you enjoy writing about a subject, make sure you know everything about it. Try and read and learn as much as you can elsewhere as well. You would be amazed how often a factoid, a quote, or anything of the sort can come in handy. I once won over a client by editing a document of his and knowing that a quote he had randomly attributed to "English proverb" was actually from Shakespeare's *Othello*. This wasn't part of the job, but the fact that

I noticed it in passing and mentioned it saved him a lot of embarrassment and led to a bonus, some five-star feedback, and an additional contract.

> **Learn More**
>
> As a freelancer you are perfectly poised to learn about anything and everything, as you will be given jobs that basically force you to do so. Away from that, you can also learn yourself, earning bigger contracts, better jobs, and getting more money and praise in the process.
>
> - **Stay Up to Date:** A lot of writing contracts focus on topical events, so it always pays to remain up to date on everything that happens in the world. A few minutes spent checking the headlines and reading the odd article will do. It's amazing how often a seemingly useless tidbit of information you learned in the morning will come in handy in the evening.
> - **Read:** The more you read, the more you know, but not if you're reading *Twilight* all day. Try to read nonfiction in your downtime. You'll pick up tricks regarding writing styles, referencing, and researching, and you might also learn a thing or two.
> - **Social Media:** YouTube, Vine, and Twitter are the way forward for many big brands and websites, and if you work for them, they will expect you to know them inside and out. Knowing who the biggest stars are, what the most popular videos are, and how to "mention" and DM helps with a surprising number of jobs. "Top Ten" videos will also supply you with a lot of useful facts that you can use to improve articles and impress clients.

The more you know, the further you can go. Don't worry if you know nothing, though, as one of the great things about freelancing is that you will be introduced to many new subjects. After researching, editing and writing on them, you will become an expert.

It may sound redundant to have so much knowledge on so many random subjects, but as an online freelancer, you won't be paid to research. You will be paid per word, that's all. You could argue that that's not fair and that the client should also compensate you for the time you spent trawling the Internet. But why would the client pay you an hourly rate to research and a per-word rate to write on a subject you know nothing about, when they could just pay an expert who would charge the same per-word rate and wouldn't need to research?

Online freelancing is very competitive, and this competition has made it the norm for clients not to pay for research and to expect you not to charge. Some less-experienced clients will, and if it is a highly specialized job and you have been headhunted, they might give you a little extra, but most of the time this does not apply.

This is why researching is a race against the clock. It's why half the time I try to wing it based on what I already know, along with a little common sense. You can also use some of the sites below, as these will cover most areas of research and can be trusted.

Wikipedia

I know what you're thinking. Wikipedia doesn't exactly have the best reputation when it comes to the truth. But you won't find more up-to-date information on an array of subjects, and 99 percent of the stuff is spot on. Also, and perhaps more important, this is where the clients go to check that what you are writing is true. There is a little "cheat" you can use when copying citations for an article that requires them. Never cite Wikipedia as a source. That makes you look like an amateur. Instead, click on the little number after the sentence, quote, or picture. This will direct you to an obscure article or book where the Wikipedia article writer got their information. You can then cite this page/book as your source. If you do this throughout the article, you will have half a dozen different sources, from medical journals to obscure academic books. It will look like you spent hours researching, even though you only skimmed through a few Wikipedia articles. This is not plagiarism or anything, so don't worry; but if the client does question you on it, be truthful and tell them you thought it would look better than simply referencing Wikipedia all of the time.

Trip Advisor

This site has a wealth of information. I have used the lists of top restaurants to help with food articles and the list of attractions to help with travel articles. I have even used Trip Advisor to help with articles on gambling, thanks to the pages on cities like Las Vegas, Reno, and Atlantic City. If you want to know anything about a city, town, or tourist destination, or if you need some info on an attraction or restaurant, this is perfect.

Copyscape

You will see many clients reference this site, and many of them will use it. Writers can also use it, but unless you're working on a rewriting job that requires 100 percent originality, you probably won't find a use for it. Still, it's good to know what the client will see when they check your work for plagiarism. Copyscape basically checks content against everything on the web, telling you how much of that content has been plagiarized from elsewhere. Bear in mind that quotes and common phrases will be flagged, but this is unavoidable. However, unless the client is an idiot, it shouldn't be an issue. Copyscape also has a couple of other features, including the ability to check two articles against each other, with the software finding any matching sentences and/or paragraphs. This is a paid service, but it works on a system of "credits," with one credit per check. These credits can be purchased very cheaply through PayPal. I personally use this service to check articles I outsource and articles I buy for my own sites. In months of doing this, I have only needed to top up my balance twice, spending just $10 a time.

Booking.com

Trip Advisor doesn't have the best information when it comes to hotels, which is a surprise. The reviews are good, and if you want to research things from the customer side, then it's okay. However, if you need info about the hotel, Booking.com is better. I have used this site to help with articles on every three-, four-, and five-star hotel in three different cities and for two different clients.

WikiTravel

Sometimes you may be called upon to write detailed travel articles, from the perspective of someone who has been there. However, you don't need to have been there to know where the airport is, to know the distance or the taxi cost from the airport to the city center, to understand the underground and overground services, or even to understand the price of food or attractions. All of this information and more is on WikiTravel, which means you can emulate the experience of someone who has traveled the world without going anywhere. Personally, I try not to lie to clients, as that has a habit of biting you in the ass at a later date. But if it means the difference between getting a job and not, and if the client is of the belief that you need to have been to a place to be able to write about it (many clients don't understand the concept of research), then a few white lies won't hurt.

Amazon

The world's biggest e-commerce site can come in handy when you need info on products. Skip the standard spiel written by the product developers and go straight to the customer reviews. One of the common jobs you will see a lot of is one asking for reviews of products. This is usually for affiliate purposes and generally requires you to write as if you have used the product. The client will not expect you to buy it, nor will they give you it for free. Your job is to read other reviews and watch videos (discussed in the following section) to get a better idea of the upsides and downsides of the product, before writing your own review. You may also be approached to write and post Amazon reviews, but this is something I would advise against. Everyone who has their own product on Amazon needs reviews to get exposure and to increase sales, and many people resort to asking freelancers to post reviews. They don't pay a great deal (after all, anyone can do it), and as well as going against Amazon rules, it is also against the rules of many freelancing platforms. By all means, write testimonials for affiliate sites, but avoid jobs where the client asks you to post those reviews yourself.

YouTube and Vine

Sometimes the easiest way to get to grips with a product is via a testimonial. Most of these are fake and paid for by the company, with the reviewer reciting from a cheat-sheet the company gave him. Still, this is what they know of their product and what they expect their customers to experience, so if you are tasked with writing a review or a testimonial, then YouTube is often the best place to research. The same goes for viral articles. There are hundreds of clients asking for this sort of content, and as well as BuzzFeed and even Cracked, the best way to get an idea of the sort of content that goes viral is to check out the most popular videos on YouTube.

19.2 — RESOURCES FOR FREELANCERS

There are a number of blogs out there about freelancing, as well as other sites that can help you. As I write this I do not have a blog of my own, as such. I do have a website based on this book, though, and one that can act as a companion to it. Links to this site, and to other blogs and websites that can help you out, are below. For the sake of full disclosure, I have only used a couple of these, so they are not essential. If, however, you like to live and breathe new ventures, to learn as much as possible, and to cover every angle, join every community, and generally be a know-it-all, then these will help.

- **Freelance with Us** (www.freelancewithus.com): This is the official site for the Online Writer's Companion, and it's also, technically, my author website. The goal is to make this website a community for freelancers, one with articles on freelancing/writing and one where I will also discuss the book, events, and anything else associated with its release.
- **Freelancer's Union** (www.freelancersunion.org): Focused on the US market, the Freelancer's Union provides a service to all

independent contractors, from agents and authors, to lawyers and more. As I am not in the United States, I have not joined myself. However, I do have friends who have used it in the past, and it is they who recommended it for inclusion in this book.

- **The Book Designer** (www.thebookdesigner.com): Another site that was recommended to me, this covers information about ebooks and self-publishers, which have been discussed in another chapter **(see Section 17.1 on page 268)**.

- **Escrow** (www.escrow.com): I have had a few issues with this service, and it is far from perfect. A client contacted me about writing a book, and as he was not affiliated with a freelancing plat-form, and as I didn't know him enough to trust him with PayPal's "chargeback" feature, it seemed like the best option. However, they charge a fairly hefty fee (paid by client, freelancer, or both), and there were a number of technical issues as well. These were fixed eventually, but not with any great haste. If you find yourself being offered a job outside of the freelancing platforms (which will happen) and you don't trust PayPal or any other web wallets, this fits the bill. However, I would only recommend it if there is a lot of money involved and if a bank transfer is out of the question. You will have to pay the site fees, but if you don't mention these to the client when using Escrow, then you should be able to get away with splitting them. If the client is the one setting the job up, then you may even find that they take the burden of those fees.

- **Freshbooks** (www.freshbooks.com): This service was designed with freelancers in mind, helping them with their accounting, invoicing, etc. It is useless in combination with freelancing plat-forms, but if you find yourself doing a lot of work away from those platforms, it might come in handy.

- **Udemy** (www.udemy.com): I don't have a lot of experience with the sites listed here, but with this one I do. I was actually approached by Udemy to develop a course about creative writing, although I doubt I was the first and I think courses can be created by anyone. They weren't paying special attention to me. There are millions of students here and a huge number of courses. If you want to brush up on your writing or create a course of your own, this could be the perfect outlet. Don't expect students to enroll instantly though, as the task of getting people to apply is down to you. If you don't have the credentials to create a course that people will be happy to join, and if you don't do your promotion first and confirm in advance that people will be interested, then there is no point in taking your time to create a course.

- **Google Docs:** I am seeing an increasing number of clients directing freelancers to Google Docs. I hated it when I first used it. It was slow, it was awkward, and I couldn't shake the feeling that when I returned to a document the following day, it wouldn't be there. In the end, it was actually much better than half of the word processors out there. The spellcheck is second to none, and for someone who types quick and often when tired, and someone whose work looks like a thesaurus threw up on it after autocorrect has finished with it, this is important. Google Docs is free—you just need a Google account—and it is collaborative.

- **Dropbox:** Another tool that clients will expect you to understand, Dropbox is used to store and transfer files. I don't work on too many jobs that require Dropbox, but there are clients who insist on it, and it is the best way to backup your data. Be sure to copy all important documents to your Dropbox folder every now and then, just in case everything goes wrong. The free accounts here are limited to a couple of gigabytes, but if you're only transferring documents then you won't be going over this. As soon as you have an account you will be able to access clients' Dropbox folders, and as long as you are not sharing any of your files or folders, they will not have access to them.

- **Tuts Plus:** (tutsplus.com): Previously part of a freelancing community known as Freelance Switch, this site is home to a number of tutorials, helping you to advance your skills in everything from coding and computer game design to business skills. There are thousands of tutorials, and while the emphasis is more on design and programming, writing is covered as well.

- **LinkedIn** (www.linkedin.com): Social networks are very dangerous to a freelancer, because before you know it, "I'm just checking my messages" can turn into a full five-hour assault of cat pictures and inane banter, and that's only if you're on my profile. They can be useful though. As mentioned elsewhere in this book, Facebook pages can be very profitable for determined designers **(see Section 5.9 on page 109)** and LinkedIn can be great for professional networking. As with all social media, though, expect a lot of bullshit and tedium, as well as a fair share of time wasters who like the idea of hiring you but don't like the idea of paying for you. You're opening yourself up to people like this if you advertise yourself on social media, and while I have gotten a few decent jobs that way, I've had far more time wasters.

- **Work Awesome** (http://workawesome.com): This is a content site focusing on productivity. It is popular with freelancers and entrepreneurs, and while I only came across it during my research for this section, it seems to have plenty of valuable content.

- **Entrepreneur** (http://entrepreneur.com): Another content site—and a hugely popular one at that—aimed at the self-employed.

Chapter 19 Summary

- There are many sites that can make your life easier.
- With the ability to research, you are not limited to the jobs you can take on.
- Use social media sparingly, and focus on LinkedIn and Facebook.
- Web wallets and Escrow can help with "offline" clients, but all of these have their flaws.
- There are millions of other freelancers, and while it's not essential in online freelancing, communicating with these can help

with the mental strains and stresses of the job while also giving you some tips.
- Check in with the book's official site if you want some updates, info on revisions, and anything else relating to the book and its author.

See Also:

- *Broaden Your Horizons (page 69 – 3.9)*
- *Connects (page 109 – 5.9)*
- *"Offline" Clients (page 120 – 6.5)*
- *Guest Posts and SEO (page 161 – 10.1)*
- *Productivity and Organization (Chapter 12.0)*
- *A Client Wants to Talk on Skype (page 201 – 13.2)*
- *Self-Publishing (page 268 – 17.1)*
- *And Finally . . . (Chapter 21.0)*

Chapter 20

TAXES

As a self-employed writer, you should be paying taxes. How much you pay and how the process works will depend on your country of origin. Unless you're operating out of a tax-free country, you should be keeping tracking of all of your incomings and outgoings.

In the United Kingdom it is fairly easy to do your taxes yourself, as discussed below. It is a little harder in the United States and other countries, but wherever you are in the world, you can hire an accountant to take the stress and hassle out of the process for you. Nobody likes doing their own taxes, and as writers tend to be the "head in the clouds" types, we usually hate it more than most. Still, if an accountant is out of the question and you want to knuckle down for one day a year and do it yourself, then there are some things you should keep in mind. In fact, even if you do have an accountant, you should still understand the process.

20.1 — EXPENSES

As a self-employed writer, you need to be claiming expenses; otherwise you'll find that every penny you have left at the end of the year will be going to the tax man. Luckily, there are many things that you can claim as a writer, and you don't need an accountant to sort this out for you. Personally, I think getting an accountant is much easier.

I was lucky enough to be put in touch with a friend of a friend who offered to do my yearly taxes for a small one-off fee, and the time and money he saved me ensured he was worth his weight in gold.

The following are what make up the bulk of my expenses every year.

Promotions

These are paid promotions for my books, but if you have any published work that you are paying to promote, or if you are promoting your website or even your freelancing page, you can claim the costs back.

Computers

Prior to being published and making it as a freelance writer, I had been using the same laptop for close to eight years. It was reliable, but a little dated. As soon as I started earning, I purchased a brand-new laptop and was able to put this on my expenses. After all, 100 percent of my work is done on this laptop.

Some of the Things You Can't Claim

- Food bills
- Clothes
- Gifts
- Non-office furniture
- Game consoles and games
- Gambling expenses
- Gadgets/electronics not related to work
- Ornaments/decorations

Office/Business/Home

You can claim rent, furnishings, and electricity costs. This applies whether you operate out of an office, a shed in your garden, or a room in your house. You can't claim all of your rent or your energy bills, but you can claim a respectable amount.

Outsourcing

As alluded to earlier (see Chapter 11.0: Outsourcing), one of the main benefits of outsourcing is that you can claim some of the cash back.

I don't usually outsource work that clients have given me, but I run some websites that I purchase content for, and I have also paid freelancers for interviews/research, editing, and more.

Research

Whatever research methods you use, if they cost you money, you can claim them on your expenses. This is a broad category and what you claim depends on how far you want to take it. There are stories of writers who have claimed everything from movie tickets and cable TV subscriptions to library rentals.

Travel

As a freelancer you may need to travel here and there to complete your work. A lot of my claims in this regard relate to my work as an author, but many of those instances would also relate to freelance writing. Fuel expenses are usually up there on all writer's expenses, and you can also claim hotel rooms, flights, train tickets, and anything else that relates to your work.

Stationery

If, like many writers, you have a stationery fetish and an ever-growing collection of notepads, pens, and pencils, then you can claim these as well. A few decades ago, one of the things at the very top of a freelancer's/author's list of expenses was stamps. That doesn't really apply anymore, but if you bought them, then claim them. The same goes for envelopes and any other costs associated with sending materials through the post and corresponding with clients.

Dinner/Drinks

There will be times when you will be given the chance to sit and talk with clients, to have drinks with them, and to go out for dinner. Such instances never happen to me, because I like to get things done quickly, I rarely take on memoir writing jobs, and I live in the arse-end of nowhere. If you do have meetings with clients, publishers, editors, or anything else that is work related, then you might be able to claim the bill or part of it. Just don't go overboard.

20.2 — HIRE AN ACCOUNTANT

You should never underestimate the value of a good accountant. If you don't know anybody personally, then do a search for a local accountant. You don't need to keep anyone on a retainer; this doesn't have to be someone who will have access to your finances and someone who could destroy you if they turned rogue. You just need someone who can file your taxes once a year, taking the stress out of a very stressful and difficult process. Even in the United Kingdom, where the process has been simplified, it still pays to hire someone who knows their stuff, because they can save you a lot of cash.

If you have made in excess of $40,000, don't stress over a few hundred quid. If that's what they charge and they're good enough, hire them. They could save you ten times as much as that. If your budget is a little tighter and you don't have the income to justify a big expense, then turn to the freelancing platforms. You can find a very good accountant on Upwork, and if you follow the rules set out in the outsourcing chapter, you don't need to pay a small fortune. As it happens, I have done this myself. As a self-published author, I was subject to a 30 percent tax from the IRS, which only disappeared when I could prove I was a tax-paying UK citizen. I was told I could get that back and hired an accountant to fill in the correct forms to do that.

Of course, I never got that money back, but that's entirely the fault of the US tax office and not the accountant who did the work.

So how much can you expect to pay in tax? Well, this is not a straightforward question. Taxes differ from country to country, and I only have an experience of the United States and the United Kingdom. However, as those will probably be the two biggest markets for this book, as my publisher is based in one and I am in the other, we'll focus on them.

In both of these countries, it is worth noting that the actual amounts will differ from person to person, reliant entirely on how many expenses you claim.

20.3 — UK: NATIONAL INSURANCE

In the United Kingdom, we pay something called Class 4 National Insurance, also known as the most ridiculous tax in history. I don't agree with this and don't see the point, because in a country that is supposedly trying to promote self-employment, this does the opposite. If you want to attract tourists to a beach resort, you don't tell them the waters are shark-infested, the sand is full of crap, and a serial killer is on the prowl. I'm exaggerating of course, but when a tax that typically takes £150 a year from those in standard employment asks for thousands from those who are self-employed, I think I'm entitled to.

With Class 4 NIC, you pay 9 percent on your earnings above £8,000 or so, and this falls to 2 percent when that figure rises above £42,000 or so. What's more, the Class 2 NIC that everyone else pays, amounting to just £2.80 a week, must be paid on top of this. Politicians need to heat their pools after all.

20.4 — UK: TAX RATES

The exact amount of tax you will pay changes all of the time, albeit only slightly.

> **UK Tax Year: 2017–2018**
>
> **Personal Allowance:** £11,000*
> **20% Basic Rate:** Between £11,000 and £32,300
> **40% Higher Rate:** Between £32,000 and £43,300
> **45% Highest Rate:** Between £43,300 and £150,000
>
> *This is a nontaxable amount; if you make less than this, you won't pay tax. If you make more, only the amount above £11,000 is taxable.

So, if you make £30,000 a year, the maximum rate you will pay will be 20 percent, and that will only be on £19,000 because of your personal allowance. This means that you will pay £3,800 in total, excluding your NIC. As soon as you go above £32,300, all money above that amount will be taxed at 40 percent. To get a better idea of what you can expect to pay, punch your details into a tax calculator, such as the one on UKTaxCalculators.co.uk. Here you will see that if you do earn £30,000, then as well as the £3,800, you can also expect to pay NICs of just under £2,000. If you earn £50,000, your total tax rate will be around £12,500, while a freelancer earning £100,000 can expect to be pumping a third of their earnings into the government coffers.

An amount like this will come as quite a shock. However, a good accountant and a detailed report of your expenses can eradicate much of that.

20.5 — UK: PENSION

National Insurance isn't as useless as I made it out to be above. I'd still prefer it didn't exist, in all honesty, but it does contribute to your pension, and for some people this is essential. Regardless of what you do or where you work, you should save for the future, but this applies even more to the self-employed because you don't know what the next month, week, day, or even hour will bring. Personally, I prefer to invest in my own way, as discussed elsewhere in this book (**see Chapter 18.0: Investing**), but a pension has its uses.

You need at least thirty years of National Insurance contributions to get a State pension, which is only around £115 a week. Assuming you earn £50,000 a year, paying Class 2 and Class 4 NIC, then you will have given the government over £101,000 minus expenses (based on the 2016 tax year). This means that you'll need to collect your pension for about seventeen years before you will break even. I don't know about you, but that sounds like a raw deal to me. Although, it's not as if you have a choice.

There are other pensions available, and while you don't have an employer paying in that pension, the government will add a little to it. The amount they add is based on your tax rate, but if you are on the basic rate, they'll top up every payment you make by 25 percent. Depending on the pension scheme you choose, you will also collect interest as it builds, making this a very useful option for self-employed freelancers.

Personally, it is not something I have done or intend to do. I would rather put my money in shares, bonds, and other investments as I don't like tying up my money for the long haul. However, for those coming out of regular employment who are used to these schemes and have come to rely on them, it's ideal.

20.6 — US: SELF-EMPLOYMENT TAX

As a freelancer in the United States, you need to apply for something known as Self-Employment Tax if you have a net profit of more than $400 for that year. A net profit is basically your total earnings minus your expenses, which were discussed in detail above. If this applies to you, you need to fill out Form 1040 Schedule SE, which is where it gets tricky.

I have had a few battles with the US tax system myself, and while I generally find all taxes annoying, the UK system is child's play in comparison. If you want to emerge from this process with your sanity intact, you definitely need an accountant—but I digress (again). So how much should you expect to pay?

The self-employment tax rate in the United States is 15.30 percent, which consists of social security and Medicare. This only applies to 92.35 percent of your earnings, though, and not if the figure you arrive at after multiplying your net income by 92.35 percent is less than $400.

There is a limit to the tax rate on the former, but not on the latter. And of course, this is not the only amount you will pay as a self-employed freelancer.

20.7 — US: TAX RATE

There are more variations in the US tax rate than there are in the UK one, and there is also no tax information available for future years.

This is a problem considering I am writing this book at least a year before it is due to hit the shelves and it will stay relevant for many years to come. The brackets in the US system begin at 10 percent and up to around $9,000 and increase to around 40 percent and over $400,000. Whether you are filing a tax return as a single person, a married (and joint) couple, a married person filing separately, a widow/widower, or the head of a household, all affects how much you will pay. On top of that, you also have the self-employment tax.

You can find the info you need on the IRS website, which is updated with the new tax rates every year.

20.8 — US: RETIREMENT PLAN

There is no state pension scheme for the self-employed in the United States, but there are schemes you can buy into of your own volition.

- **401(k):** One of the more popular ways you invest for your future, the amount you can sink into a 401(k) depends on age, employee status, and a few other factors, but generally you can invest more here than in other schemes. There are many benefits, and while some of these are negated by annual fees and setup fees, it's still a very beneficial scheme. You can even take out loans against your investment, which might come in handy during those weeks when you're struggling to find work or when you have fallen ill.
- **SEP-IRA:** A "Simplified Employee Pension" is one of the more basic schemes, allowing you to set aside $250 of every $1,000 you earn up to a certain amount. That amount changes, but it is generally around $50,000. The beauty of this scheme is that you can choose to deposit as little or as much as you want, but this might be a bad thing if you struggle with self-discipline and can see yourself depositing the bare minimum or nothing at all.
- **SIMPLE:** Don't you just love it when a good acronym comes together? This is a Savings Incentive Match Plan for Employees, which was designed with the self-employed (and with small

businesses) in mind. To be honest, this seems to work better if you have employees, an office, and an actual business, but it is still a viable option for self-employed freelancers.

Chapter 20 Summary

- As a freelancer, you are self-employed and will need to do your own taxes or hire someone else to do them for you.
- Keep a record of all outgoings and incomings.
- Expenses are essential, and without an extensive record of all of these, you could be in the red at the end of a tax year.
- Taxes differ from country to country and year to year. Try to stay up to date.
- In the United Kingdom, National Insurance is a killer for self-employed persons, but as it works on profit, you can still limit the damage it does with your expenses.
- Although not essential, there are a number of pension plans, retirement plans, and more available.

See Also:

- *Payment (page 95 – 5.2)*
- *Deadlines (page 118 – 6.4)*
- *Suspensions, Rules, and Disputes (Chapter 9.0)*
- *Enjoy Your Money, Prepare for Taxes (page 261 – 16.8)*
- *Investing (Chapter 18.0)*

Chapter 21

AND FINALLY . . .

As a freelance writer, you are afforded the rare ability to complain about a dream job. For me and others like me, this is what I always wanted to do. Yet try telling me that when I've been awake for fifty-plus hours writing the same old crap because I have a bulk batch of articles to complete and rent to pay. I can't imagine footballers will complain about living out their childhood fantasies and getting six-figure sums every month, but if you show me a freelance writer who's doing what they always wanted to do and doesn't complain, moan, or suffer just a little bit, then I'll show you someone who drowns their demons with substance abuse.

As a freelancer, you will meet the best and worst people, and you'll have to be nice to all of them. Imagine waking up in the morning and beginning a day that sees you bump into a postman who flips you the bird, a traffic warden who shits on your windscreen and charges you for the trouble, and a boss who spits in your face, calls your work shit, and then demands that you stay overnight to correct it. Imagine that when you're tired and on your last legs, you have to deal with the demands of a spouse or family member who has no idea what you have just been through, does not spare a thought for the time of day or your mental condition, and assumes that they are the only person in your world as they run off a list of demands that need to be done there and then. That's what your clients will do, and that's why this job is so hard and so stressful.

You will meet a lot of horrible and demanding people, and you'll find yourself working for a number of them. I have a friend who likes to enquire about my clients and my freelancing, a friend who knows what many of them say and ask, a friend who has actually been there when some of those demands have been sent my way. He often says to me, "I don't know how you haven't completely lost your mind and killed everyone yet."

The truth is, I'm okay with it. It takes a certain mentality to make it in this game and to put up with all that shit. But they're not all like that. There are some amazing clients out there, and once you struggle through the fist few months, you can limit yourself to dealing only with these clients. Also, deep down—when you're getting annoyed because a client is being horrible and illogical and you can't lash out or even correct them for fear or pissing them off and suffering the backlash—I remember that this is a job that pays well. It is a job that allows me to research an array of subjects, to write everything from articles on kitchen refurbishment and slot machines to descriptions of tea blends and chocolate. It is a job that puts me in touch with some very well-connected people, a job that never stops opening doors, and a job that allows me to work in my boxer shorts if I want (and I so often want).

When everything is going wrong, when you feel like you want to murder your clients, remember that not only will things get better, but things are already pretty fucking good.

Of course, if you're here to make a quick buck—if being a writer is not and was never your goal in life—you will struggle to see the good side. Freelance writing is to a writer what nonleague football (or amateur soccer if you're from across the pond) is to a professional player. It's not the best possible scenario, but you're still getting paid to do what you love and what you have always wanted to do.

21.1 — THE ABYSS OF LONG-TERM SUCCESS

While regular jobs and a regular income is probably your main goal, once you get to that point it can be very difficult to balance your career. There will come a time when you are working all hours of the day and turning down new offers of jobs left right and center. In those times, you are far too busy to stand back and enjoy your success or your newfound wealth. These are the newborn years, because you're a walking, talking zombie who gets little sleep, sees little sunshine, and doesn't stop thinking about the thing causing all the stress.

Then you finish the jobs, and you collect the money. You're happy, but only briefly because only then do you realize that you have nothing else to do. The jobs you turned down begin to look pretty appealing at that point. You have to start the process all over again, applying for new jobs, working toward those days of endless stress and no sleep, only to despise them when you finally get there.

Unfortunately, the trick is to ensure those days never end. Don't worry, though, eventually you'll be numb to them and will even begin to tolerate them. To do this, you need to balance your work. I've already mentioned **(see Section 6.4 on page 118)** how you should never give a client an accurate deadline and always prolong it, so that you're working multiple jobs a day and are never spending too much time on a single one. You should also find time to apply for jobs and to respond to interviews, because eventually those jobs will dry up and you'll be stuck.

Upwork Study

According to an independent study that was (in part) conducted by Upwork, there are more than fifty-four million Americans working as freelancers. This means that more than a third of the US workforce classifies themselves as either full-time or part-time freelancers. Of course, this includes everyone from plumbers, builders, and other contractors, to entrepreneurs and those who freelance to earn extra on top of their full-time job, and it doesn't mean that a third of all working Americans are on a freelancing platform. However, it does bode well for the future, as more and more employees are going it alone and these platforms are growing constantly because of it.

Fortunately, you can afford to be even stricter with your negotiations **(see Section 4.3 on page 81)**. Don't back down. Don't take less than what you think you deserve, and always push for a very long deadline. That way you can take the job immediately but not start until everything else has dried up. If you do this a few times, when your first batch of jobs dries up, you'll move onto this fresh batch. In your first year, there will not be a time when you need to stop applying for jobs.

After that, things get a little easier. You should still try and keep the jobs coming in, but by this time you should have developed relationships with long-term clients and they will usually have something for you to do. As I write this book, it has been eight months since I have had to apply for new work. In that time, I have worked with a number of long-term clients, and just when it seems one of them has given me all they can give me, a client from last year, or even two years ago, emails me out of the blue and gives me something.

This is because it is a necessity to work with dozens of clients in your first year. You haven't been given the time to develop long-term client relationships, so you'll have to keep cycling through client after client. Some of them might give you a $50 job and will show up months later with something much more substantial. Others may give you a $5,000 contract, only to never contact you again after it's finished.

That doesn't mean that after a few years you won't need to apply for anything ever again. There will come a time when even that work dries up. It might not seem like it will, but believe me, it will. But that's the beauty of having been doing this for so long. Someone is always sure to pop up out of the blue and ask for something. And if not, getting a job at this stage is much easier than it used to be, because many top-level freelancers are tied up with long-term jobs, and there are few of them applying for each job that is available. That means that as soon as one of them does apply, they standout.

Trust me on this, as difficult as it seems when you're just beginning, and as tiresome, frustrating, and stressful as it is during that first year, it does get easier. Of course, then you have to deal with complacency and boredom, but such is life—I can't help you with that.

21.2 — ABOUT THE AUTHOR

I encountered a few problems when writing this book, one of which was the fact that I had freelanced under an alias—a name different to the one on the front of this book. Technically, my success belongs to a different name, and the one you will see on the spine has made no waves as a freelancer. I have used that name as a client, though, and prior to the publication of this book, I also made the decision to change my freelancing names to correspond with this one. I didn't do this to attract more work. If anything I need the opposite. I get a lot of requests that I can't handle, and because I still hate saying no and disappointing people (even after all of the shit I have received and gone through), I often talk myself into wasting my own time. The reason I changed the name was to provide a contact, a voice—for you to know that the person who wrote this book really did use those sites and (maybe) continues to do so. By the time you read this book I won't be as highly ranked on those sites as I once was, simply because I am limiting how much I use them. If all goes well, I'll reduce my freelancing to part time. If I'm still a high-ranked, very active freelancer when you read this, then you have my permission to be disappointed in me.

If you want to get in touch with me, or learn more about this book, its imprints, and the advice contained within, then checkout my website at www.FreelancewithUs.com. I'll try my best to populate the site and to answer any questions that you might have, but bear in mind that between my obligations as a freelancer and an author, I don't have a lot of free time. It's easy to look down on a writer that doesn't respond to your query or doesn't go out of his way to do so, but believe me when I say it's not out of ignorance. Although it might be because I don't like you very much.

If you are a client and you are looking for a good writer, just check out Upwork and see what you come up with. If you read through the outsourcing section and follow the rules there, you can get someone who is good and professional, instead of someone who will piss you about and then deliver substandard work. As for me, you probably wouldn't want me working for you. I would give you my best and I would be nice to you, no doubt about that, but I might then go and write a book about you behind your back.

ACKNOWLEDGMENTS

The past few years have been crazy. For much of the last decade it seemed like my life was on pause; then someone hit fast-forward and everything became a blur. I have been very lucky in many ways, but I've also worked endlessly and that has cost me some valuable time with my partner and my family, while also sending me a little insane.

This book marks the culmination of that period in many ways, but I won't bore you with the details. I do want to thank everyone who has been there and has supported me in that time though. This includes my partner, who has received many mentions in this book and has found her way into every dedication and acknowledgment to date. That's because without her, I'm not sure any of this would have been possible.

She's at the top of the list, but it's a very long list, so I'll forgive you if you skip this section.

I should begin with my parents. They waited just as long as I did for me to find success as a writer and an author. But while life can be kind, it can also be a bitch. My mother fell seriously ill at the same time that things began going well for me, and it seemed like the better things got for me, the worse they got for her. So, to my mother, I love you, and I owe you more than I could ever repay.

I also owe a lot of thanks to my only brother. He never stopped playing the role of the older, protective sibling, and he has given me two wonderful nephews, Aiden and Harry, and one beautiful niece, Leah.

My in-laws also have my sincere gratitude. Because even though they live a thousand miles away, and even though we don't share the same language, they have welcomed me as one of their own.

This book wouldn't have been possible without my clients, the good and the bad. I have ranted a lot, and I have discussed many bad experiences with clients that have been rude, demanding, unreasonable, and illusive. That doesn't mean all of my experiences were bad, though, and I have worked with many fantastic clients over the years. So, for being a credit to the service, for being a friend as well as a client, for giving me long-term contracts and never giving me a reason to hate you or my job, I owe my gratitude to all long-term clients. These include Khaled, Adrian, Sebastien, Charles, Chelsea, Alex, Nichola, Polly, Jonathan, Betvin, Ravi, Suresh, Tanya, John S, Itai, Lasse, Marcus, and Angus.

I am also indebted to my agent, Peter, who helped me piece together the proposal for this book and to sell it; to my editor, Kelsie, and everyone else at Allworth Press; and to Alan Gray, an old friend, colleague, and employer who has a heart of gold and is always willing to help.

And just because I feel like I have thanked everyone else, I should also thank Beatrice, Rincewind, Sheldon, and Hugo, my pets. Because even though I've woken up every morning with cat hair on my face, in my mouth, and even up my nose, and even though they like to squeeze between my lap and my laptop, demanding attention in the real world when dozens of clients are demanding attention in the virtual one, my days would have been decidedly less interesting without them.

INDEX

ALLWORTH PRESS
NEW YORK

BOOKS FROM ALLWORTH PRESS

The Author's Toolkit, Fourth Edition
by Mary Embree (5 ½ x 8 ½, 272 pages, paperback, $16.99)

Abused, Confused, and Misused Words
by Mary Embree (6 x 9, 232 pages, paperback, $14.95)

Business and Legal Forms for Authors and Self-Publishers, Fourth Edition
by Tad Crawford (8 ½ x 11, 176 pages, paperback, $24.99)

The Business of Writing
edited by Jennifer Lyons (6 x 9, 304 pages, paperback, $19.95)

The Fiction Writer's Guide to Dialogue
by John Hough Jr. (6 x 9, 144 pages, paperback, $14.95)

Promote Your Book
by Patricia Fry (5 ½ x 8 ¼, 224 pages, paperback, $19.95)

Propose Your Book
by Patricia Fry (6 x 9, 288 pages, paperback, $19.99)

Publish Your Book
by Patricia Fry (6 x 9, 264 pages, paperback, $19.95)

Starting Your Career as a Freelance Writer, Second Edition
by Moira Anderson Allen (6 x 9, 304 pages, paperback, $24.95)

The Writer's Guide to Queries, Pitches, and Proposals
by Moira Anderson Allen (6 x 9, 288 pages, paperback, $19.95)

The Writer's Legal Guide, Fourth Edition
by Kay Murray and Tad Crawford (6 x 9, 352 pages, paperback, $19.95)

Writing What You Know
by Meg Files (6 x 9, 212 pages, paperback, $16.99)

To see our complete catalog or to order online, please visit *www.allworth.com*.